THE ONLY WOMAN IN THE ROOM

Women and Politics in the Pacific Northwest

Series editor: Dr. Melody Rose, Marylhurst University

This series explores the many roles women have played in Northwest politics, both historically and in modern times. Taking a broad definition of political activity, the series examines the role of women in elected office and the barriers to their role in the electoral arena, as well as the examples of women as advocates and agitators outside the halls of power. Illuminating the various roles played by diverse and under-represented groups of women and considering the differences among and between groups of women, acknowledging that women of the Northwest do not experience politics in a single, uniform way, are particular goals of this series.

PREVIOUSLY PUBLISHED:

Remembering the Power of Words: The Life of an Oregon Activist, Legislator, and Community Leader
Avel Louise Gordly with Patricia A. Schechter

With Grit and By Grace:
Breaking Trails in Politics and Law, A Memoir
Betty Roberts with Gail Wells

Up the Capitol Steps:
A Woman's March to the Governorship
Barbara Roberts

"The Only Woman in the Room"

THE NORMA PAULUS STORY

Norma Paulus
with Gail Wells *and* Pat McCord Amacher

Oregon State University Press   Corvallis

Library of Congress Cataloging-in-Publication Data

Names: Paulus, Norma, author. | Wells, Gail, 1952– author. | Amacher, Patricia, 1953– author.
Title: "The only woman in the room" : the Norma Paulus story / Norma Paulus ; with Gail Wells
    and Pat McCord Amacher.
Description: Corvallis, OR : Oregon State University Press, [2017] | Series: Women and politics
    in the Pacific Northwest | Includes bibliographical references and index.
Identifiers: LCCN 2017003878 | ISBN 9780870718953 (original trade pbk. : alk. paper)
Subjects: LCSH: Paulus, Norma. | Politicians—Oregon—Biography. | Women politicians—
    Oregon—Biography. | Legislators—Oregon—Biography. | Women legislators—
    Oregon—Biography. | Feminists—Oregon—Biography. | Lawyers—Oregon—
    Biography. | Oregon—Politics and government—1951- | Oregon—Biography.
Classification: LCC F881.35.P38 A3 2017 | DDC 328.73/092 [B] —dc23
LC record available at https://lccn.loc.gov/2017003878

∞ This paper meets the requirements of ANSI/NISO Z39.48-1992
(Permanence of Paper).

Oregon State University Press
121 The Valley Library
Corvallis OR 97331-4501
541-737-3166 • fax 541-737-3170
www.osupress.oregonstate.edu

Contents

Foreword

For nearly six decades I have had the good fortune to know, work, and socialize with Norma Paulus, one of the most remarkable people I have ever known. I admit to a well-founded bias in her favor. I am confident that, after you read this biography, you will share my immense admiration for Norma.

In the fall of 1959, returning from active duty in the US Air Force, I enrolled at Willamette University College of Law. For some time Norma had been attending law school part-time while working as a legal secretary at the Oregon Supreme Court. She'd previously worked as a legal secretary in Burns, Oregon, for the Harney County district attorney. Consequently, we both became members of the law class of 1962—fewer than sixty fledgling law students, only two of whom were women.

Norma quickly established herself as an intelligent and energetic classmate. She was well regarded by her fellow students and the faculty. Norma was an excellent law student, passed the bar, and began practicing law in Salem with her husband, Bill Paulus, whom I had long known—he and I had sung in the youth choir and served as acolytes in our church (St. Paul's Episcopal) and participated together in youth activities in Salem schools and the local YMCA.

Some time in 1965 I decided to run for the Oregon House of Representatives. I invited a few close friends to join my election campaign. Norma accepted the challenge, and I was grateful she did. She was a wonderful campaigner—strategy, door-to-door, lawn signs, and the other election activities of the day. Among other tasks, Norma headed up our lawn-sign detail—no small effort. The task was to select locations for several hundred signs, secure permission from the homeowners, put the signs in place, and keep track of them throughout the district. Norma tells the story of how, one day, while she and her two young children, Liz and Fritz, were placing signs, a woman approached her and said how good it was for her to help her husband's campaign. Norma quickly responded, "He's not my husband, just a friend." Norma became a trusted adviser on my subsequent political campaigns.

In 1970, as I ran for the state Senate, Norma put on a highly successful campaign for a seat in the House. The campaign was hard-fought, and Norma was victorious. Thereafter she and I worked together writing and passing legislation that we thought was important to Oregon. From her House seat, she ran for secretary of state and won handily—the first woman in Oregon history to be elected to statewide office. Later she was elected superintendent of public instruction—another first for an Oregon woman. She capped her years of public service by becoming executive director of the Oregon Historical Society.

Norma has always had a down-to-earth, practical approach to solving problems both large and small. One example of the latter: when her old car's ignition was wearing out, she devised a handy substitute from a Popsicle stick—and it worked! She showed a similar practicality throughout her career, working with like-minded colleagues from across the political spectrum to secure rights for women, protect Oregon's natural environment, and reform public schools.

Public service was Norma's lifetime goal. I believe she served the people of Oregon as well as anyone who has ever been in public life, and better than many. Her integrity, persistence, intelligence, patience, and loyalty set her apart. She would have made a great governor—one goal that was unfortunately denied her.

If I could have one wish for all of us, it would be that everyone could have a friend like Norma Paulus.

Wallace P. Carson Jr., 40th Justice of the Oregon Supreme Court
2015

Tribute

One definition of leadership is simply to go first. Norma Paulus embodied that definition so well that she created firsts: First woman to graduate from Willamette Law School without receiving a college degree. First woman to win the Moot Court Competition at that law school. First woman elected to statewide office in Oregon. First woman to serve on the Northwest Power Planning Council. First woman to serve as superintendent of public instruction. To attain these formidable accomplishments, Norma Paulus had to be willing to go first, to give of her talents and energy, and to trust that the giving would matter. These are the qualities that truly embody Norma Paulus.

Our word for it is "generosity." While we of all people are not naïve about the motives and costs of attaining public office—and the often immoderate ego it requires—we, as her children and as citizens of Oregon, are direct beneficiaries of Norma's tremendous generosity. In all her years of service, she never imagined she did it alone, nor did she ever cease to serve. And we, and all of Oregon, have benefitted from her grace, her smarts, and her courage.

Perhaps it is an innately human endeavor to preserve the clear memory of our elders' lives and accomplishments. As the daughter, son, and daughter-in-law of a remarkable woman, we feel especially beholden to that impulse. Not only have we received many personal gifts from the life of Norma Paulus, we have been front-row witnesses to her unfailing dedication to, and delight in, the well-being of the citizens of the state of Oregon.

We leave it to others to analyze her place in history, to examine her impact, and to acknowledge her achievements. As Norma's memory declines and becomes altered by age, we wanted to help tell her story as she might have done. As we and others helped to distill her life and pack it between the covers of this book, we did our best to represent Norma's words, her feelings and ideals, and her distinctive voice.

With much love and gratitude, we dedicate this book to Norma Jean Petersen Paulus.

Elizabeth "Liz" Paulus
William "Fritz" Paulus
Jennifer Viviano

Note on Sources

Norma Paulus always intended to write her own autobiography. To that end she recorded many hours of oral history for the Oregon Historical Society (OHS) between 1999 and 2010, amounting to nearly four hundred transcribed pages. While she is a superb storyteller, as the transcripts richly affirm, Norma felt she needed help in writing a sustained narrative of her life. In late 2010 she hired Russell Sadler, radio and television journalist, newspaper columnist, and chronicler of Oregon's late-twentieth-century political landscape, to co-write her autobiography.

Over the next year and a half, Sadler interviewed Norma several times, and he also talked to many of her friends and colleagues. He left the project in early 2012, after writing a preliminary draft of a chapter covering Norma's childhood. By that time Norma was nearly eighty, and family and friends were noticing that her energy and memory were both waning. She was still committed to capturing her life and legacy in an autobiography, but she was finding it more and more difficult to participate in the writing of it.

In 2013 Norma's children, Liz Paulus and Fritz Paulus, and Fritz's wife, Jennifer Viviano, asked the authors to take over the telling of their mother's story. They asked us if we could manage the task using the sources that already existed, including Sadler's preliminary work, for which Norma expressed gratitude and appreciation. When we saw his good notes, we were grateful, too, for the head start he gave us.

So we took on the task with zest, and also with a healthy skepticism of the veracity of memory—anyone's memory. We relied on Norma's oral histories to frame her life, and we confirmed nearly everything she said by means of extensive research in newspaper archives, government documents, and interviews with her colleagues, friends, and family. Our mission was to create an affectionate portrait of a remarkable woman who led a public life in a singular era. *The Only Woman in the Room* is an authorized biography that relies heavily on oral history. The strands of her story were gathered and woven together by two writers who, like Norma, are storytellers first and foremost. It does not claim to be a comprehensive or definitive historical work, but rather a lively and authoritative account of Norma Paulus's life and times, one that evokes her voice and is faithful to her legacy.

Here are the major sources we used:

▶ Oral history interviews with Norma Paulus, conducted by Clark Hansen. Interviews are dated April 19, 1999; June 2, 1999; July 1, 1999; July 30, 1999; October 2, 1999; October 5, 1999; October 27, 1999; November 11, 1999; March 23, 2000; April 13, 2000; July 6, 2000; November 2, 2000; April 13, 2003; February 3, 2010; February 10, 2010; February 17, 2010; and February 24, 2010. A total of twenty-six tapes are recorded; the transcript is 390 pages long. Recordings and an electronic file of the transcript are on file at Oregon Historical Society.

▶ Oral history interview with Norma Paulus, conducted by Linda Brody, Oregon Historical Society. Interview dated January 14, 1982. The transcript of thirty-two pages obtained from Fritz Paulus and Jennifer Viviano is in the possession of the authors.

▶ Initial work by Russell Sadler, including twenty-one interviews conducted with Norma Paulus and others. Interviews are dated October 15, 2010; November 2, 2010; December 17, 2010; March 3, 2011; March 8, 2011; March 11, 2011; March 15, 2011; April 8, 2011; April 22, 2011; May 5, 2011; June 2, 2011; June 23, 2011; August 18, 2011; October 26, 2011; November 9, 2011; November 30, 2011; December 14, 2011; December 18, 2011; December 19, 2011; January 17, 2012; and February 10, 2012. Recordings—there is no transcript—were obtained from Fritz Paulus and Jennifer Viviano and are in the possession of the authors. Sadler's work also included a four-page "Tentative Outline, version 1.1" and a ninety-eight-page first draft, "Copy for First Readers."

▶ Willamette University Archives. Records included many newspaper clippings, House of Representatives floor notes, campaign materials, copies of speeches and articles by Norma Paulus, correspondence, and other records. Specifics of these sources are noted in the endnotes.

▶ Oregon Historical Society archives. Records included many newspaper clippings and campaign materials, books and articles especially on the Rajneeshee episode, copies of speeches and articles by Norma Paulus, correspondence, and other records. Specifics of these sources are noted in the endnotes.

► Oregon State Archives, records on Norma's time as secretary of state. Specifics of these sources are noted in the endnotes.

We consulted many other books, newspaper and magazine articles, websites, and other records and materials when we needed more information about a specific time or event in Norma's life. Specifics of these sources are noted in the endnotes. Websites cited in the notes were visited in September 2015 unless otherwise noted.

During 2013 through 2015, we conducted interviews with

Larry Austin

Bill Bakke

Bob Burns

Wallace P. Carson Jr.

Nancie Fadeley

Dave Frohnmayer

Rod Harvey

Gretchen Kafoury

Hector Macpherson

Chet Orloff

Bob Packwood

Peter Paquet

George Passadore

Liz Paulus

Fritz Paulus

Paul Petersen

John and Gerri Pyrch

Joyce Reinke

Henry Richmond

Del Riley

Ozzie Rose

Dick Roy

Nels Thompson

Jennifer Viviano

Norma and her brother Harold Petersen at the oil derrick site near Lawen, Oregon, circa 1938. Family archives.

Chapter 1
The Early Years

> On our way to Eden—the lush green farmlands we had heard
> about in Oregon—we ran out of money and stopped in the
> mountains of Idaho to work in a sawmill cutting lodgepole pine.
> Some of my earliest memories were of spring walks up trails
> in the forest to the tune of tinkling bells. My mother tied bells
> to me to scare away bears while my sister Polly and I picked
> huckleberries for pie. Our journey to our new home ended 13
> miles outside of Burns, about a mile and a half off the main
> country road. The land was completely flat. Wright's Point,
> a long flat, high bluff, was the only relief. No trees, no hills,
> nothing but sagebrush and rattlesnakes. Even though the sun
> would always be shining, it was bitterly cold in the winter—and
> blazing hot all summer.
>
> —Norma Paulus

Norma Paulus made her entrance into this world in an auspicious and startling fashion. According to the often-told family story, she drew her first breath on top of the kitchen table in a Nebraska farmhouse. Her mother had labored for many hours without progress, and she was exhausted. She overheard the doctor warning her husband that this baby was so large that it might have to be cut out of her in pieces. Ella Petersen had borne three healthy babies, and she was not about to lose this one. She pushed for all she was worth, and the squalling girl who popped out tipped the scale at thirteen pounds. The way Ella used to tell the story was that, when Norma finally emerged, "she was so big I thought she'd walk across the floor."[1]

The Petersens, Paul and Ella and their growing family, were prosperous then—successful farmers, well respected by the other German American Lutheran families in their rural community of Belgrade, Nebraska. But hard times were on the way. In the year of Norma's birth, 1933, thirty-eight dust storms were recorded, up from fourteen the previous year. Paul and Ella farmed corn and raised dairy cattle on four hundred acres, and had fashioned a life of comparative comfort. According to family lore, Norma's father was the county's first automobile owner, and the first to put his team of horses to work pulling it out of the ditch Ella swerved into the first time she drove it. Like everyone they knew, the Petersens worked hard, and their toil had paid off, until the winds came and blew everything away.

All the surrounding families were in the same trouble, and all of them were moving on. Norma's father didn't want to leave, but there was really no other choice. Norma's mother always told her that he paced the kitchen floor of the farmhouse in search of an answer until finally, in the middle of an autumn night in 1936, he woke Ella with his decision. "Get up," he told her, "We're leaving."[2]

They piled the farm truck high with their possessions, including Ella's prized oak dining-room table. The Petersen brood then consisted of three sons and two daughters: Harold, fourteen; Polly, thirteen; Gale, eleven; Norma, three; and the baby, Paul Junior, eighteen months. Their meandering route took them through Wyoming, where they camped along the Green River, and on up to Idaho, near McCall.[3] They spent four or five months in Idaho, and then packed up again and moved on. They ended up in Eugene, Oregon, right around the hop-picking season. Like the small children of many such families, Norma recalled toddling along rows with strings supporting hops or beans, although she was too young to do much more than explore.[4]

When hop season ended, Paul found a job selling insurance. The family settled into a small frame house near the banks of the Willamette River, joining other families in a neighborhood on the east side of Eugene. Paul Junior recalls a good-sized porch on the front of their house, with lattices nailed to the bottom. The Petersens' dog met an untimely end under that porch after he was run over by a black-and-tan Model A Ford. He crawled under the lattice and then died, and the poor creature could not be buried until Paul Senior could dig him out.

Despite their poverty and their father's struggle to make a living, the children found that the riverside community was not a bad place for adventure. Norma's big brothers took her wading in the soft mud of the shallow water, and she played with the neighbor family's girl who was just her age. Paul Junior recalls ruining his white sailor suit for Easter Sunday when his friends persuaded him to investigate tar barrels at a nearby gravel pit.[5]

Paul Senior had a job, unlike many, but he was hard-pressed to bring money home when he only got paid on commission. In 1938, he approached a local veterinarian with a sales pitch, and was sold a bill of goods instead.

Left, Norma's brothers, *(L–R)* Gale, Paul, and Harold, next to buildings that comprised their home and oil derrick near Lawen, Oregon, circa 1938. Family archives. *Right,* Petersen family photo *(L–R):* Harold in WWII sailor's uniform, Gale, Ella with baby Richard, Polly Clark, Chuck Clark; front row, Paul and Norma; Burns, Oregon, circa 1942. Family archives.

The doctor serenaded Paul with a tempting get-rich-quick scheme. He knew a farmer out east, he said, who was convinced there was oil on his land, south of Burns, Oregon. The farmer's plan was to form a corporation and round up investors to fund the enterprise. Assuring Paul of his firm intention to invest in the scheme, the doctor said Paul could do the hands-on work of building and drilling. With perhaps a touch of nostalgia for his years working the land urging him on, Paul agreed to sign on.

He borrowed an old truck, and Ella and the children packed up their household yet again, leaving the green valley behind and heading east. Traveling over McKenzie Pass, Paul Junior got sick and was banished to the rear of the truck, where he clung to the tarp tied over their possessions.[6] Norma's sister Polly, then fifteen, cried the whole way. Having visited the endlessly flat, barren site for the derrick with her dad prior to their move, she believed she was being banished to the ends of the earth, far away from her friends at school.[7] That the family's new home was near places with names like Poison Creek Canyon and Barren Valley attested to the contrast between the fertility of the valley they had left and the dusty brown desert where they finally unpacked their worldly possessions.

Norma was too young to know any difference. She was barely five years old, and her life still revolved around observing her older siblings and knocking around with her younger one. "I remember playing with Paul in the ditches where the water ran out, and pushing our little trucks and cars around in the hot sand," she recalled. "We'd go into the buildings and crawl around where the equipment was. I remember seeing my brothers going out into the desert to bring loads of sagebrush for the boiler in a wagon."[8]

The oil enterprise was a huge undertaking. Paul had served in the Army Corps of Engineers in World War I in France and had learned there to reconstruct bridges knocked out by German troops. Enlisting whatever help he could get from sons Harold and Gale and the farmer who owned the land about thirteen miles south of Burns, Paul built the derrick, a cook shack, and a crude bunkhouse for the family's sleeping quarters.[9] There was an outhouse, of course, but no electricity or water. There was no well for water, either, and no containment method available in the desert. The family had to make do with a tank that stood by the kitchen to hold water Paul brought from the neighbors' wells.

The biggest problem with the Petersens' new home wasn't the hastily cobbled-together living space or the lack of amenities. The true difficulty they faced in the unforgiving desert climate was transporting the older children to school. In summer the dust was a foot thick, and in winter the road froze into deep ruts. Traversing the frozen road was no small feat, but on a good day it was at least passable. With the advent of the spring thaw, however, it became a daily ordeal. Polly was soon sent to live with a woman named Mrs. Carrico, who lived near the high school, while the boys made their own arrangements, consisting mainly of giving up on school and helping on the derrick. Harold and Paul Junior, who at five years old was too young for school, line-trapped jackrabbits for the bounty of a nickel for each pair of ears, often making more money off a bag of rabbit ears than Ella made working for thirty-five cents a day in a local restaurant. Unfortunately, the stringy beasts were all but inedible— the boys hacked off the valuable bits and threw the rest to the vultures—but Harold and Gale soon became adept also at bringing down deer for the table.[10]

As for carving a living out of this hostile climate, oil prospecting failed to provide the answer, although Paul was not the only one to fall victim to wildcat oil-drilling dreams in Harney County. A February 1920 article in a publication called the *Oil Trade Journal* details the blighted hopes and dashed dreams of West Coast wildcatters as early as the 1910s: "Unverified reports tell of some wildcat operations in Oregon, both in the Rogue River Valley and farther east around Burns, in Harney County," the reporter writes. "These are being carried on by small local concerns, and geological opinions have not generally been favorable."[11] A contemporary summary of Harney County's "oil rush" charts the persistence of wildcatters who carried on in the face of little to no encouragement from US geological surveys of the area. One pair of drillers in 1922 penetrated the desert to a depth of 3,700 feet, finding only marsh gas, before suing the investors who'd hired them for back wages.[12]

Paul suffered a similar disappointment as a wildcat driller, but without the means to sue for remuneration. After months of toil, all that shot out of the earth, up to a height of 1,400 feet, was steaming 180-degree artesian well water. The drill also hit shale and brought up fish skeletons, a sign of the desert's former life as an ancient seabed.[13] Though Paul didn't want to believe it, the doctor responsible for his family's hardscrabble life at the oil rig was proving to be a scoundrel. As the Petersens grew poorer, the doctor seemed to grow more prosperous, visiting the derrick in a new auto and wearing fine new clothes. It's entirely possible he knew of other wildcat failures in Harney County and had targeted Paul as someone new to the region who wouldn't have heard about them. Soon it was clear the man had sold more shares in the derrick than it was worth, and it wasn't long before Paul learned the doctor had pocketed the money and disappeared. To add to Paul's mounting woes, the derrick was vandalized one night, its drill cords cut, irreparably crippling the operation.

The daily battle to get the children to school was becoming insupportable anyway, and the family prepared for relocation once more. By then, in about 1940, Polly had married Chuck Clark, a West Virginian who had come to Burns with the Civilian Conservation Corps and he was later hired to build the Harney County Courthouse. He might have met Polly when he camped near the derrick with the rest of the Corps. In the evenings, Paul Junior recalls, Chuck brought his accordion over to entertain the Petersens. When the courthouse was finished in 1942, Chuck stayed on in Burns, hiring on with the Oregon & Northwestern Railroad. The railroad had been completed in 1929 as a private carrier of Ochoco Mountains timber for the Edward Hines Lumber Company, Burns's largest employer, located a few miles southwest of town. As newlyweds, Chuck and Polly moved into a little house off of Burns's Riverside Drive. When the Petersens moved into town, they rented the basement of the larger house next door. With no children of her own, Polly played an important part in raising her younger siblings.

Paul took a job grading roads with the county, and later worked for the city water department. The vision of striking it rich kept a hold on him. No matter what job he was working in town, he continued to visit the derrick whenever he could, pulling up the odd bucket in search of oil, just enough to keep him tethered to the dream. Apparently, moving his family back to the green Willamette Valley, where there was more opportunity and a friendlier environment, never struck him as a viable option. "I think what happened was

Left, Norma and her brother Paul with their dog Sweet Pea near Lawen, Oregon, circa 1938. Family archives. *Right,* Norma riding the family horse with her brother Paul near Lawen, Oregon, circa 1938. Norma Paulus Papers, Willamette University Archives and Special Collections.

my father just kind of gave up on moving us again," Norma said. "I know he was a very smart man, but he still went out to the derrick all the time, bringing up buckets full of oil and sure they were going to hit it big any time."[14]

In addition to his road job, Paul made a little money on the side drilling water wells, and Harold contributed to the family earnings by setting pins at the bowling alley. While living in town made it easier for the younger kids to go to school, the family still had nothing in the way of material comforts or disposable income. The basement space they all inhabited cost $35 a month. The family car was a beat-up pickup with exposed springs in the seat. Paul Junior recalls wearing hand-me-down shoes with cardboard fitted into the soles to improve the fit and impede the elements.[15]

Like many Americans suffering during the Depression, Norma's parents revered President Franklin D. Roosevelt and believed his New Deal would save the country. When Harold brought home a console radio purchased with his pinsetter wages, Norma and her dad listened as intently to FDR as they did their other favorites: Jack Benny and Rochester, Fibber McGee and Molly, the Lone Ranger, and the Green Hornet.

The radio became a true family essential when Pearl Harbor was attacked by the Japanese on December 7, 1941. Since it was Sunday, the Petersens were at home. Norma was eight years old, and from her perspective it was the worst thing that had ever happened. The eldest boys were already gearing up for the coming conflict, while Paul, haunted by his stint in World War I trenches, tried to contain his worry that the boys would end up in similarly heavy combat. On the day of the Pearl Harbor bombing, he told Harold and Gale they were to go to Boise the next day to enlist in the navy, where he believed they would at least have a clean bed and decent meals. Within the month, Harold was in training to become a radio technician for the navy, and Gale had begun training as an electrician. The boys left in short order, after trying to work out a code with their dad in order to communicate their whereabouts by mail, but the rigors of censorship undermined their effort. The boys were assigned to different ships, an aircraft carrier and a transport ship (LST). After the war, when they came home for good, the brothers figured out that their ships had been moored side by side in the Philippines.[16]

Burns weathered the war years like most small towns in the country: its citizens patriotically bought war bonds, hoarded ration stamps, collected rubber and tin, and recycled everything. Norma's Girl Scout troop filled a boxcar with paper. People gossiped about who might be buying what on the black market. Schools held air-raid drills; air-raid wardens marshaled the townspeople on safety and awareness. The Petersens hung a flag with two stars in their window to let the world know their family had sent two boys to war. Ella sent fruitcakes off to her sons for Christmas. One of the cakes came back to her a few years later, flat as a pancake. At night the Petersens gathered at the radio to hear President Roosevelt and Winston Churchill broadcasting messages of encouragement and inspiration. They listened to Walter Winchell's messages, sent out, as he began each one, to "Mr. and Mrs. America and all the ships at sea." Like so many who lived through those years, Norma carried the vivid memory of those voices with her throughout her life.[17]

The war was ever-present even in the barren landscape surrounding the town. The army sent soldiers to the Harney County desert to train them to fight in northern Africa. Pup tents popped up everywhere, along with a United Service Organization center hastily arranged by the women of Burns for the soldiers' leisure hours. The presence of so many young strangers filled the quiet air with novelty and excitement, and provided much grist for the rumor mill when Burns's girls began keeping company with the eager young men. Many mothers kept their daughters safely indoors with strict instructions not to speak to the boys in uniform.[18]

Harold and Gale came through the war relatively unscathed. Ella said she had a sixth sense about things, and while the boys were off fighting, she often assured her worried husband that they were all right, because if anything had gone wrong, she would just know.[19] But much had changed while the boys were gone. A fourth son, Richard, had been born in 1942, and the family had moved out of the basement into rooms on the top floor of the big old house. Their little sister and brother had grown from young children into adolescents, and, in Norma's case at least, big things were happening. Pearl Harbor had been the catalyst for change in her life, lifting her eyes to higher horizons the moment her brothers left for the Pacific Theater.[20] The war opened a new door onto the world for her, and she stepped through it, immersing herself in all that learning had to offer.

LOVE OF LEARNING

The Petersen children made up a passel of Nordic-looking towheads, immediately recognizable to anyone in Burns. Anywhere they went they would likely hear, "You're one of the Petersens."[21] From early on Norma stood out, a bright, curious chatterbox. Before she started school, the only books in the house were some old ones on the subject of geology, from which she taught herself the rudiments of reading.[22] When she entered first grade, Norma discovered the first and perhaps most important of her many gifts: an insatiable love of learning.

It wasn't until a few years later, when she noticed her parents sharing an exasperated smile at her expense, that Norma realized something about herself: "I talked a lot, and I asked a lot of questions." Her first teacher, Ruth Shaw, had noticed it immediately. In second grade, Norma, with her lunch bucket, was pulled out of her classroom and promoted to third grade, without a word of explanation to her or her parents. Norma learned later that her teacher finally became fed up with the way Norma's hand shot up with every question posed to the class. "I just loved school, and I was driving her crazy," Norma said. "She didn't know what else to do with me."[23]

Once she figured out she was being advanced and not demoted, Norma, though smaller and younger than her classmates, flourished at her new grade level. By middle school, her teacher and the principal, Henry Slater, escorted her to the school library, gave her a list of book titles, and told her to sit down and read. The first title was Richard Blackmore's 1869 historical romance, *Lorna Doone*, followed by a score of other classics of the eighteenth and nineteenth centuries, books that would not be assigned to her fellow students until much later in their high school years. Norma worked through the list, discussing the books with Mr. Slater as she finished them. Each list was followed by another, with Norma's independent study occupying most of her school day, even to the exclusion of other classes. She didn't find the regimen strange or unusual, although she was grateful to be singled out for this wonderful gift of reading to her heart's content. Soon she began helping out in the library as well, shelving books and minding the circulation desk.[24]

Left, Norma (on far right) with other girls in flag uniforms with batons, Burns, Oregon, early 1940s. Norma Paulus Papers, Willamette University Archives and Special Collections. *Right,* Majorette and high school senior Norma Petersen, photographed in the Hecht Studio, Burns, Oregon, 1950. Norma Paulus Papers, Willamette University Archives and Special Collections.

By the second semester of eighth grade, Mr. Slater approached Norma and another advanced student, Helen O'Connell, and asked them to work afternoons in the school office, in a kind of makeshift school-to-work program. Norma engaged this assignment with relish, discovering an innate enthusiasm for organization. Her new task provided an opportunity Mr. Slater had probably not foreseen when she and Helen came across their own well-above-average IQ scores in the filing cabinets.[25]

Norma loved her teachers and felt their encouragement, and she kept in touch with some of them throughout her life. "Ruth Shaw was living in the Willamette Lutheran Home in Salem when I ran for secretary of state in 1976," she recalled much later. "She organized the whole place for me, and Henry Slater volunteered to be my campaign chairman in Harney County. I saw my fifth-grade teacher, Austa Carlon, off and on, most of her life and was very good friends with her daughters."[26]

Norma twirled a baton for half-time entertainment at basketball games, all decked out in a patriotic red-white-and-blue costume that her sister Polly sewed for her.[27] Norma's skills with the baton stayed with her, inspiring enthusiastic reactions from crowds gathered at campaign events when Norma ran for the legislature. At age fifty, Norma twirled her baton at a fund-raising event to pay off the campaign debt from her run for secretary of state.

When Norma entered high school in 1947, it opened up new vistas for both academic and extracurricular enjoyments. "I was young for high school, undernourished and scrawny," she said, "but I had five Phi Beta Kappa key holders as teachers. Some of the members of the school board were very well educated themselves, and they wanted the best education for the students of Harney County—despite having to pay more to get such excellent teachers in this rural area."[28] She was involved in everything.[29] She was editor of the school newspaper, a member of the gymnastics team, and the pep team's drum majorette, garbed in what passed for Scottish Highlands apparel in eastern Oregon. She became yearbook editor and the senior class president. She performed in school plays, planned school dances, and twirled her baton along with cheerleaders for all four high school years. The only school activity out of her reach was music. The Petersens had no money for instruments or lessons, and certainly had no piano in their parlor.[30]

By then the family was complete. Although Harold, Polly, and Gale were out on their own, Norma and Paul Junior were still at home with the youngest Petersens, Richard and Gerri, born in 1942 and 1946. The family's poverty bothered Norma more as she grew into adolescence. She was embarrassed by the houses they lived in and didn't want her friends to come for visits. The house they moved to when they left the oil derrick was old and rundown. The crowded basement they all occupied consisted of two tiny bedrooms and an enclosed porch where her older brothers slept. When they moved into the upper level, there was more room: three bedrooms and one bath upstairs, a room for Paul and Ella, one other room, and a kitchen,[31] but from the outside it was still just a ramshackle house. When Norma began dating, she arranged for her young men to meet her at Polly's house.

The last dilapidated house the Petersens occupied in Burns was a great source of worry for Ella. It had a woodstove at first and then an oil stove, which was "such a tinderbox she was always afraid we'd burn up." Norma recalled many nights when Ella sat up, keeping vigil while her family slept. A few years later, after the family had moved out, the house did burn, killing two children who were asleep in Norma's old bedroom.[32] Ella's sixth sense proved uncannily correct once more.

Yet the Petersens' poverty did nothing to hold Norma back socially. She recalled that the young people, poor and less poor alike—there were no truly rich Burns citizens—socialized together without a trace of snobbery.

We really had a great group. There was the Burns group and then there were the really fine young people connected to the ranches. A lot of young men worked at the mill. But young and old would go to the Poison Creek Grange Hall on Saturday night. And the band, which often consisted of a banjo player, somebody playing the piano and a fiddler, was up on the stage, and people put their whiskey bottles on the stage so when they danced around they could stop and take a swig, or go out in the pickups and take a drink. Now, I went out during intermission and when the bottle was passed you didn't say no. You might put your tongue in it but you didn't say no. It was a matter of hospitality and sharing. Everybody drank out of the same bottle and then you'd go back and dance. Also people brought their babies, and the little boys had the white shirts on and blue jeans just like their parents. If a 5-year-old boy came over and asked you to dance, you'd dance. If you didn't it was an insult to the family. That's how kids grew up there.[33]

Norma's daughter, Liz Paulus, confirms that Norma would have perceived her Burns milieu as devoid of snobbery, with her characteristic assumption that everyone was as outgoing and interested in people as she was. Her mother, Liz says, "does things because she doesn't know they can't be done. She didn't know any different—to her there was no social distinction."

Bob Smith was a member of Norma's social circle, the best friend of her first fiancé, Orville "Corky" Corbett. Smith would go on to serve in both the Oregon and US House of Representatives, and would be a key mentor for Norma during her first term in the House. Both boys were a few years older than Norma. Although she and Smith weren't close friends then—she recalls him as just a "tall, quiet kid"—Norma and her friends would go up to the Smiths' family cabin on Emigrant Creek to drink whiskey and shoot guns. Norma caught other glimpses of a world beyond Burns on jaunts with chums: to John Day and Prairie City for the scenery, to Boise with a girlfriend whose aunt lived there, to the Idaho penitentiary to visit a girlfriend's older brother.

When she was a sophomore in 1948, Wayne Morse came to Burns High School and spoke to the students at an assembly. A former University of Oregon law professor who became the law school's youngest dean at thirty-one, Morse had been elected to the US Senate in 1944 as a Republican. He became an Independent in 1952 before switching again, to the Democratic Party, in 1955. Norma listened intently as Morse spoke, with no inkling of how his career would influence and color her own. "I was absolutely mesmerized," she said.

I had never heard anyone like him. He talked about the Constitution and about rights. . . . I didn't know I had any rights. I knew I
had a lot of obligations, but nobody ever told me I had any rights. It
was my first real inkling of politics. When Morse died in 1974, I was
asked to be one of the people to stand in the State Capitol Rotunda
when his casket was lying in state. He was such a powerful figure.[34]

When Norma was seventeen and a high school senior, she and Corky
Corbett became engaged. This was what girls her age did then, especially if
they had not the intention or means to go to college. Corky was five years
older than she, and his family, which owned one of two Burns drugstores, were
among Burns's less-poor citizens. He had served briefly in the navy and was
attending Oregon State College in Corvallis. Norma went to Portland with
Corky's family to attend OSC football games, which were held in Portland at
that time. She and the Corbetts would stay the night at the Imperial Hotel on
Southwest Broadway downtown, a luxurious venue the likes of which she had
only read about in novels.

Although Norma was leading a more varied social life than ever before,
her schooling was still foremost in her mind, and her teachers were her most
important mentors and guides.

I had two years of Latin from Miss Nydegger. That would come in
handy in unexpected ways and sooner than anyone imagined. I loved
Latin and English. My math teacher, Mr. Roby, could do equations
with his right and left hands at the same time. I had a great drama
coach and performed in some of our school plays. Our speech
coach took us to Corvallis for competitions. We had the time of our
lives. We came over the Cascades and into the lush Willamette Valley. It was like another world from the high desert—quite a contrast
for kids from Burns where nothing grew but sagebrush. It was so
beautiful and green we wanted to get out and roll in it. We saw green
and yellow skunk cabbage in a bog along the road and we had to
have some of it. Our speech coach warned us it would smell, but we
would not let him continue until we picked an armful.[35]

A LIFE-CHANGING OPPORTUNITY

Early in her senior year, Norma received an opportunity that would change her life. Harney County district attorney Leland Duncan was about to lose his secretary, who was newly married and planned to move away with her husband. Duncan contacted the high school teachers who taught clerical skills and asked them to provide a list of capable girls who might be interested in an office job. Norma was the first and only candidate they suggested. She later believed the teachers were concerned that a lack of money would deny a girl so bright the chance to go to college. They helped her brush up on her typing and shorthand skills, and Norma was hired. She soon found herself going to school in the morning and reporting to work at the DA's office in the afternoon.

The job was an education in itself. In Harney County, the DA was allowed to conduct a private practice in addition to fulfilling his duties as county prosecutor. Duncan was retained on contract and estate work involving large ranches, which gave Norma a familiarity with matters of probate. Driven by her own curiosity and aptitude for independent research, Norma educated herself on property rights by studying deed records in the county clerk's office.

Her toil in high school Latin, used more frequently in legal proceedings back then, paid off nicely. She helped draft wills, she processed paperwork for Sheriff Eldon Sitz, the Burns-based Oregon State Police trooper, and she typed reports and warrants. Alan Biggs, a traveling circuit court judge from Ontario, often came to town without a court reporter, so Norma had a hands-on tutorial in that capacity. When federal district judge Alger Fee came to preside over cases, she helped him empanel juries. On rare occasions when a woman was incarcerated, Norma served as bailiff and took food to the inmate on weekends. She attended autopsies with the district attorney to take notes. One autopsy was of a young man who had died under suspicious circumstances. Another was of a middle-aged woman Norma knew who had been battered to death by her husband.

Back at school, she had been elected class president, an honor that obligated her to plan the Senior Skip Day. While previous senior classes had gone to Suttle Lake in the Cascades near Sisters, Norma and her committee decided it was time for them to see the ocean for the first time. They were able to convince three or four teachers to chaperone a trip to the Taft Hotel in Lincoln City.

Norma graduated from high school at seventeen with a 3.9 grade-point average, a record that won her several college scholarship offers. That path was not for her, however: her parents had no money to cover any expenses, no matter how small, beyond what she was awarded.[36] Instead, Norma went to work full-time for the district attorney, earning $220 a month—no small sum in 1950. As a good credit risk, Norma was able to borrow money for a used Ford. Her father taught her to put a small sum away from every paycheck, and then when she had enough, to buy a savings bond she could cash in later.

In 1952, at nineteen, Norma was a full-fledged working and taxpaying member of the Burns community. There, the economy was driven, as in many Oregon towns, by the post–World War II housing boom. Logging, railroading, and ranching were the prevalent means of making a living. Though the town was small, with a population of about three thousand, it contained several successful enterprises, including a post office, two jewelry stores, lots of restaurants and saloons, a variety store, women's and men's clothing stores, grocery stores, and one hotel, the Arrowhead.

Many Burns residents of European descent could trace their roots back to the Oregon Trail. Burns was also the home of many Basques as well as the Paiute Indian tribe. The Paiutes had inhabited the area surrounding Burns, including Malheur Lake eighteen miles to the southeast, for thousands of years. Ancestors of the Basques had come to southeastern Oregon in the late 1800s, finding the climate of Harney County excellent for raising sheep. Norma's closest girlfriend, Rosie Garatea, was of Basque ancestry; her mother ran a small hotel for retired Basque shepherds.

Norma frequently encountered Harney County lawyer Tony Yturri in court. Yturri was one of the first Basques to graduate from an American law school; he went on to be the first Basque elected to the Oregon legislature. He would become a valuable friend to Norma during her own legislative years. They became reacquainted during her freshman term in the House, when she was appointed to a high-profile statewide commission Yturri chaired that was charged with modernizing Oregon's criminal laws.[37]

Paul Petersen lived to see his bright daughter's growing independence before he died suddenly of a massive coronary on April 30, 1951. Norma was not at home—between work and her active social life, she seldom was—and Paul Junior was by then logging for Edward Hines Lumber Company up north in Seneca. Paul and Ella were still raising their youngest children, Richard, nine, and Gerri, four. Paul came home from work that day complaining to Ella of feeling ill. Paul Junior believes he went upstairs to dose himself with Epsom salts, as was his practice. Tragically, Gerri found her dad in the bathroom, gasping for breath, and ran for Ella. Paul died quickly, before help could arrive.

POLIO

In the late summer of 1952, Norma became Harney County's twenty-seventh victim of the nation's worst polio outbreak in history.[38] Since the late 1800s, periodic polio outbreaks had spread throughout the country, mostly during the summer months. There was no vaccine in those days, and, like most Americans, people in Burns believed the virus was being transmitted through water—in this case a swimming pool, fed by the mill pond at Hines Lumber, that was frequented by young and old. (The highly contagious virus is usually transmitted through contact with unchlorinated water that is contaminated with the feces of an infected person.[39]) Severe outbreaks during the 1940s and 1950s sparked a massive public-health effort that resulted in the development of the first effective polio vaccine in 1955.

In the fall of 1952, Norma's usually robust and athletic body began to fail her.

> I first noticed I had a problem during this period in late September when I walked to the post office to pick up the daily mail for the office. I noticed that when I would step up on the curb it would take me two or three attempts to land my foot on the sidewalk. I didn't think much about it. . . . The doctor gave me some sort of relaxant because he thought my heart was beating too fast. I took that medicine and wandered through my work day for a couple of weeks.

One weekend Norma rode with her fiancé and his mother to their cabin in the Ochoco Mountains. Norma sat between Corky and Mrs. Corbett, "and I remember answering questions from them and turning my head from one to the other, and it was like pulling a spoon through thick dough." Later that week she was sitting in the grandstand at the Harney County Fair rodeo with some girlfriends, watching the calf-roping event, and she had to lie down on the bleachers.

> I went home and then to work the next day, but by the middle of the afternoon I didn't feel well, so I told Mr. Duncan I had to go home. On my way, it became difficult to walk because my chest muscles and my legs were hurting. I told my mother I was sick and went upstairs. I got this intense headache. It was so intense I thought, "I must call Mom. I must call Mom and tell her about this." But the

headache was so bad I couldn't. I don't know how many hours I lay there like that, but it was a long, long time.[40]

The next morning Norma fell down in the kitchen. Ella called the hospital. A doctor came to the house and started trying to move Norma's limbs, pushing against her stiff muscles. He recommended that Norma be tested for polio. "My sister took me to the small hospital in Burns to do the tests," Norma said. The nurse on duty was Ruby Hershey, who was also Norma's baton-twirling teacher. Hershey said, "Oh, Norma, not you, too!"

"They did a spinal tap," Norma said, "which was almost as bad as the disease, and they came back and said, 'Yes, you have polio, and you are going to have to go to Portland because the Boise hospital is full." She asked the family's doctor, Clifford Weare, "Is this going to be a bad case or a light case?" He replied, "Norma Jean, I'm just positive this is going to be a light case."[41]

Norma was heartened by Dr. Weare's confidence. Because the town's sole ambulance (which was also its hearse) was transporting another polio patient, Corky's mother offered to drive Norma to the hospital in Portland. Mrs. Corbett had the backseat removed from her big Chrysler and replaced with a makeshift cot. Then she collected Norma and her sister Polly, and the three of them drove to the Holladay Park Hospital in northeast Portland. At that time the hospital was dedicated to mental-health patients and drug addicts, but because the city's hospitals were overcrowded with polio cases, Holladay Park's second floor had been converted to a polio ward. Norma was assigned a room facing west. From her window she could watch, fascinated, as the drawspan on the Steel Bridge went up and down.

At first she was kept in isolation. A nurse came in every few minutes and asked her to wiggle her toes, which she could do, but she could barely move her hands and arms. Although she wasn't paralyzed, she couldn't hold up a magazine or brush her teeth while lying flat. After a short while she was moved to a big, airy room with a woman in her thirties who had a family at home. This patient was in a rocking bed that could raise her up vertically and bring her down flat, designed to maintain her breathing. There was another woman in the room in her early twenties whose legs were paralyzed. Norma would stick her good legs out of the bed, and this roommate, with her good arms, would grab Norma's feet and pull their beds together so they could play cards.

Norma kept her spirits up through her ordeal by focusing on Dr. Weare's encouraging diagnosis. She was convinced—perhaps channeling her mother's sixth sense—that she wasn't going to be permanently paralyzed. She was soon assigned to a good physical therapist who taught her exercises, which she performed faithfully in the hospital, as an outpatient, and after she went home. When she was discharged from the hospital, Norma stayed with a cousin of Ella's she didn't know she had; Cousin Tootie took care of Norma in her home and drove her to her outpatient therapy. For one exercise, she sat in a chair with old newspapers on either side of her. One after the other, she took the pages in her hands and crumpled them as tightly as she could. She focused every ounce of energy on regaining her strength.

Within a few weeks of starting her outpatient therapy, Norma was back at work. She could walk, but she could not climb stairs because her spine had become crooked. So she would sit down at the bottom of a set of steps and move up one step at a time on her backside—a daily ritual that caused a mild stir across town.[42] Norma didn't have to wear a brace, but for two years she slept on a board covered with a folded flannel sheet instead of a mattress. She did her exercises every morning and night without fail. Her spine gradually straightened, and Norma was cured—living proof, she is convinced, of Dr. Weare's prophecy and her own confidence.

Norma's illness gave her time to do some spiritual soul-searching. The Petersens were nominally Lutheran, and as Norma often noted, their portrait of Jesus on the parlor wall shared equal prominence with one of President Franklin D. Roosevelt. Church was not a dominant part of their family life; neither Norma nor her family attended more than casually. During her long recovery from polio, however, and at her friend Rosie's behest, Norma decided to convert to Catholicism. The decision wasn't cataclysmic to her life, then or later, as her children attest, although she chose to be married in the church and to baptize her children as Catholics. But, at nineteen, on her own and debilitated by polio, the choice may have proved helpful as she focused on her struggle to regain her strength.

WIDER HORIZONS

Soon after she returned to work, Norma's boss, Leland Duncan, died of a brain tumor. His replacement, appointed by the governor, was Portland lawyer James M. Burns. His new job required Burns to exchange city life for what might have seemed a tedious rural existence. Years later, introducing Norma at a state bar convention, he would tell the story of his first glimpse of her. "On his first day on the job," Norma recalled, "he opened the office door, and the first thing he saw, he said, was me sitting at a desk, reading a *New Yorker* magazine and smoking a Parliament cigarette. He said he decided then that living in Burns might not be so bad after all."[43]

Duncan's estate proved complicated to settle; it could not be accomplished until his private practice's probate cases in Harney County were closed. Duncan's family hired Brian Goodenough, a Salem lawyer, to come to Burns and finish the probate. After witnessing Norma's probate expertise, he asked her if he could put her on the estate's payroll to help him, paying her a small salary; her boss agreed to the arrangement. The moonlighting required a monthly visit to Salem, with financial data from the county assessor's office to be reported to the Oregon Tax Commission so estate taxes could be calculated. It was on one of these visits that Goodenough remarked on what a smart thing it would be for Norma to leave her hometown and move to Salem. He promised he could find her a good job there.

Norma was already thinking about leaving. She was no longer engaged— her fiancé had broken it off, prompted, Norma suspected, by the qualms of his mother. Mrs. Corbett wanted a cultured, accomplished wife for her son, Norma said, and may have thought a hometown girl with a high school education would never measure up. After she got over being dumped, she went out with a few other young men, but soon realized that none of them were suitable marriage material. Her father was dead, she had survived polio, and Burns was starting to feel like a very small pond.

Norma had discussed the subject more than once with her friend Rosie Garatea. The two girls had shared most of the adventures of their young adult lives. When they were eighteen, they had flown to California with another high school friend, Patsy Weiss, to visit Patsy's aunt. Like many people in Burns, Norma and her friends carried silver dollars and tipped the cab drivers with them, a custom the San Francisco cabbies found outlandish.[44]

By the time Goodenough made his offer, Norma felt she was ready to leave Burns behind, and Rosie agreed to join her. First Norma considered a job offer from Tony Yturri, who'd asked her to come to Ontario, a small town on the Oregon-Idaho border, and work for him. "But I had this strong feeling my destiny would be in Salem," she said. "So I loaded my possessions in my old Ford, said a round of farewells to my friends, and moved to Salem."[45]

WEB OF CONNECTIONS

Norma began her life in Salem as the guest of the Goodenoughs, who lived in a lovely Victorian house on Court Street. When Rosie was ready to make her move, Norma rented an upstairs apartment for the two of them in a house

Goodenough owned on Winter Street. Rosie was an experienced bookkeeper and found work immediately at Master Service Station.[46]

After weighing a couple of job offers, Norma went to work for two lawyers, Eugene Laird and Peery Buren, who shared an office in the Pioneer Trust Building downtown. Brian Goodenough's office was also in that building, as were the offices of other prominent Salem firms, including those of the Rhoten family and the Carson family. Norma began to be aware of the web of connections among Salem's political and business elite. Peery Buren's sister, Maxine Buren, was a reporter for the *Oregon Statesman*, published in Salem, and his brother was the doctor for the prominent Paulus family. The name meant nothing to Norma then, but she learned that the Pauluses owned a fruit-packing business and were leading Salem citizens. Nearby buildings housed the firms of Otto Skopil, who later became a federal judge, and Bruce Williams, a well-known trial lawyer. "The Salem bar had a large number of quite extraordinary people," she said. "Talented, quality people, who were very impressive to a dirt-poor girl from Burns."[47]

A couple of years after Norma took her job with Laird and Buren, Goodenough came to see her with another idea. The chief justice of the Oregon Supreme Court, Earl C. Latourette, was losing his secretary—the woman who had filled the role for a long time was retiring. Here was a rare opportunity, Goodenough told Norma, and she ought to apply for the job. The supreme court was a great place for a legal secretary to work; summers were mostly off, unless the judge called you in for a little filing, and there were other perks so wonderful that the secretaries tended to stay on the job until they retired.

Norma said she was tempted but uncertain of her qualifications. Goodenough assured her she was well qualified. The only question was, would they hire a twenty-three-year-old secretary? She would be far younger than the others in the pool. Goodenough promised a glowing recommendation and Norma agreed to apply, carefully keeping it a secret for fear of losing her current position. She prepared for her interview with exquisite care.

> I stayed up late with some girlfriends getting just the right outfit. I still remember exactly what I wore: It was a navy blue linen dress that buttoned down the front. It was quite fitted with long sleeves and a white brocade collar. I wore a white hat with navy trim and white gloves. I walked into Judge Latourette's large office timidly.
>
> "Come in here, little lady," he said. So I walked in and sat down very primly.

"Now, you're, uh, Miss uh, let's see, Miss Petersen and you want a job," he said.

"No sir," I said. "I don't want a job. I have a job. I want this job."

"You look awfully young to me," he said. "How old are you?" I told him I was 23. "Well," he said, "you just look too young."

"Youth is generally considered to be an asset, sir," I replied. I had rehearsed that with my girlfriends the night before.[48]

Latourette asked Norma to tell him about herself. She told him about working for the Harney County district attorneys, Duncan and Burns, and she included the part about taking notes at the autopsies. This seemed to impress the judge. Then he asked her about her family, and especially about her father, and why he had moved the family to Burns all those years ago. "After we talked for some time, he sat quietly for a few minutes. Then he looked at me and said, 'Go downstairs and tell Fred Sercombe, the clerk, that you're going to come to work. I'll see you in August.'"[49] Norma couldn't believe her luck. She had landed a privileged, secure, and prestigious job with the Oregon Supreme Court's chief judge, and it paid $400 a month!

She soon grew to love her new position. Her days were filled with diverse, extraordinary experiences. She performed the regular duties of an ordinary secretary, typing and taking shorthand, revising documents sent down by the justices, and keeping track of case assignments. Beyond these, she found herself on a new and fascinating educational path. She conducted research in the supreme court library to draft and revise her boss's opinions, which required citing and quoting other cases. She sat in on many oral arguments. Because the law library was heavily used by Portland and Willamette Valley law firms who had no such resource of their own in those pre-Internet days, Norma came to know many law students, clerks, and lawyers. She knew she was living in rarified air, far above the scrub and sage of her home turf.

Life for the judges was "very isolated, a true ivory-tower existence," said Norma.[50] Judicial ethics prevented them from fraternizing with members of the bar, particularly those who had cases before them.

So the top floor of the Supreme Court building was a very quiet place. The offices were very large—large windows, tall ceilings, 15-foot French doors. There were seven judges and seven secretaries. Every judge had a clerk, but the clerks were housed on another floor of the building. So on the whole top floor there were just 14 people and oftentimes they weren't all there at the same time. It could be quite lonely. I think that may have been hard on new judges who were used to being with a lot of lawyers, in and out of court and bantering back and forth and having coffee with other people. There wasn't much of that.[51]

The job was not all work. Justice Latourette had the habit of inviting his fellow judges in for a drink at the end of the workday. He also performed frequent marriages in his office, offering a drink to all attendees afterward so they could toast the bride and groom.[52] For these reasons he kept a personal bar and needed to replenish it from time to time. His clerk, a young Mormon man, wouldn't touch liquor or buy it for someone else. So Latourette opened his billfold and sent Norma to the liquor store with enough money for an assortment of spirits.

Norma grew to suspect that her new boss had been a bit of a rake in his younger days. When he hired her he was divorced from his first wife and married to a beautiful, blonde, much-younger woman. But Norma never felt an inkling of anything that could be construed by present-day standards as sexual harassment, even though the judge told her later that he had hired her because she had good-looking legs. He was always kind to her, and she repaid him with her greatest respect and affection.[53]

After about a year with Justice Latourette, Norma was asked to come to his office after work for a word with him and a colleague she knew and liked, Justice Hall S. Lusk. Norma had some time to stew over the judge's summons. Had she made some terrible mistake? Was she about to lose her job? When she entered Latourette's office at the end of the day, Norma became even more alarmed by the serious expressions on the men's faces. Quietly hiding her anxiety, she listened as they told her why they'd asked her to come. They believed she needed to attend law school, and they knew a way she could make it happen. She let out her breath and sat up straighter.

There was a law on the books, Justice Latourette explained, that enabled veterans of World War II and the Korean War whose education had been interrupted to challenge a college curriculum with testing, preparatory to getting into a professional school. Latourette had studied the statute and concluded that it also could be applied to someone in Norma's situation, because it didn't require that the person be a military veteran.[54] More important, it meant that she could be admitted to law school without an undergraduate degree.

Such a flood of relief and joy! Norma had long dreamed of going to college, particularly since moving to Salem and finding a place in that new and very elite world. Moving in a larger pool of intelligent, high-powered people, she had learned some things about herself. She knew she was smart, no question about that, and probably better-read than the average college graduate. But credentials mattered in this new world, and she lacked the basic credential of a college degree. What was more, she knew her Nordic good looks along with her lack of formal education pegged her in some people's minds as the stereotypical dumb blonde. She'd learned to forestall such prejudice by conducting herself in a more reserved manner, aiming to appear anything but frivolous. The pose ended up making her feel uncomfortable and not at all like herself—an odd feeling for the popular, outgoing Norma Petersen from Burns.

Norma had stewed over all this for so long that when the judges put forward the idea of law school, she recognized it immediately as a glimmer of new hope. To attend college as an undergraduate, she would have had to quit her job and work part-time or at night. Now there was a new avenue to consider. Anyone could go to college, she thought, but not everyone could go to law school. Not only was she fascinated by the law, she was becoming well-versed in the procedural aspects of it. Best of all, Willamette University's law school was right across the street from the Oregon Supreme Court.[55]

How could she turn such an opportunity down? She decided to go for it. Unfortunately, Justice Latourette did not live to see the change he set in motion for his secretary's life; he died suddenly in 1955, after she had worked for him little more than a year.[56] Norma was to feel his loss keenly for many years, but she trained her focus unerringly on the prize he had set before her. She traveled to Portland for two days of examinations and passed them easily. When she walked into the office of Dean Seward P. Reese, flush with her success on the challenge exam and newly confident about her extraordinary plan, the dean was less than enthusiastic. He told her that, in fact, she could not be enrolled as a special student unless she was at least twenty-four years old. Norma was twenty-three.

On her twenty-fourth birthday, March 13, 1957, Norma went back to see Dean Reese. He agreed to admit her, but only for one semester, and only for two classes. It would be a probation, he said: if she earned As in both classes, she could come back. Norma had been an A student her whole life, and she quickly agreed to the terms.[57] She was in! Later she realized the dean had an ulterior motive:

> I didn't know it was just a way to get rid of me. I later learned Dean
> Reese was not interested in having a woman in his law school and
> certainly not a woman who had not been to college. Well, not

knowing any better, I certainly would not have challenged Dean Reese. Back in those days nobody talked about rights. You just talked about your responsibilities, and it never occurred to me to challenge the rule on the grounds of discrimination or unfairness.[58]

THE SOCIAL SIDE OF SALEM

Norma and Rosie lived in their Winter Street apartment for a year before Rosie decided to marry her young man and move back to Burns. Norma found a new place with a divorcee who had a new house out in the northeast part of town. But it was a bit of a drive, so she relocated to an apartment on Chemeketa Street with new friends, including Gloria Sanders, Gloria's sister Doris, and Sharon Brown, whose family owned Keith Brown Lumber Company.[59] When the time came to pay her tuition, however, Norma had no choice but to sell whatever she had of value. Tuition for special students was especially high. Norma cashed in the savings bonds her father had advised her to buy when she first went to work. Her only other possession of value was her blue Ford. She sold it without regret and paid her tuition, but she realized she needed to move closer to work and school.

She rented a cheap room close to campus. Her landlady was elderly, and peculiar. Norma came home one day to find most of her wardrobe piled on the front doorstep. The landlady, unrepentant, explained she had too much clothing for a young girl, and she, the landlady, had decided to donate the excess to the Salvation Army. The last straw was when Norma woke from a sound sleep in the dead of night to find the woman leaning over her. Norma knew she had to get out of there.[60]

One of her classmates was Al Laue, a veteran whose wife, Sheila, was a devout Catholic and an amateur actress who had campaigned unsuccessfully for the legislature as a Democratic candidate in 1956. Her voters' pamphlet portrait shows a woman of glamour with a serious demeanor, adorned with pearls, large-framed glasses, and a knowing smile. Al and Sheila Laue were parents to seven children and had recently moved into a rambling old mansion downtown near both the capitol and the law school. Needing help with their mortgage, the Laues invited Norma to move in with them. They had another tenant, Billy Smith, who worked in the highway department's paint section. His willingness and skill in dealing with the Laue children earned him the nickname of Uncle Billy.

The Laues were among the founders of the Pentacle Theatre. The Pentacle, which opened in a West Salem barn in 1954, was the first theater-in-the-round in

Oregon. Sheila starred in Pentacle's productions, and also was the grande dame of large, noisy, epically long parties every weekend at the Laue mansion. The Laues introduced Norma to a life more glamorous than she had ever known.

> Coming from Burns, thrown into this untidy but sophisticated, stimulating environment was a wonder to me, a whole new world. I was living in the midst of all this—the law clerks and students, the Pentacle Theater, the law firms, the Drama Department at Willamette—it was so extraordinary. There I was, fighting with these smart, educated, worldly people over the Sunday *New York Times*—the theatre section, of course!—or the latest James Bond paperback. But they loved to hear me tell stories about Burns, and all the different characters out there. They were all bright, honorable people, fun people. Most of them didn't have much money. Many of the law clerks had come from schools out east specifically to see what kind of a place Oregon was, to have produced Wayne Morse, the UO law school dean and senator who spoke at my high school on that day that seemed to me like a lifetime ago.[61]

At twenty-four, slender, pretty, and fashionably turned out, Norma never lacked for suitors. Both at school and at work she was surrounded by young men who would have noticed her anywhere. As one of very few female law students, Norma attracted more attention from men than ever before. She wasn't too surprised then when, coming out of the law school library after studying on a Sunday afternoon, she saw a handsome, well-dressed young man lounging on the balustrade. He stood up and stuck out his hand. His name was Bill Paulus, and he was a law student, he told her. He had heard she was working at the supreme court while putting herself through law school, and he just wanted to welcome her, on behalf of his fellow students, to Willamette.

Norma may have suspected that Bill didn't just happen to be lounging there. He had noticed Norma a few weeks before, when she and her girlfriends had gone to the law school hangout, Dick Orey's Tavern, for a beer. Norma was attired in white slacks and a tight-fitting white sweater, and Bill spotted her from across the tavern as he shot pool. She noticed him too, casually, as she looked around the crowded room. Afterward, Bill's discreet inquiries yielded the information he needed to stage an encounter with the attractive new girl. Norma thought it was a nice welcoming gesture.[62]

Then Bill asked her out to see a movie, and Norma accepted. She was already dating a young law clerk, Nick Zumas, who, like Bill, was handsome and intelligent, but there was no understanding of a deeper commitment on either side. At the time of this first date, Norma was still staying with the landlady who had tried to give away her clothing. The landlady knew Bill's family—everybody in Salem knew the Pauluses—and so, when she opened the door to Bill and said, "Well, are you here to take Norma out or are you going to marry her?" it almost scared him away.[63]

> We decided not to go to a movie. We decided to go to the Oak Room in the old Marion Hotel. We were the only ones in there. Bill had just cashed his GI Bill check and we played Bobby Darin's "Mack the Knife" and danced to it until the bartender told us we had to stop. We might have had something to eat, but all I can remember was sitting around that jukebox, talking and dancing.[64]

Norma liked Bill very much, but she also liked Nick. She continued to see both of them openly, no strings on either side. When the time came for the law school's annual fall dance, Bill invited Norma to go with him, but he was too late—she had already promised to go with Nick, and she couldn't possibly renege on a date. Bill took the news equably. The dance was in full swing when Bill finally made his entrance with a well-built blonde woman on his arm. Her name was Miss Mickelbust, Norma recalled. Maybe Bill's striking companion was his attempt at one-upmanship, but to Norma's knowledge he never saw the woman again.

By then Norma and Sheila Laue had become fast friends and confidants who shared a Friday ritual: after Al and Uncle Billy came home, Norma and Sheila would leave the men in charge of the children and duck out across the alley to the Stagecoach Bar. They would have a drink and discuss the news and gossip from their converged social circles, the law school and the Pentacle crowd. On one such Friday night, Norma told Sheila she was feeling pressure to make a choice between Nick and Bill. Sheila agreed it was about time; people talked of little else, and it was getting a little embarrassing. One drink led to another, and then to a third. Norma vowed she would ask Bill to marry her. Sheila, for all her liberated ways, was shocked at this idea.

> Sheila tried to dissuade me. She favored Nick, but really she thought it was just awful that I was going to propose. I mean, how many

women do that? I demanded that she give me the keys to her car so I could drive to Bill's house. I walked up the stairs to his apartment, and I opened the door. He was sitting at his desk studying, and I just stood there. I said, "Bill Paulus, will you marry me?" He didn't say anything for a long time and I just stood there. Then he said, "Well, I'll have to think about it." So I turned on my heels, started crying, got back in the car, drove home and by this time Sheila was there with all the law clerks and students and Billy and Al. Sheila had rushed home to tell them what an idiotic thing I was about to do.[65]

Norma was inconsolable, certain she'd ruined her life, her relationship with Bill, and her reputation. She rushed past the revelers and up the stairs, flinging herself on the bed. Uncle Billy came up to try and comfort her, but all she could do was cry. Then she heard a crash from downstairs: it was the front door being flung open. She heard Bill Paulus's voice booming out: "When's the wedding?" Norma composed herself and came downstairs in a much better mood. That was Friday night, and some people were still there Sunday night.

As the party wound down, Bill and Norma were helping the Laues and Uncle Billy clean the kitchen when Bill revealed his dream to his fiancée. As newlyweds, he told her, they could go to Alaska, where Bill could provide free legal services to disadvantaged people, such as Alaskan natives. He made it sound like the most romantic adventure with which to start their new life. Norma was taken aback. "I don't remember what was in the papers at the time about the plight of the natives in Alaska, but I was just stunned," she said. "Alaska? That was the last place I wanted to go. 'Can't we just stay home,' I asked, 'and work with our own tribes?'"[66]

A WEDDING IN BURNS

Not long after Bill accepted her proposal, Norma began to understand the sort of family she was joining. Bill's parents had two homes; they lived mostly in San Jose but maintained their Salem house. After Bill told them the news and the engagement was announced, Norma came back to the Laues's one night to find Sheila in raptures. Jeryme English, the society editor at the *Oregon Statesman*, had telephoned to request an interview with Norma, or at least a comment. Norma had never heard of Jeryme English, and she couldn't fathom why a society editor was interested in her or the forthcoming wedding. Sheila had to explain that the Paulus family was well known in Salem as the founders and

Norma and Bill Paulus on their wedding day in Burns, Oregon, August 1958. Family archives.

owners of Paulus Brothers Packing, the largest independent canner of fruits and vegetables west of the Mississippi. A wedding in that family was bound to be a big social event.[67]

Bill graduated from law school in the spring of 1958. His father, William Paulus, and his five Paulus uncles all attended the graduation ceremony. The six of them invited Norma to lunch, without Bill. The men asked her about herself, about her plans for the wedding, and promised they would all attend. Although they were none too pleased to hear that the wedding was to take place in the Catholic church, as lunch was served and everyone began to relax, Robert, the eldest brother and the original founder of the cannery in 1924, told Norma they had all agreed that she bore an uncanny resemblance to their late mother, Elizabetha, who was herself a devout Catholic.

They told Norma the story of the deal their mother had made with their dad, who was not Catholic. Elizabetha had told her husband that he could raise his sons any way he wished, but as for her, she would raise their daughters in the church. Since no daughters were born, church had never been part of the Paulus family's traditions. Nevertheless, in this vetting of Norma by Bill's family, she had passed with honors.

Then it was Bill's turn to meet Norma's family and see where she grew up. Because he loved to golf, Norma thought he might enjoy meeting her old friend, Billie Batchelor, who worked in the clubhouse at the Valley Golf Club in Hines. Bill had been nursing a stomach ulcer, which he jokingly attributed

Photo of Norma announcing the Paulus–Petersen marriage on the society page of the *Statesman Journal*, 1958. Edris Morrison. Norma Paulus Papers, Willamette University Archives and Special Collections_Personal Clippings Scrapbook_003j.

to Norma, and had lost weight. When Norma introduced Bill to Billie as the man she intended to marry, Billie set up two glasses of whiskey on the bar, even though it was only 11:00 a.m. Bill took one look and told her he couldn't possibly drink the stuff because of his ulcer. Billie's eyes lit up, and she leaned forward. "All you do," she said confidentially, "is get some sheep's tallow, render it over a slow fire on the back of the stove. Then you drink it when it's warm and it just plugs all those holes."[68]

At the Burns Elks Club that night, Bill was the center of attention. Norma had warned him ahead of time, "Now, if somebody buys you a drink, you must drink it. If a woman asks you to dance—which is very likely—you must dance. I don't care what she looks like, who she is, or how drunk or how tall or how short she is, you have to dance with her. That's just the Code of the West over here." All night long, people came up to Bill and slapped him on the back and related stories about Norma and the Petersens. "She's poor," they told him, "but she comes from good stock."[69] Tales like these became a permanent part of Bill's répertoire.

Norma and Bill were married in Burns on August 16, 1958, in a Catholic ceremony conducted by Father Reedy, who, Norma loved to say, was the only priest granted a special papal dispensation to wear cowboy boots in the pulpit.[70] Norma booked all the rooms in Burns's best motel for their many out-of-town guests: friends from school, law clerks Norma knew from her job at the supreme court, the Pentacle crowd, and assorted other friends from Salem. Each of the Paulus uncles drove over the mountains from Salem in a large, luxurious automobile, and a friend of the family named Ellis von Eschen drove a pink Lincoln Continental. The people of Burns had never seen such an assemblage of fine autos. On the eve of the wedding, a steady stream of locals cruised by the motel parking lot in their humbler vehicles, just to take a look at those cars from west of the mountains.[71]

Al and Sheila had been put in charge of the flowers. In the spring they'd planted dozens of gladioli at Sheila's father's farm up the Santiam River canyon, planning to transport the flowers to Burns, where the climate was too harsh to grow them. Al and Bill packed the long showy stems in dampened boxes and drove them out to Burns before dawn on the wedding day. There was a near-disaster with the flowers, but everything turned out all right:

> The wedding reception was held at my sister's house. Her next-door neighbor was Mrs. Corbett, whose son Corky had jilted me years earlier because his mother never thought I would amount to anything because I couldn't afford to go to college. The Corbett's lawn and my sister's lawn were contiguous, no wall, no fence, no barrier except for one large brick outdoor fireplace between the two houses. Just after dawn, Al and Uncle Billy arranged all the glads in vases and put them on the outdoor fireplace and went out to breakfast. When they returned, they found Mrs. Corbett had turned on her lawn sprinklers to water her lawn, and, not incidentally, all the vases of flowers. Al and Uncle Billy rushed in and rescued the drowning flowers, which survived, but they were not as pert as they were when they arrived. But they still looked good on the white tablecloths when the reception began.[72]

After the reception, the newlyweds left for their honeymoon at Crater Lake and San Francisco. Norma's going-away ensemble included a chic cloche hat. The trunk of their car contained an ice chest and two bottles of Mumm's champagne that Bill's mother had been saving for them. About twenty miles out of town, Bill pulled over at a maintenance station for the highway department. Surrounded by huge piles of red gravel, Bill and Norma drank the

first bottle of Mumm's. They arrived at the Crater Lake Lodge at about nine
o'clock that night.

STUDENT AND HOMEMAKER

Bill and Norma settled in Salem, and Bill worked at establishing a law practice
with his longtime friend Dan Callaghan. Norma returned to her job and her
studies. Law school was a slow slog for her, because initially she could take
only those classes that were offered in the morning before she reported to
work. When she ran out of morning classes, she asked her boss (who by that
time was Justice William McAllister, Latourette's successor) if she could adjust
her lunch hour from 11:00 to 12:00 in order to take eleven o'clock classes. The
judge approved, and by the time Norma had finished all the classes in that time
slot, it was 1960, and she was pregnant with her first child.

For their third wedding anniversary in August 1961, with baby Elizabeth
just a few months old, Bill planned a celebration that they really could not
afford: dinner at the Benson Hotel in downtown Portland. When they were
settled at their table at the high-toned London Grill restaurant, Bill told Norma
he had a surprise. He had borrowed enough money from one of his uncles to
allow her to quit her job and finish school as a full-time student. Norma was
ecstatic, and relieved that her goal was finally in sight.[73] "It was the most exciting moment of my life," she later said, "and nothing that has happened before
or since can even come close to it." [74] She quit her job and focused on school
and motherhood. In her last year of classes, she took fifteen hours, the allowed
maximum, during the first semester. In the second semester she petitioned to
take twenty hours, and her request was granted.

Norma's full-steam-ahead approach to completing her degree hit one
speed bump when the time came for her to participate in the annual Moot
Court Competition, in which senior law students show their mettle in mock
trials. The competition was to take place in the afternoon, and because she
didn't have a sitter for Elizabeth, who was a few months old at the time,
Norma asked to be excused. Her professor insisted that all students had to
make their oral arguments for the moot court, even if, like Norma, they had
A grades in the course and knew their cases inside and out. All right, she said.
If that was the rule, she'd find a way to do it. Then, as she turned to leave, the
professor flung an offhanded remark at her departing back: it wasn't as if she
was likely to win, anyway. "And that made me so mad," she said. "I can close
my eyes . . . there's two times in my life that I got so mad I could have lifted a
refrigerator. You know? When you get this spurt of adrenaline? I remember

Norma's graduation from law school with daughter Elizabeth, May 1962. Family archives.

stomping out there and thinking, 'Okay, if that's the way you want it, buster, that's the way you're going to get it.' I walked out of there and I knew I was going to win."

She got a sitter, and she went to the moot court oral arguments, and she won. "I won the first round, then I won the second round, then I won the third round, and then I won the last round. The judges said, 'She's won the

P. 8, Sec. 1, Capital Journal, Tues., Mar. 27, '62

Housewife Nears Law Goal

By RAY INOUYE
Capital Journal Writer

Norma Paulus stands scant steps away from a goal she forged 12 years ago. She can reach it this June, when she is scheduled to receive her degree from the Willamette University College of Law.

It's been a long time coming, though, and a pair of detours— in the form of marriage and motherhood — have crossed her route. She's got new goals now.

It was in 1950 that Mrs. Paulus, now the wife of William G. Paulus, Salem attorney first set her sights toward the law profession.

As an 18-year-old fresh out of Burns High School, Mrs. Paulus was hired as secretary by the Harney County district attorney.

In the sagebrush section of Eastern Oregon, the district attorney augments his income with a private practice. There have been less humble beginnings for law-school graduates, but Mrs. Paulus considers herself lucky.

BACKGROUND BROADENS

"I was able to build a background on all phases of law," she recounts.

Since then, she has gravitated to other jobs in the field, including one as legal secretary for Oregon's chief justice.

She had served in this position for a year, when Earl C. Latourette, then the chief justice, encouraged her ambitions to attend Willamette's law school.

Mrs. Paulus, who had no college experience, was admitted to the school as a "special student," one whom officials deemed qualified for entrance because of experience and other factors.

She studied on a part-time basis for five years. Her hus-

COUNSELOR ALSO COOKS — Mrs. Norma Paulson combines duties as a Willamette University College of Law student and an attractive mother of one, as shown in her choice of reading matter. Here, she puts aside a collection of state statutes to plan the evening's dinner. Mrs. Paulus, named recently as the law college's top second-year student, is the wife of William G. Paulus, Salem attorney. (Capital Journal Photo)

While the March 27, 1962, Capitol Journal article "Housewife Nears Law Goal" lauds her accomplishments as a top law student, it also clearly assumes that even highly experienced and trained women of the era were housewives first. Norma Paulus Papers, Willamette University Archives and Special Collections_Personal Scrapbook_32.

argument hands down.'"[75] Her final hurdle left in the dust, Norma was set to graduate in spring 1962, with full honors.

A few weeks before her graduation, the *Capital Journal* published a profile of the young woman who had come to Salem twelve years before, with a dream long deferred that was about to come true. The reporter detailed some of Norma's accomplishments since beginning law school in 1957, including her stellar grade-point average.[76] A two-column photo accompanying the article shows a smiling Norma, "the law student and attractive mother of one," holding two large books: a collection of statutes that, according to the caption, she's about to put aside, and a large cookbook she'll use "to plan the evening's dinner." That photo became a family joke, because Norma is the first to admit that she is not a gifted cook.

The reporter said that Mrs. Paulus's goal after graduation was "to try and qualify for the State Bar," and to "find time for research and other things afterward." She regards her studies as "an insurance policy," the reporter wrote, and secondary to her real career: "My family's my main concern. They deserve a lot of attention. A career in law is out." The sentiment was genuine; Norma was happy as a wife and mother. It also reflected the conventional aspirations of a person who had brains and career potential but who also happened to be female. "Time helped alter her 12-year goal," the reporter wrote soothingly, "and a husband-daughter combination is making the change stick."

Although a good human-interest feature, the reality was less storybook-simple. Norma passed the bar, and then in 1963, her son, Fritz, was born. As she told Oregon Historical Society interviewer Clark Hansen in 1999,

> I had two small children and wanted to find some way to keep my hand in law but still be at home. An appellate practice allowed me to do that because you don't have normal people for clients, you have lawyers for clients. I was offered some jobs by law firms and because of my work with the Supreme Court and then down in the Pioneer Trust Building as a secretary I knew most of the lawyers in town. . . . It was fun to work with them to research the cases and write the briefs and argue them before the Supreme Court, which I thought was kind of interesting and unusual because the last time I was in the building I was a secretary. In 1964, I became involved in politics because of Wally Carson who is now the Chief Justice. As I became more involved and more visible, I was appointed to things that involved civic decisions, and I was still practicing law.[77]

Along with motherhood and marriage, her appellate practice kept Norma busy and satisfied, but only briefly. Ever a civic-minded person, Norma naturally attracted opportunities that would soon call her to use her legal education in a bigger arena.

Norma in front of Oregon State Capitol as a recently elected legislator, 1971. Family archives.

Chapter 2
Freshman in the House

> Wally and I both graduated and passed the bar in 1962. It wasn't too long after that he called me on the phone and told me he was going to run for the legislature and asked me if I would help him. So I got involved. It was every day all day working on that campaign, on the phone with my two little kids. I remember when we were putting signs up I had Elizabeth and Fritz with me and somebody went by and saw us and they called Wally's office and said they didn't think it was right that he had his wife and two kids out putting up signs.
>
> —Norma Paulus

By the time Norma began to think about entering public life, a woman running for office was not unheard of, but it was still something of a public spectacle. Women candidates were queried as often about fashion and family as they were about politics and campaign agendas. In an era when newspapers still dominated political discourse, much of the coverage of women in public life appeared in the so-called society section, which has today gone the way of hot lead type in most daily newspapers.

The double standard irritated Norma Paulus, but it didn't stop her. She was of an era (the Great Depression) and temperament (pragmatic and not overly reflective) that did not feel the need to make an intellectual distinction between women's public and private spheres. She focused on practical concerns. Norma Jean Petersen had learned early to do what needed to be done and not fuss about it. One of those urgently needed things was education for young children, especially gifted youngsters like her own. She remembers a conversation with a preschool teacher who'd accepted her daughter Elizabeth, then a precocious three-year-old, into her class. Shortly afterward the teacher called Norma and asked her to come in and talk about an issue with Elizabeth.

> "I thought, 'What has she done?'" Norma said. "The only thing I could think of was, she wasn't used to playing with other kids and

she'd poked someone. She never did that at home, but then she'd never been around other kids very much. I was just panicked."

The teacher confronted Norma with concern on her face. "Mrs. Paulus," she said, "surely you must know." Norma swallowed. "What do you mean?" she asked.

"Surely you must know that she . . . reads."

"Well, I just burst out laughing," said Norma. "It was such a relief! I told her, 'Yes, I know; I don't remember Elizabeth ever not being able to read, and frankly I'm not worried about it.'"

Well, it was causing problems, the teacher said. "All the other children see her reading books, and they want to read, too."

Norma shook her head. "I'm sorry," she said, "but frankly I don't know what to tell you."[1]

Norma could see that Elizabeth needed more than her preschool teacher could provide. There was no publicly funded early-childhood education and nothing for talented and gifted children. In a few years the cause of publicly funded kindergartens would be taken up by the legislature, spearheaded by Democratic representative Betty Roberts, who would become a close colleague and friend.

Norma must have recalled her own small-town education in Burns, which had been unconventional but effective in developing her particular gifts. She carried her gratitude for her teachers throughout her life. After moving to Salem, Norma had become acquainted with a remarkable schoolteacher named Mary Eyre. Eyre—like Norma a graduate of Willamette University (class of 1918)—had recently retired after forty years of teaching history and government at two Salem high schools. Eyre chaired the local chapter of the League of Women Voters and was active in Democratic politics. Norma admired her civic engagement and her advocacy for education, women's rights, and open government.[2] Eyre's outspokenness was one influence that inspired Norma to get active on behalf of other families as well as her own.

Norma had become friendly with other young mothers who wanted something more for their children. "A good many of these women were highly educated; they had graduated from Eastern schools," she said. "They were the wives of doctors and other professionals. They came to me and asked if I would represent them in the legislature."

Norma did not have their educational background. In fact, she didn't have an undergraduate degree at all—something that has bothered her at times throughout her life. (It was, she said much later, the main force that drove her to

Liz, Norma, Bill, and Fritz Paulus on tandem bike, 1970 campaign photo. Doug Raines. Family archives.

go to law school. "It wasn't because I had such a burning desire to be a lawyer. It was because I felt so inadequate because I hadn't been to college." Did she ever overcome that feeling? "I don't know that I ever did."[3]) Despite all that, she did have a law degree, and the women regarded her as the best qualified of them to approach the legislature to get funding for talented and gifted children.[4]

"They'd put together a bill, and they asked me to go and represent them before a legislative committee," she said. "They brought me all this material and I went up to the legislature with them."[5] As it happened, on the day Norma and her group arrived, the hearing they'd planned to attend had been cancelled. But they ran into Representative L. B. Day, a Marion County legislator and Teamsters Union official,[6] who was at that time a Democrat. (Day switched his affiliation to Republican after the 1967 regular session.[7])

"I went over to him and said, 'Hey, look, these women say there's a hearing here and what are we supposed to do and where is it?' He rustled up the fellows. I testified on that bill and we got it out of the committee and that was the beginning of the Talented and Gifted Program."[8] Norma's encounter with Day foretold a productive relationship that would include a collaboration on Oregon's historic land-use legislation a few years later.

HELPING THE CARSON CAMPAIGN

At about this time, Norma signed on to help her classmate Wallace P. ("Wally"), Carson Jr. in his first campaign for the Oregon legislature. Wally and Norma had graduated from Willamette Law in 1962, although Norma had been attending longer because she'd started out as a part-time student. Norma was also acquainted with Wally's father, Wallace P. Carson Senior, who headed a law firm in the Pioneer Trust Building, with offices adjacent to those of Malcolm Marsh and Ned Clark, where Norma worked after she graduated from law school.[9] Wally was also a boyhood friend of Bill Paulus's—they'd gone to St. Paul's Episcopal Church together and sung in the choir.[10]

The Carson family had deep roots in Salem politics and law. Wally's great-aunt, Ann Rafter (Anna M. Carson), was one of the earliest women to graduate from the Willamette School of Law, the first of a line of Carson women to do so. All of Wallace Senior's siblings, including two sisters, had trained in the law, and one of the sisters, Catharine Carson Barsch,[11] had been Oregon's assistant attorney general. Norma and Bill had settled into a deep, easy friendship with Carson and his wife, Gloria. "I found that Norma who grew up in Burns, could pull her own on any level, intellectual, political and certainly in fighting back," said Carson. "We thoroughly enjoy and love Norma Petersen Paulus and have for years. So please take into account that whatever we tell you, we're horribly biased."

When Carson decided to run for the legislature—he was recruited by legendary Republican operative and future US senator Bob Packwood—he saw in Norma Paulus a distinct political asset. It was true, she was still a Democrat, having been raised in a house where pictures of Jesus and President Franklin D. Roosevelt had roughly equal billing.[12] And she was a woman lawyer, but for the Carson family that was barely remarkable. Perhaps more important for the campaign, party identities were not so ideologically rooted in those days. Norma's practical progressivism harmonized well with Carson's own.

At that time the local organization of both political parties was loose and informal in Oregon, in contrast to the tightly structured political machines that dominated in some other cities and states.[13] "As a result, the party structure had not been particularly helpful in assisting candidates for state office," Carson said. "Maybe that's not a bad thing. But the candidates had to put together their own team." Norma would later refer to this phenomenon as "the star system"—meaning a candidate had to have the star power to hold the center of a campaign because she couldn't depend on a strong party fabric. "You had to have your own organization," she said. "I was never elected or defeated by a party throughout my political career."[14]

After attending a seminar outlining Packwood's strategies for winning elections, Carson and his supporters organized what was called a "kitchen cabinet" consisting of Norma and Bill, Carson's law partner Dave Rhoten, and local Republican movers and shakers Hal and Jordis Schick. "We were so naïve, we didn't know you had to get a Karl Rove[15] from out of state to organize your campaign," said Carson. "We were home-grown, and it was great fun. We didn't spend much time talking about whether we were conservative or liberal. We were practical." Norma became an instrumental part of Carson's campaign. "[She] was one of the stars of that campaign," Bob Packwood recalled much later. "I resolved that, if I ever needed another candidate in this district, she is the one I want."[16]

Packwood was a big proponent of grassroots, door-to-door campaigning, and lawn signs were a signature Packwood strategy. "Norma had the not-too-enviable job of getting these lawn signs placed around the community," Carson said, "and she did a marvelous job." He recalls the time Norma was roaming the neighborhoods with both her children, hammering in lawn signs, "and one woman came out of the house and said she thought it was awfully nice that the candidate would allow his wife and kids to help with his campaign." Norma recalls that incident slightly differently: "We were putting up signs and I had Elizabeth and Fritz with me, and somebody went by and saw us, and they called Wally's office and said they didn't think it was right that he had his wife and two kids out putting up signs."[17] Norma was amused but not surprised at the assumption that she was the candidate's wife.

Carson won the election and entered the House in the 1967 session. "I liked campaign work," Norma said. "I found it exciting, and I found that I was very good at it."[18] After some soul-searching, she had switched her registration to Republican, for immediate and practical reasons. As the primary election neared, Bill said to his wife, "It doesn't make much sense for you to work for a candidate and then not be able to vote for him." More likely a deeper reason was that she'd found her philosophical home. "The Republicans were the ones that were exciting," she said. They were the good thinkers, the moderates. They were the ones who wanted to be in government for all the right reasons."[19]

DIVING INTO COMMUNITY SERVICE

Oregon's established political leaders—Salem mayor Dr. Vern Miller, Bob Packwood, and even Governor Tom McCall—were starting to pay attention to

1970 legislative campaign photo of Norma inspecting a Marion-Polk Boundary Commission map, a precursor to the concept of Oregon's Urban Growth Boundaries. Doug Raines. Family archives.

the bright young woman who had helped elect Wally Carson. In 1967 Mayor Miller[20] appointed her and Carson to the Salem Human Relations Commission.[21] "Salem was being faced with the first changing of Oregon's complexion, with the burgeoning Hispanic population," Norma said, "and the Russian Old Believers, who were becoming part of the valley's population. We were trying to get the cities and counties to offer one-stop services for transients and Hispanic families, and also trying to find interpreters for them." The commission also dealt with problems arising from Salem's many mental-health and penal facilities.

Governor McCall then appointed Norma to the Marion-Polk Boundary Commission, one of the first such bodies in the nation. Fellow members were Ned Clark,[22] Ed Stillus, a mortician from Woodburn, and a farmer from the Dallas area. The commission's charge was to monitor and manage growth at Salem's urban-rural edges.

Norma also volunteered to cochair the Salem Hospital's annual fundraiser, the High Fever Follies,[23] with Eunice Crothers, whose husband Morris Crothers, a hospital physician, had been in the state House since 1963.[24] He was to become one of Norma's key champions in her first legislative campaign in 1970. "He was very much my mentor," she said. She recalled a time before she'd even thought of running for office, when her husband Bill was testifying before a House committee on which Crothers sat. At the end of the hearing, the chairman asked members if they had further questions. "And Morris leaned over and said, 'Yes, Mr. Paulus. I want to know when you're going to let your wife run for the legislature.'"[25]

Norma plunged happily into her community service work. She found it very satisfying to develop practical solutions for poor migrants, families of inmates, and farmers squeezed by urban sprawl. She said at the time she wasn't thinking of these activities as stepping-stones to elected office.[26] Yet the idea must have been stirring in her mind. Maybe it was the zest of campaigning that captivated her, and maybe also her growing awareness that political power could be used for good.

In 1970, after two terms in the House, Wally Carson decided to run for the Senate. To Norma it looked like opportunity knocking. "I went to him and told him I was going to run for his seat." They lunched together in the Oak Room of the venerable Marion Hotel, Salem's main eatery and watering hole for legislators, reporters, lobbyists, and other political types.[27] Carson told her, "Norma, Marion County will not elect a woman."

Norma paused for a moment. From the level of public service at which she was already engaged, the leap into an elective campaign did not seem so far. She had helped run a successful campaign already. She was becoming more visible in the community. She was getting encouragement from Oregon's winningest political strategist, Bob Packwood, who had served in the House alongside Carson. Norma had accompanied Carson to one of the noted Packwood "campaign schools" back in 1966. "Bob Packwood told me a number of times," she said, "that the biggest asset in his career was that he tapped into the resource of well-educated women when nobody else was doing that.[28] So [running for office] just seemed like a natural consequence of my involvement. Plus I wanted to have something to say about what was happening in the state."

Norma leaned across the table and smiled. "Wally," she said, "I think I can get myself elected."

In early 1970, she declared her intention to seek a Republican nomination for an Oregon House seat. In February the *Oregon Statesman* reported that Norma Paulus, "Salem housewife and attorney," had filed for Marion County Position 4, the seat vacated by L. B. Day, who had joined the staff of US interior secretary Walter Hickel.[29] Both Salem newspapers, the *Statesman* and the *Capital Journal*, ran in-depth articles on the background and qualifications of Norma and the other two Republican hopefuls, a farmer named Sam Brown and a horseshoer named H. Tex Shively. The *Statesman* article noted that Paulus advocated "reasonable" gun control, a motel/hotel tax, better administration of the welfare system, and opening of the gasoline tax for general use. She also favored state-supported kindergarten, better education for special-needs kids, and stronger consumer-protection laws.[30] "We strongly favor the nomination of Mrs. Paulus," the *Capital Journal* editorialized in May 1970. "She has particularly strong views about racial equality and improving education. . . . We prefer her judgment, values and priorities and believe she has the ability to make a major contribution."[31]

After Norma won the primary in May, she selected Salem insurance agent Barney Rogers as her campaign manager for the general election. Rogers was a childhood friend of Bill Paulus's and knew Gerry Frank, Mark Hatfield's longtime aide and a Republican notable in his own right.[32] Norma followed Bob Packwood's playbook and recruited campaign workers from her wide network of friends. "I tapped into all these people," she said, "most of them close friends of mine who were really bright women, and they found it exciting. They had all kinds of talents to bring."[33]

In the general election she faced a young up-and-coming Democrat named Mike Dye, who, like Norma, was a new attorney and very good-looking. "A handsome man," Norma recalled. "He was the hottest ticket on the Democratic side." Dye had cultivated labor unions in his campaign and had the support of many union members. Norma was not plugged into any similar organizations capable of delivering votes in a bloc. She knew she would have to run a strong grassroots campaign—combing the neighborhoods, getting her name out to the public, winning over voters one by one.

For this task, Norma found a valuable asset in her neighbor, Ann Lyman. Lyman organized hundreds of meet-and-greet coffee gatherings in homes throughout the county and quickly earned the title "The General." Here is one of her typical invitations, hand-calligraphed, with an elephant drawn in pen and ink:[34]

Rally 'Round the Candidate
Join the grass roots movement
Meet the people
Shake the hands
Wednesday, August 23rd, 5 pm to 7 pm
Vote to Come

Other women designed Norma's campaign leaflets, bumper stickers, and handouts. One came up with a striking logo: Norma's name reversed out of a black circle, with a six-petaled daisy. The logo, simple and elegant, didn't need to be printed in color, which satisfied Norma's frugal nature.[35] They made thousands.

1970 legislative campaign photo in front of the family station wagon, "Blister." Doug Raines. Family archives.

We made it in all different sizes; little squares, big things, small things, little tiny stickers and they became so popular with school kids. The kids would come to the campaign meetings and beg their moms to bring the stickers home so they could put them on their

Colleen Walton's VW bug plastered with campaign stickers, 1970. Family archives.

notebooks. One of my friends had a little beetle Volkswagen, and her kids begged her to let them cover the Volkswagen with these stickers and she agreed to it, "if Norma would take them all off after the election"—which I did with the kids. They covered this Volkswagen and she was beginning in the real estate business so she was all over town. So they were all over.[36]

Norma made the rounds of Marion County speaking at civic clubs, business and professional groups, chambers of commerce, women's groups, schools, the county fair. She cut ribbons at grand openings and waved from floats at neighborhood parades. She appeared with Mike Dye at an October candidates' fair at North Salem High School. A *Capital Journal* photo shows her being escorted down the hall by a phalanx of young male students. In her high-heeled boots and upswept hairdo, she looked fetching and hardly older than her escorts.[37]

The various renderings of her honorific title in newspaper accounts reveal a society coming to grips with how to treat women in public life. Most stories from her campaign days call her "Mrs. Paulus," even as they refer to men by their last name only. Even after she was elected, some newspapers continued to refer to her as "Mrs. Paulus" (or, later, "Ms. Paulus), or even "Norma," while styling male legislators as "Rep. So-and-So" (for example, "Reps. Paul Hanneman and Bob Smith and Mrs. Paulus").

Here, for example, is a *Statesman* account of her inauguration, written (typically for the time) by the society page editor, Jeryme English: "Attending their first opening session as freshmen members, . . . Mrs. William G. Paulus, chic in a green knit outfit, joined by her husband and two children, Elizabeth and Fritz. . . . Norma has the distinction of being the second woman ever to be elected to the State Legislature from Marion County." [38] Not until she was well into her second term was she was routinely referred to as "Rep. Paulus," alongside her male colleagues.

This uncertainty in the stylesheet mirrored a world of varied opinions about a woman's place, sometimes asserted in a stinging way. The mayor of Silverton had been glad to escort Mark Hatfield, Bob Packwood, and Wally Carson up and down Main Street and introduce them to Silverton's merchants. When he refused to do it for Norma Paulus, she was dumbfounded.

"I told him, 'But you know you and I agree on all these issues,'" she said. "He was just lovely to me in his home and at social gatherings, but he would not escort me on the street" because it wasn't proper for a woman to be running for office.[39]

It wasn't only men who felt that way. Ann Lyman's neighborhood coffees were targeted at women who did not work outside the home. These voters were essential to Norma's victory. "Most of these women were better educated than I," Norma said. "Most of my friends had gone to college and had seen their husbands through school or professional business. And they were the hardest sell. Some of these educated women in my own age group were my biggest obstacle."[40] This, too, stung. "When I would tell them, 'I'm going to run for the legislature and I want you to help me,' the first thing they would say is, 'What does Bill think of this?' Of course, it was fine with Bill. He was my biggest supporter! But they didn't know how our marriage worked. They could see it did, but they didn't understand it."[41]

Their reaction made her realize she was "dumb lucky" to have Bill's unqualified support. "In the era when my husband and I were married, very few women worked outside the home," she said, "and there were just a handful of us that were lawyers. The women's movement hadn't come into full bloom yet."[42] It was true; Oregon's women's movement lagged a little behind those of more populous states and cities, and the main legislative action on women's issues still lay ahead. The 1973 and 1975 legislative sessions

Campaign fundraising tea in the Paulus home with Norma and Tom McCall, a mentor and friend throughout her early political career, 1970. Gerry Lewin, courtesy of the *Statesman Journal*. Willamette Heritage Center, 2016.023.0033.173.

in particular would see great gains in legal protection for women's rights, and Norma would be in the thick of it. Even so, in 1970 there was plenty of conversation about certain issues. An important issue was abortion, which was illegal or restricted in most US states, including Oregon;[43] the landmark *Roe v. Wade* decision legalizing abortion in all states was still three years in the future.

Asked about the abortion issue by an *Oregon Statesman* reporter, Norma's opponent Mike Dye said he opposed lifting restrictions on abortion. Norma sidestepped the question by saying the courts were considering the constitutionality of abortion laws, so the matter was probably moot. Her answer was both truthful and politically strategic: why take a position on a highly divisive question that isn't key to the campaign? In the same interview, Norma changed the subject to talk about her consumer-protection ideas—a classic example of rhetorical redirection.[44] The *Statesman* endorsed Norma Paulus.[45] Later, when it mattered, Norma committed to a full pro-choice position.

THE GOVERNOR WEIGHS IN

About three weeks before the election, House speaker Bob Smith, who had been watching the race closely, telephoned. "Norma, we've got a labor poll that shows you losing. How can we help you?" Norma was taken aback: "I just can't believe that!" she said to Smith. She thought about the offer for a short moment, and then said, "An endorsement from Tom McCall would really help." The governor, besides being Oregon's Republican-in-chief, was popular across party lines, and his ideas on land use, the environment, and most other issues echoed Norma's own.

McCall was contacted. He would be happy to send a letter to voters under his name, as long as the envelopes were hand-addressed. Why? Because the common touch was one of McCall's most valuable political assets. A letter that looked mass-mailed would reflect poorly on both him and Norma. This was a job for The General. Ann Lyman commandeered the Paulus dining room for four days and nights and recruited an army of scriveners. "Bill and I would leave in the morning," said Norma, "and we would come home at midnight, and here would be a different round of men and women hand-addressing these letters, and there'd be big jugs of wine on the table."[46] Thus it was that every registered Republican in Marion County got a hand-addressed letter from Governor Tom McCall a few days before the election.

Norma beat Dye by a comfortable margin: 23,383 votes to 20,128. She became the second woman to be elected to the legislature from Marion County.[47] Immediately, letters of congratulation poured in from constituents hoping to make a favorable contact. Here is one from Robert MacVicar, president of Oregon State University, postmarked November 6, the Friday after election day:

> My dear Representative Paulus,
>
> Congratulations on your election day victory! You undoubtedly are pleased and very greatly relieved to have the campaign behind you.
>
> Hopefully your service in the legislature will give us an opportunity to get better acquainted. We have many common interests and would like to work with you for the betterment of Oregon. We

at Oregon State University stand ready to assist you and your associates in every way possible.

A BRIEF REST

The campaign had taken a toll on Norma. "I'd lost a lot of weight, and I was absolutely exhausted," she said. In September she'd had some unpleasant news from her doctor: she needed a hysterectomy. Bad timing, she told the doctor, "I can't get off the campaign trail." A few days after the election, she went in and had it done. "Then I stayed home until the inauguration. And the lobbyists who wanted to lobby me came and lobbied me in my house."[48]

She entered the House as a member of the majority party. In the Senate the Democrats were the nominal majority, but their power was curbed by a cadre of conservative "coalition Democrats" who tended to side with Republican proposals.[49] In addition, many of the leaders in both chambers represented areas outside the Willamette Valley: Stafford Hansell was from Hermiston, Lynn Newbry from the Medford area, and House speaker Bob Smith from Norma's hometown of Burns. These non-urban representatives tended to be more conservative than those from the valley's urban corridor. "I used to put it like this," Norma said. "If you look at the Willamette Valley as kind of like a bathtub, the legislature was controlled by the ring around the bathtub."[50]

Even so, she recalls that the representatives worked mostly in a bipartisan spirit. Even sharp disagreements tended to turn on pragmatic rather than ideological concerns. At that time, legislators were elected at large from within counties, which, Norma said, tends to moderate extremes of opinion. "My constituency was very mixed. I had a monastery and a nunnery, a strong Catholic community, a strong farming community, organized pulp and paper workers, the business community, the Russian community, the Hispanic community, and then downtown Salem, with its university and its affluent population. It was a very mixed bag"—and she had to represent everybody.

After single-member districts became the rule in 1973, she represented south Salem's District 31.[51] Norma has outspokenly criticized single-member districts: they split counties into neighborhood zones, reinforce political and economic dividing lines, and encourage extremism in representatives who answered only to their narrow slice of the electorate. "They also allow the political forces to target people with more concentrated money," she said, "which leads to more special-interest legislation. I just deplore that kind of politics."[52]

Norma at her first legislative seat, circa 1971. Gerry Lewin, courtesy of the *Statesman Journal*. Willamette Heritage Center, 2016.023.0041.002.

SETTLING IN

Norma quickly made friends and forged alliances among her House colleagues. Speaker Bob Smith was a key supporter. Others were Stafford Hansell from Hermiston and Bob Ingalls from Benton County. Through Wally Carson, now in the Senate, she met Senator Hector Macpherson, representing Linn County, and she renewed her acquaintance with L. B. Day, who by then had left federal service and was secretary-treasurer of the Teamster-affiliated cannery workers union.[53] Day and Macpherson were working hard to develop a comprehensive land-use planning system for Oregon, an effort that Norma would soon join.

Some of her male colleagues didn't quite know what to make of her. A few may have thought they were mentoring a rookie, giving her advice and showing her the ropes. She didn't see it that way. "I didn't need that kind of advice. I needed allies on issues."[54] Here, for example, is one piece of advice: "Be calm, serious, considerate. Rap the hammer with determination, forget your [*sic*] a mother—be one of the boys. HOW COME YOU DIDN'T WEAR A LONGER SKIRT? YOUR KNEES ARE SHOWING."[55]

Second-grade artwork by son Fritz, 1971, which Norma later framed and hung in her office. Family archives.

Some undoubtedly let her attractiveness go to their heads. When she gave Oregon's "birthday speech" in the House on February 14, 1971,[56] she was bombarded with floor notes praising her style and appearance. Dick Eymann wrote, "Most beautiful and most distinguished speaker this season." Gordon Macpherson complimented her and asked for a copy of her speech.

Norma had set out to make a good impression on her fellow legislators, and she was succeeding. She was a good extemporaneous speaker—"throughout my career I've had very few written speeches"—but she knew better than to pop off her mouth at every opportunity. She was a respectful debater. "There were a lot of old hands that I really respected—Stafford Hansell, Bob Smith, and others. I chose my speaking opportunities very carefully."[57] She did her homework, stuck to the topic, developed her ideas thoroughly, and presented them skillfully. "I think I demonstrated that I could look around the corner a little bit as far as what was needed, and could persuade my fellow legislators on both sides of the fence to support me." These skills boded well for her political future[58] and earned her loyal and lasting friendships.

Speaker Smith appointed her to the House Judiciary Committee.[59] Norma was one of only seven lawyers in the House,[60] and she and Smith both felt it was the logical place to deploy her skills. "That was a real workhorse of a committee," she said. "We had such a huge volume of bills go through, and there were so few of us lawyers." Her colleagues included Gordon Macpherson, who'd become a fan, and her old mentor Morris Crothers. "It was a really good committee," she said. "I enjoyed each and every one of the men on there. We became really good friends."[61] She also served on the Natural Resources Committee and was vice-chair of the Fish and Game Committee.[62] In addition, Governor McCall appointed her to a statewide commission working on revising Oregon's criminal law code.[63] The commission, which included legislators and private citizens, had been created by the 1967 legislature to overhaul and modernize Oregon's criminal laws.[64]

The criminal-code commission was a high-profile appointment for a freshman legislator. Norma was the only woman on the panel, which was chaired by Tony Yturri, a long-serving state senator from Malheur County Norma had known since childhood.[65] Other members included Wally Carson; John Burns, president of the Senate; Lee Johnson, then Oregon attorney general, who went on to become an Oregon Appeals Court judge; Herb Schwab, a lawyer and judge who had recently helped establish the Oregon Court of Appeals; and Norma's friend and supporter Robert Chandler, editor and publisher of the *Bend Bulletin*.[66] "It was a powerhouse group," she said. "All the counts of murder, all the counts of burglary—for every crime on the books, we had to systematically go through the criminal codes for the past 100 years. It was an arduous, difficult task, and it took all the brainpower we had."[67]

The panel's work was enshrined in a revised criminal code, enacted by the 1971 legislature. The commission then prepared a new criminal procedure code during the 1971–1972 interim session; that code was turned into law by the 1973 legislative assembly.[68] "Of all the things that I've ever done," Norma said, "that probably was the most rewarding, because of the way in which it was done and the people that I served with."

Because of her heavy judiciary commitment, education had to take a backseat for a while. Norma made a deal with Mary Rieke, a fellow freshman Republican, who had served on the Portland School Board and who also had a passion for improving education. "We decided, as neophytes, that we'd . . . keep each other apprised of our different bailiwicks. I'd keep her informed about the Judiciary Committee," and Rieke would keep Norma informed about doings in education.[69] The women also shared an interest in changing inheritance laws to end discrimination against widows. "She and I drafted a bill in 1971, introduced it, got it down the legislative hopper," Norma said, "but since we were novices, we didn't know how to marshal our votes and how much effort it took." The bill failed, but they brought it back in the 1973 session and got it passed. "We were much smarter by then," said Norma.[70]

Working with Rieke and other legislators on a wide variety of bills, Norma was solidifying her positions on many issues. She voted "yes" on a bill to extend voting rights to eighteen-year-olds.[71] She voted "no" on a bill that would require public employees to pay union dues. She voted "no" on a bill to legalize "casino night" fund-raisers for nonprofit organizations[72]—regarding it as the thin edge of a wedge that would eventually drive legalized gambling into Oregon. The measure passed.[73]

SEASONED AFTER A SEASON

Norma proved herself an extraordinarily effective new legislator. The City of Salem honored her with a Distinguished Service Award for her work on the Human Resources Commission. In February the Oregon Federation of Business and Professional Women awarded her one of eight Golden Torch leadership awards. And at the end of the session,[74] she was named the outstanding freshman in the House by members of the press. That honor led to a fellowship from the Eagleton Institute, administered by the Center for American Politics at Rutgers University, devoted to improving the quality of political leaders nationwide.[75] The fellowship covered a week at an exclusive political workshop on Singer Island in Florida, where the philanthropist John D. MacArthur donated land for a park now named after him.[76]

Norma and Bill traveled to Florida with Wally Carson, who had been named outstanding freshman in the Senate, and his wife, Gloria. It was the summer of 1971.[77] Carson tells this story about the trip:

> We stopped in Atlanta. Everybody stops in Atlanta; even when you go to Heaven you have to stop in Atlanta. That's a Southern joke. Well, anyway, we stopped to visit a Navy officer from Bill's days in the Navy.[78] His wife was quite Southern, and she said, "I've never met a lady legislator before. " She was just agog. I called Norma a "lady legislator" till she told me to stop.[79]

Unsurprisingly, Norma was the only woman participant. She came to find out that she was the first woman ever to attend the Eagleton Institute gathering. "For the first three days I was there," she said, "everybody assumed my husband was the legislator. I guess they thought I was sitting and taking notes for him while he was out playing golf."[80] At the end of that summer week, she knew she'd left her freshman days behind. She had studied hard, worked hard, and learned much.

When she'd first considered running, all she had known about the legislature was what she'd observed in advocating for her children. Once elected, she found that the process made intuitive sense. "Being a lawyer was a tremendous help for me," she said, "for two reasons. One, it gave me credibility as a woman. Two, if you understand our system of jurisprudence, it's so much easier to become effective in the legislature right off the bat, because you understand what the law is and how it works, the machinery that's used to make it."

She also learned quickly to read the underlying political currents—grasping how things actually get done, not just how they're supposed to get done. "Some of the old hands would make end runs around me and never tell me they were doing it," she said.

> It had never occurred to me that people dealt this way. My policy always was to go find my known adversaries and say, "I'm going to introduce a bill to outlaw snowmobiles," or whatever it was, "and I know you will be opposed, but I want you to know that I'm going to do it, and this is why." I felt then I was raising the level of the debate. It was not personalities you'd want to bring to the House floor, but legitimate arguments, pro and con. And I don't care what the issue is; there are always legitimate arguments pro and con."[81]

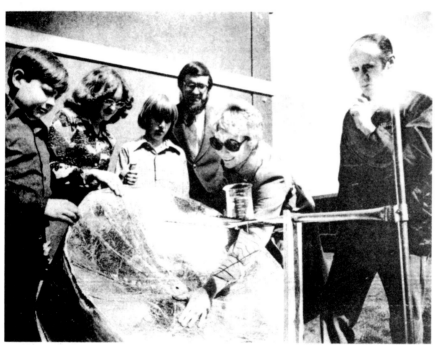

Tapping the Sun State Rep. Norma Paulus wears dark glasses for protection as she tests sun's heat trapped in home-made solar energizer at Judson Junior High School in South Salem Thursday. Rep. Paulus is interested in legislation promoting solar energy research. Students and teachers participating in the Judson solar machine experiment are (from left) Mike Parker, Linda Cox, Rusty Moss, Al Rudeen and Richard Nunez. Rudeen is a Brush College Elementary School teacher whose class worked on Judson project. (Statesman photo by Ron Cooper)

Norma visiting Salem's Judson Junior High School students' solar energizer used to heat water. Published on March 21, 1975, the article was part of her campaign for legislation to encourage the development of solar heating. Ron Cooper, courtesy of the *Statesman Journal*. *Statesman Journal* digital archive, front page, 3/21/75. Norma Paulus Papers, Willamette University Archives and Special Collections_Personal Clippings Scrapbook 1974–75_046.

Chapter 3
Champion of the Environment

> The threat to our environment is no longer only from industry.
> It's you and me. It's the motorized vehicles that now can take
> people virtually everywhere. What's needed is some kind
> of restriction. We're the victims of reverse migration, with
> hundreds of thousands of persons going out into the woods or
> to the beach every weekend.
>
> —Norma Paulus

Education was the cause closest to Norma's heart when she entered politics. The advancement of women became a passionate concern throughout her public life. Oregon's environment was the third star in her crown of convictions. Her environmental ideals were pragmatic, rooted in her impoverished upbringing and her deep respect for the productive capacity of Oregon's lands and waters. She could not abide waste, whether it took the form of paving over prime farmland for suburban neighborhoods or something as seemingly trivial as excessive packaging of grocery items.

She made headlines in her first campaign for the legislature by carrying a sack of groceries into a Rotary Club meeting where she was scheduled to give a campaign speech. "I took fifty dollars of my grocery money and went to Roth's IGA and bought examples of all the bad packaging that was just coming onto the market," she said. "When I was giving my speech, I started taking these things out of a brown bag. And then I'd have to stop and pound and hammer them to take them out of the plastic." Norma continued calmly with her speech as she wrestled to separate each item from its packaging. She placed goods and packaging in separate piles on either side of the lectern. "By the time I finished my speech," she said, "the plastic was this high"—holding her hand at about shoulder level—"and I said, 'Have I made my point?'"

Her audience was, of course, all men—women could not belong to the Rotary Club in those days. "So I said to them, 'You, as husbands, as people watching your purse strings, you ought to go home and help your wife deal with this problem, because it's costing you money.'"[1]

This presentation was an early example of the showman-like flair that Norma had learned in her dancing and baton-twirling youth. Never the shrinking violet, she brought an attention-getting pizazz to her public appearances. In a similar presentation to a gathering of women supporters at the YWCA, she revised her pitch to highlight women's power to change the world from within their traditional sphere.[2]

"I want to show you what we as responsible women can do about our environment," she said, and again she drew one over-packaged grocery item after another from a brown bag. As she wrestled the wrappers off, she ticked off a long list of things her listeners could do to help the environment: Commit to recycling. Refuse to buy nonreturnable bottles and cans. Buy white toilet paper instead of the colored kind, which doesn't decompose as fast and clogs septic tanks. Don't let the store clerk put your apples and oranges in individual sacks. Don't buy nonnutritious sugared cereals. Don't patronize cleaners that won't take back their hangers. "Become militant," she said. "That way you'll get your point across that you're sick of all this excess and waste you're paying for."

Yet she also told her audience, "Put your bras back on, kiss your husbands, and be responsible women when it comes to your environment." Perhaps without being fully aware of it, Norma was signaling her uneasiness with the rising "women's lib" movement.

BOTTLES, BICYCLES, AND BEACHES

Norma's 1970 legislative campaign had stressed two of her three passions: education and the environment. When she entered the House as a freshman legislator in 1971, she was poised to become an effective, bipartisan player in the most environmentally notable sessions in Oregon history. She joined like-minded Republicans and Democrats to pass an unprecedented number of laws protecting the environment.[3] They addressed such issues as the siting of nuclear power plants and disposal of wastes, restrictions on automobile and industrial air pollution, and gradual phase-outs of open-field burning in the Willamette Valley and of billboards alongside state highways. Lawmakers opened Oregon's highway trust fund to bicycle-related investments, and approved special tax assessments for open-space lands.[4]

That session's most memorable bill was House Bill 1036, the Bottle Bill—the first in the nation that required deposits on beer and carbonated soft-drink containers and banned detachable pull-tabs as can closers.[5] Norma was a cosponsor.[6] While this version of the Bottle Bill was touted as one of

Governor McCall's key achievements, an earlier version in the 1969 legislature had died for lack of the governor's support. The first bottle bill, HB 1157, was introduced by Paul Hanneman, Republican House member from Cloverdale, on the north coast.

The idea for the bill came from a constituent, Richard Chambers, who detested litter and made a practice of picking up trash when he went hiking and kayaking. He routinely brought home large bags of other people's throwaways, consisting mostly of beverage cans and bottles.[7] Chambers wanted a law that mandated a deposit on beer and pop containers. "Chambers came to me as soon as he found out that I was going to run for the legislature and that I had this strong environmental campaign," Norma said. "He came and explained that it was his idea, and Paul Hanneman introduced the bill for him, and he provided all the information and all the background."[8] Recognizing in Chambers a kindred spirit, she quickly agreed to support Hanneman's bill if she were elected.

Deposits on soda and beer bottles were common in the early decades of the twentieth century. It was cheaper for beverage companies to wash and reuse bottles than to buy new ones. After World War II, metal cans became cheaper, and steel and aluminum companies began to market nonreturnable containers to beverage bottlers as a way of increasing business.[9] Hanneman's bill, HB 1157, went beyond Chambers's idea and banned all nonreturnable pop and beer bottles.[10] After raising considerable alarm from packaging industry lobbyists, the bill was amended to impose a five-cent deposit on these bottles. The bill came within three votes of passing in the House,[11] but Hanneman's pleas to the governor's office for support went unheeded.

To a later reader, this may seem out of character for a governor whose championing of the Bottle Bill would define his environmental legacy. But McCall was a man who understood timing, and he understood that, in 1969, the issue wasn't yet ripe. The governor was planning to introduce his own version of the bottle bill in the 1971 legislature.[12] In the meantime, McCall planned to endorse an industry-backed anti-litter program called S.O.L.V. (Stop Oregon Litter and Vandalism), which container-makers hoped would blunt support for a mandatory deposit.

McCall's motives for these machinations were complicated. The governor understood perfectly well that S.O.L.V. was a diversionary tactic, but he wanted to appear to support it in order to "keep the Bottle Bill's opponents busy"[13] while he gathered his energies behind a 1971 revival of the bottle bill—this one with his name on it. The Bottle Bill that reemerged in the 1971 legislature as HB 1036 had the resounding endorsement of the governor. This version of the bill called for both outlawing nonreturnables and imposing a minimum five-cent deposit on them.[14] For most Oregonians, Norma believed, a system of deposits and returns made simple common sense. "When McCall got on the bandwagon about the Bottle Bill, he said, 'I'm going to put a nickel on the head of every can and bottle in Oregon.' And we all said people could do just what everybody had done in the early war years—they'd return bottles for the deposit, and Boy Scouts and Girl Scouts could go out and make money" from holding bottle drives.[15]

This time around the bill had better prospects. The governor's endorsement had pulled in support from previously reluctant legislators and also from environmentally minded citizens, such as the members of the newly organized Oregon Environmental Council.[16] Opponents of the bill came forward with many reasons why it shouldn't pass. Some grocery stores, for example, alleged that dealing with all those empties would be an intolerable financial burden. One prominent groceryman, John Piacentini, offered a powerful rebuttal to that claim. Piacentini owned the convenience store chain Plaid Pantry. He supported the Bottle Bill—in fact, he was already offering a half-cent return on any soda or beer bottle. Piacentini invited Oregon's beer and soda drinkers to bring in their bottles and cans and "bury me in litter."[17]

"To have a businessman that was actually doing this was very powerful testimony," Norma said. It helped, she added, that Piacentini's Plaid Pantry stores were well regarded, especially by older people—the cheery little stores reminded them of the old-fashioned neighborhood groceries they had grown up with. "Now here was John Piacentini doing the same thing, but in another era." The bill also had a powerful booster in Orville Roth, co-owner of the Roth's Friendly Foodliners supermarkets in and around Salem. Roth had already banished nonreturnable beer containers from his Lancaster Drive store and was preparing to carry the policy throughout the chain. "We'll be issuing an ultimatum [to beverage companies] that either they'll have the returnables or we won't carry their product."[18]

Norma was well aware that S.O.L.V., a purportedly grassroots anti-litter group, was financed by the industries that were trying to kill the Bottle Bill. After Piacentini's testimony, she got up and issued a roundhouse attack on S.O.L.V. "I said it was started and funded by the beer companies, the very people who were trying to kill the Bottle Bill. I said S.O.L.V. was not environmentally concerned; S.O.L.V. was started just as a red herring to draw our attention away to make the public believe that the beer companies were going to solve the problem, and that it wouldn't."[19] Soon after her broadside, she received a visit from Kessler Cannon, the governor's top environmental aide. Cannon took her to task for her bluntness. The governor wanted this bill as much as she did, he told her, but there was no need to antagonize the opponents unnecessarily. "He said, 'Norma, why are you saying this? We're trying to win them over and now you're taking them on.' I said, 'Well, I'm sorry, but the truth is the truth.'"[20]

Her outspokenness on the Bottle Bill propelled Norma to a stature and visibility unusual in a freshman lawmaker. "State Rep. Norma Paulus was talking about the bottle bill at a dinner party in Salem the other night. She was one of its sponsors," wrote Doug Baker in the *Oregon Journal*.[21] Clearly admiring Norma's forthrightness, as well as her more physical charms, he continued, "She is a remarkably persuasive woman, Mrs. Paulus. Nature seldom packages beauty and brains in a single politician. Mrs. Paulus, an appellate attorney, is endowed with both qualities." Baker mentioned the beverage industry's funding of S.O.L.V. and commended Norma for recognizing this sponsorship for the diversionary tactic it was. "The statuesque blond lawmaker understands the problem," Baker wrote, "and she knows how desperately the beverage people have tried to sell their anti-litter campaigns."

When the Bottle Bill passed the House with a wide margin—fifty-four votes to six—the container-industry lobbyists redoubled their efforts. "They came with their alligator briefcases and their alligator shoes," said Norma. "They came from the bottle companies, they came from the glass companies, they came from the beer companies. They got out of their Learjets and they went right to the legislature, ready to give as much money as they could to stop the bill." She added, "It's hard now for most Oregonians to picture that, but that's what happened."[22]

By this time the bill was in the Senate's Consumer Affairs Committee, chaired by Democratic senator Betty Roberts. After many contentious hours of hearings, one of the bill's opponents moved to revise the definition of "beverage" to make it less specific. "That should have raised a red flag in my head," Roberts recalled. But, thinking a goodwill gesture might defuse some of the opposition, she agreed to the amendment.[23] In her book, *With Grit and By Grace*, she tells what happened next:

> On voting day I walked onto the floor of the Senate and saw containers lined up on senators' desks. Every kind of beverage was there, from canned milk to squeeze-bottle lemon juice to canned baby formula to cooking oil and more. I knew the trap had been

set. When I spoke on the bill, the senators began asking if the items they displayed would be covered. I realized this as a ploy to create confusion and thereby defeat the bill.

When one of the bill's opponents moved to re-refer it to Roberts's committee—confident it would die there—Roberts knew she had to act fast. After the Senate adjourned for lunch, she announced, as was required, a quick meeting of the committee. She rounded up two members who she knew supported the bill and told them to report to the committee room. The other two members, both "nay" votes "wandered off for lunch," wrote Roberts. She and the first two members restored the former, more-precise definition of "beverage," passed the amended bill, and sent it back to the Senate floor for another vote.[24]

When the bill came back to the Senate floor with its original definition of "beverage" restored, opponents realized their ploy had not worked. Subsequently, someone in the opponent camp approached at least two legislators, including Roberts, with offers of campaign cash in exchange for help in killing the bill. For Roberts, the offer came in an anonymous phone call. She told the caller she was not interested, and hung up. In a speech the following day, she told the Senate of the attempted bribe, saying, "We may not be able to keep the environment and politics of Boston, Washington, D.C., and New York clean, but I'd prefer to keep Oregon's environment and politics clean." "After that," Norma said, "everybody was afraid not to vote for it, for fear they'd be complicitous."[25] The Senate approved the Bottle Bill with a vote of twenty-two to eight.[26]

Norma always understood the Bottle Bill as a step toward a larger environmental vision. She understood and shared the average Oregonian's revulsion to seeing garbage all over the roads, trails, and waterways. "That was the reason the Bottle Bill passed—it was because of litter, in the minds of the public. But those of us who were more visionary—people like Betty Roberts and me—were viewing it as a first step toward a real recycling and energy-conservation policy."[27] She and Roberts, she noted, were children of the Great Depression. "We used to recycle pop bottles and everything all the time. For us it was about conservation of natural resources, not just litter."[28]

Governor McCall was ecstatic about the success of the Bottle Bill and well pleased with the rest of 1971 legislature's environmental accomplishments: "The ecological package seemed almost divinely inspired, led off as it was by the 'B' legislation of bonds, bottles, billboards, bicycles, and boats; not to mention provision for monumental coastal and Willamette Valley [environmental] studies and [a] heftier department of environmental quality."[29]

LEARNING ABOUT LEADERSHIP

By the end of the 1971 session, Norma's standing with the environmental community was as high as it could be—remarkable, she knew, for a mid-Willamette Valley Republican lawmaker, and a freshman at that. When the Oregon Environmental Council ranked the 1971 legislators according to their environmental voting record, only three legislators were given "perfect" scores (twenty-two out of twenty-two correct votes): Nancie Fadeley, Keith Skelton, and Norma Paulus.[30] Norma was pleased that the legislature had done so much for the environment, but her other passion—education—had taken a backseat. Like her Democratic colleague Betty Roberts, Norma vowed to keep pushing for publicly funded kindergartens. "That program got knocked in the head this year," she told the *Capital Journal*.[31]

By the end of her first term, Norma had learned a lot about how power flows through a legislative body, through its normal rules and channels and also through the less obvious pathways forged by alliances of ideals and interests, forceful personalities, feuds, arm-twisting, jawboning, capitulation to circumstance, and, occasionally, a genuine change of heart. "As a new, freshman legislator in 1971," she recalled, "I was more interested in my own bills and everything like that. It wasn't until the 1973 session that I got involved in the power struggles."[32]

One big thing was different: the House was now controlled by the Democrats. The 1973 session would go down in Oregon history for sweeping legislation on women's rights, land-use planning, revision of the criminal code, and other important issues. It was also memorable for being a long, sprawling, and exhausting session. Norma later described her service in the 1973 legislature as an "unbelievable, frantic and even bungling experience."[33] The reason, she believes, is that the Democratic leaders under House speaker Richard Eymann ran a looser ship than the Republicans had under the measured and careful Bob Smith. "I thought, and I still think, that Bob Smith was the best Speaker we ever had.[34] If he ever lost his temper, I never saw it. He respected the [established legislative] process, and he controlled the process very, very well." He never bent the rules, she said—never manipulated the composition of committees, for instance, to get his own way.

"For example, the Bottle Bill," she said. "Bob Smith was opposed to it. I'm sure he was, because there were strong lobby groups that would have been his natural allies that were opposed to it. Yet we passed that bill in 1971, when both houses were controlled by the Republicans. I don't believe it could have passed in 1973, when there were more Democratic votes for it, including Dick

Operation Recycle: Some Do, Some Don't in State Government

6—(Sec. I) Statesman, Salem, Ore., Fri., Sept. 6, '74

By ALLEN J. MORRISON
Staff Writer, The Statesman
(Story also on page 1.)

State agencies are trying, with varying enthusiasm and success, to live up to a 1973 Legislative resolution urging the state to recycle waste paper.

Rep. Norma Paulus, R-Salem, who was chief sponsor of the recycling legislation, conducted a tour of state agencies Thursday morning to learn how her bill is being implemented.

Accompanying her were William Bree, coordinator for the Department of Environmental Quality's Recycling Information Office; Betsy MacInnis, with the State's Energy and Resource Allocation Office; John Mathews of Clayton-Ward recycling firm, and newsmen.

Mrs. Paulus said some state agency heads and employees apparently are under the mistaken impression that it is a voluntary recycling program. "This is very interesting because it is supposed to be mandatory."

It was also learned during the tour that about half of the 1,000 30-gallon recycling cans originally purchased by Clayton-Ward Co. have disappeared. Neither that firm nor state agency heads, including General Services Division, knows what happened to the cans, costing about $6 each.

Mrs. Paulus noted on her preliminary inspection tour that some agencies are setting a good example in the recycling program while others are giving it "token compliance." Agencies cited as good examples included General Services Division, including the State Printing Office, Department of Veterans' Affairs, and state universities outside the Salem area. The big Highway Division is not cooperating in the program, said Clayton-Ward.

At State Accident Insurance Fund (SAIF) in the Labor & Industries Building, the management apparently regards recycling as voluntary, said Mrs. Paulus. Yet, she noted the Executive Order, signed by Gov. Tom McCall, makes it mandatory and sets down an administrative procedure to implement the program through cooperation with janitorial services and recycling groups.

A chief janitor of SAIF said only about half of the recyclable paper is finding its way to processing plants. Part of SAIF's non-compliance is apparently attributed to that agency's current relocation to a new building in the Civic Center area. When the agency is moved it will have space enough to implement a double waste basket system that is more effective.

Mrs. Paulus explained that several state offices have effectively used the double waste basket system, using one marked canister for recyclable paper and the other for cigarette packages, carbon paper, typewriter ribbons and other non-recyclable items.

At the State Printing Office, the touring delegation learned that state agencies have traditionally over-ordered in their materials, believing they are saving money by not reordering later. This increases the demand for paper and is really a waste of money and time, printers say. The state is starting to get on the right track, said Mrs. Paulus, by limiting orders, using both sides of paper and by instituting recycling.

Mrs. Paulus and others hope that private companies and other government agencies beyond direct legislative control will enter the paper and other recycling programs voluntarily, not only because it would save money but would also extend the life of overburdened landfill operations.

Clayton-Ward Co. issued a report in July on the recycling program, showing that the state made $21,000 from selling waste paper. Actually the amount was greater because some state agencies have individual contracts to dispose of computer cards and other more valuable papers, the firm noted.

However, the report concluded that the legislature or the Executive Department should appoint a full-time coordinator to insure that the maximum recycling effort is reached with minimum cost.

Bill to keep farm land along river wins vote

SALEM (AP) — Legislation designed to preserve the Willamette Greenway without taking land along the river out of farm use won approval Tuesday from the House Environment and Land Use Committee.

The bill, HB 2497, prohibits condemnation by the state of any land along the river that is used for farming. The state would be permitted to acquire the land when it is taken out of farm use.

This would prevent development of the riverbanks.

The bill now goes to the House floor.

Rep. Norma Paulus, R-Salem, is the chief sponsor of the legislation, prompted by the action of the Highway Division last year in starting condemnation proceedings against several farms.

The division wanted the land for state parks along the river part of the Willamette Greenway — a concept to preserve the river and its banks in a natural state.

Rep. Paulus said the Highway Division misinterpreted the intent of past legislatures when it began condemnation proceedings against farm land.

The legislation is opposed by some backers of the Willamette Greenway, who said that waiting until land is taken out of farm use will cost the state large sums of money because of rapidly rising land costs.

2-6-73 Statesman

Rep. Paulus Bill Would Restrict Off-Road Styles

Rep. Norma Paulus, R-Salem, plans to sponsor legislation to establish restricted areas for use by off-the-road vehicles such as snowmobiles.

She said that under present laws, authorities only can tell drivers of the vehicles where they can't go.

"I want to change the law so that the agencies can tell the operators of such vehicles where they can go," she said. Authorities would be directed to set up special permit zones for use of snowmobiles and other off-road vehicles on public lands.

She said regulations are needed to protect wildlife areas.

Statesman 6/2

Control Sought Over Turbine Plant Sites

By ROBERT E. GANGWARE
Statesman Business Editor

Legislation to bring selection of jet turbine power plant sites under state control popped up at the Oregon Capitol Wednesday in the wake of Salem's controversy over Portland General Electric's new Bethel generating plant.

Three Marion County legislators are sponsoring the bill to put the location of plants like Bethel under the same law that pertains to nuclear power plants. The sponsors are Sens. Keith Burbidge and Wallace Carson and Rep. Norma Paulus, all of Salem.

They said they are not only introducing the bill but are doing further research to see if it could be given a retroactive provision to make it apply to the Bethel site.

This was the main development the day after PGE was granted an air discharge permit by Mid-Willamette Valley Air Pollution Authority, thus getting the official go-ahead for completing the Bethel installation in time to generate power this fall.

But there were other developments. East Salem Environmental Council, major foe of the Bethel project, started consideration of a possible appeal to the courts to overturn the permit.

(Additional details page 9.)

Throughout her career Norma was involved in and concerned with environmental issues, as demonstrated in this sampling of articles on this and the next page. Norma Paulus Papers, Willamette University Archives and Special Collections_Personal Clipping Scrapbooks.

Eymann. . . . That's because the Democrats didn't know how to control the process." Passing major legislation, she added, is "very, very difficult. It's much easier to kill a bill than to pass one. All you have to do is be tenacious and know the system really well, and have one or two people to help you in key spots." If Bob Smith had wanted to intervene and manipulate the process in 1971, she said, "the Bottle Bill would have been history. It would have been defeated. But he didn't—he voted 'No' himself, but he set the committees up and let the process go forward." In contrast, the 1973 session "was not that way at all, and they couldn't shut it down. They didn't know how to stop it."

10—(Sec. I) Statesman, Salem, Ore., Fri., Feb. 9, '73

Rep. Paulus Seeks Greenway Without Farmland Destruction

By ED GROSSWILER
Associated Press Writer

A proposal to preserve the Willamette River Greenway concept without destroying prime agricultural land will be placed before the Oregon Legislature.

Rep. Norma Paulus, R-Salem, told the House Environment and Land Use Committee Thursday that a bill will be introduced providing for state purchase of scenic easements on riverfront property now used for farming.

"Scenic easements could be used to preserve the naturalness of the river's edge," said Mrs. George VanLeeuwen of Halsey, representing riverfront owners.

She said farmers would support the idea of scenic easements.

The Willamette River Greenway has run into difficulties because farmers have protested efforts by the State Highway Commission to condemn agricultural land for inclusion in the greenway system.

The Greenway was the brainchild of former State Treasurer Robert Straub and Gov. Tom McCall. The purpose is to preserve a strip of green along as much of the 500 miles of river as possible.

Some 200 miles of the river has been identified by the state highway division for possible acquisition, but less than 50 miles has been purchased.

The Oregon Highway Commission is awaiting legislative direction before proceeding with any acquisition by condemnation. Purchases now are being made only from willing sellers.

Rep. Paulus, who will introduce the easement bill with Sen. C. R. Hoyt, R-Corvallis, said "Farming should be within the greenway concept as long as use of the farmland is not intensified."

A scenic easement would require the farmer to maintain a strip along the riverbank in a natural condition. It would not be available for use by the public, but could be viewed by recreationalists on the river.

Mrs. VanLeeuwen said zoning in Linn County already prevents prime agricultural land from being converted to other uses.

George VanLeeuwen, her husband, told the committee, "I feel scenic easements and zoning will accomplish the real preservation of the river."

Earlier in the committee hearing, Dave Talbot, state parks director, described how the decision was made by the State Highway Commission not to purchase scenic Cape Kiwanda on the Oregon coast.

The committee is considering legislation directing that the state purchase the Cape.

Rep. Steve Kafoury, D-Portland, asked Talbot if the commission would ignore a legislative resolution direct-

Concern had been expressed at an earlier committee hearing about how the legislature should go about directing that the state purchase the Cape.

It has been for sale for several years and is now under option to Portland General Electric Co. which is studying the possibilities of the area around the Cape for construction of a nuclear power plant.

Riverway Cost Hearing Asked

Rep. William Gwinn, R-Albany, asked the House Environment and Land Use Committee Thursday to hold a hearing on potential costs of the Willamette River Greenway.

officials at the hearing did not comment on the estimate.

"The legislature should consider the costs that this monster is going to create for the state of Oregon."

REGISTER-GUARD, Eugene, Ore., Wednesday, J

6-6-73

Official favors restrictions on helicopters in wilderness areas

From Wire Service Dispatches

SALEM — A Multnomah County commissioner Tuesday suggested that if the Legislature is looking to the not-too-distant future helicopters ought to be added to the list of off-road vehicles to be limited from intruding on persons seeking solitude in wilderness areas.

Don Clark, county commissioner, testified before the Senate Transportation Committee in support of HB2282, the bill to limit motorcycles, snowmobiles, and other vehicles to certain designated areas. He said the day is not too far off when these vehicles will need to be controlled.

Clark said an increase in private ownership of helicopters and their increasing use would make them the same sort of threat to wilderness solitude as land vehicles are now. He said the day when helicopters would be frequent violators of the back country silence was not far off.

Rep. Norma Paulus, R-Salem, principal sponsor of the bill, testified that the bill has been changed somewhat from its original version.

She said the state is limited in directing the federal government to set restrictions. The amended bill directs the governor to enter into agreements with the federal government on restriction of federal lands to off-the-road vehicles.

She said that 52 per cent of the area of the state is federally-owned.

She added that the bill — which would take effect after Jan. 1, 1975, would provide an impetus for federal enforcing agencies to "get off their duffs and do what their directives say."

Opponents say the bill unnecessarily restricts public use of public lands.

Rep. Gary Wilhelms, R-Klamath Falls, said his mail has been 10-1 against the bill, which he said he felt was unenforceable.

Rep. Roger Martin, R-Lake Oswego, said a survey in his district showed more than 50 per cent of those who responded favored controls on recreational vehicle use.

In other legislative developments:

● Persons convicted of driving while under the influence of alcohol would get a minimum six-day jail term under legislation approved by the Senate Tuesday. The measure returns to the House for concurence with Senate amendments.

It would require judges to impose the minimum sentence in cases where the defendant's blood alcohol level was measured at .15 per cent — representing about eight ounces of liquor consumed by an average sized person within an hour. The 1971 Legislature passed a law with similar intent, but the Oregon Supreme Court ruled that its wording made the jail sentence optional.

● A measure that would have allowed state employes to run for the Legislature was defeated by the Senate Tuesday.

Contingent upon voter approval, the measure would have removed constitutional restrictions against state employes serving in the Legislature.

A proponent, Sen. Wallace Carson Jr., R-Salem, said all state employes should have the right to serve.

But Sen. Lynn Newbry, R-Ashland, opposed the measure, citing the example of an executive department employe finding himself in a position to act on his own department's budget.

Carson gave notice of possible reconsideration.

The Oregon Constitution was amended in 1958 to allow educational employes to serve in the Legislature.

● The Senate unanimously passed and sent to the House a measure that would give retirement benefits to permanent legislative employes. Sen. Norman Howard, D-Portland, said the measure — sponsored by 24 senators — would "correct an old mistake of excluding these loyal employes."

● A bill that would permit gambling in charitable organizations was referred back to committee with specific instructions in Senate action Tuesday. The proposed amendments would specify that the gambling take place on premises that "do not have gambling as the primary purpose or its profits as the primary source of revenue."

Capital Journal, Salem, Ore., Thurs., May 24, 1973, Sec. 2, Page 19

State will get Cape Kiwanda yet, say solons

Environmentally-minded legislators still are confident Cape Kiwanda will end up in public ownership one way or another — before the legislative session ends.

They say this despite the 34-23 House defeat Tuesday of a resolution which asked the state to buy the scenic coastal headland near Pacific City.

Their hopes were buoyed Wednesday when the House revived the Kiwanda issue and voted to send HJR21 back to the House Environment and Land Use Committee for re-working. They say this saved the resolution.

But the real decision on state purchase of Kiwanda hinges on those who control the purse strings — members of the Joint Ways and Means Committee.

A bill calling for the state to appropriate $500,000 toward the purchase of the cape has been in a Ways and Means subcommittee for several months now. No action has been taken on it because the committee chairman is waiting for a final vote from the House on whether the lawmakers think the state should buy the cape.

Subcommittee chairman Rep. Harvey Akeson, D-Portland, says, "I see no need to go out on a limb and commit money for something when the legislature hasn't decided for sure what it wants to do."

He thinks he has the votes on his subcommittee to send out the Kiwanda bill with a "do pass" recommendation.

Two lawmakers have asked Atty. Gen. Lee Johnson for an opinion on whether the state owns Cape Kiwanda.

Rep. Keith Skelton and Sen. Betty Roberts, both Portland Democrats, say the state may own the cape because it is surrounded by dry sand.

The 1969 Oregon beach law says that the state owns the dry sand areas along the coast. There is a strip of dry sand behind the cape.

The resolution defeated Tuesday was sponsored by Rep. Norma Paulus, R-Salem. She tried desperately to save it when she discovered ther was considerable opposition to the resolution. But her political maneuverings didn't work.

Rep. Paul Hanneman, R-Cloverdale, spearheaded the strongest opposition. He lives only about a mile from the cape. He says he wants to see the cape placed in public ownership, but disagrees with Mrs. Paulus on how much of the cape area the state should acquire.

Hanneman wants to limit the purchase to the cape proper — about 75 acres — and he has a resolution in the House Environment and Land Use Committee requesting that. Mrs. Paulus wants the state to

By
Larry
Roby
Capitol Journal
Writer

acquire the cape and adjacent area for development as a state park.

Mrs. Paulus says the highway commission shouldn't have to negotiate for a specific amount of area at the cape. If the commission is told by the legislature to purchase a specific acreage, she says, the state will have to use condemnation proceedings, "and I'm sure nobody wants that."

Hanneman is miffed because the environment committee didn't consider his resolution in the first place.

"We could have averted the whole fiasco on the floor Tuesday if somebody had discussed HJR 20 (the Hanneman resolution) with me," he says.

Hanneman also fears that under the Paulus resolution, the state would develop the area adjacent to Cape Kiwanda into a typical state park complete with picnic tables and benches.

Mrs. Paulus doesn't think the parks people have to develop the Kiwanda area in the traditional park system scheme.

Nobody, including the chairman of the House Environment and Land Use Committee, Rep. Nancie Fadeley, D-Eugene, knows what that committee will do now with the returned Paulus resolution.

It appears that all sides prefer a cooling-off period of about a week.

"If the resolution is kept alive," Mrs. Paulus says, "the Highway Commission might get the message to start re-negotiating on Kiwanda."

Last year the commission recommended against buying the cape. It said the area is too dangerous. In recent years, 14 persons have slipped from the cape into the ocean and have been killed.

The issue of the Cape Kiwanda purchase was clouded for the past few months. Portland General Electric Co. (PGE) held an option to buy that land from McMinnville banker, B. A. "Barney" McPhillips.

PGE was studying the possibility of constructing a nuclear power plant near the cape. The company gave up that idea last week.

Hanneman favored PGE's acquisition of the land with the idea that PGE would donate the cape proper to the state. That would mean the state wouldn't spend money for thecape.

Hanneman says he still is "looking for another PGE" to buy the land and donate the cape to the state.

"Any further purchaser is out of his mind if he doesn't offer the cape proper to the public," Hanneman says. He's confident there will be no commercial development of the cape while the state is trying to decide what to do.

Rep Fadeley said she doesn't consider the negative vote Tuesday in the House a rejection of Cape Kiwanda. She thinks the no vote was against the state meddling in purchases to be made by the highway commission.

She agrees that the legislature shouldn't tell the highway commission specifically what it should buy for parks development. But she considers Cape Kiwanda a special case.

She plans to send another resolution back to the House floor for another expression on the Kiwanda issue.

Mrs. Fadeley, a strong environmentalist, says she has received several calls from people asking what they can do to help save the cape.

"If the legislators receive communications from the people back home telling them of the importance of this issue," she says, "we can have some favorable action."

"I just can't believe that Cape Kiwanda will be lost," Mrs. Fadeley said. "I can't accept the idea that a treasure such as this will be permitted to slip through the fingers of Oregonians."

That contrast in leadership styles may have helped confirm Norma in her Republican identity, despite her Depression-era Democrat upbringing and her consistently progressive views. The best leaders, she believed, put their own biases aside to serve the common good, like Bob Smith did.[35]

CAPE KIWANDA

Norma was a key player in the 1973 effort to preserve a stretch of cliff-studded coastline along Oregon's northern coast for the people of Oregon. The rugged and staggeringly scenic Cape Kiwanda was in private hands, but its owner, McMinnville banker B. A. "Barney" McPhillips, wanted to sell it. The cape and surrounding acreage had been in his family for several generations, and the yearly property taxes of around $12,000 had become burdensome. He was offering 302 acres of headland, beach, cliff, and upland for about $1 million.[36] Governor McCall was keen on acquiring the cape and its environs to preserve it from development. Norma agreed with McCall's vision, urging that the state buy the whole 302-acre property. Not only did public sentiment favor preserving the picturesque site, she said, but "if the state doesn't act, private interests might grab the land and turn it into the 'coastal condomania' feared by the Governor."[37]

State parks officials had discussed the matter with McPhillips in 1972. But the talks broke off when the Highway Commission[38] decided that the cape was not a good candidate for a state park. Its heavy surf and steep terrain were a public nuisance and a potential legal liability; several people had fallen to their deaths from the cliffs over the years. (Clearly the public was using the site already, as McPhillips acknowledged.[39]) The land was both wild and fragile, unsuitable for development into a destination campground accommodating thousands of campers and hundreds of cars and RVs. Finally, a geological analysis had determined that the cape was eroding very rapidly.

"From a preservation or scenic standpoint," wrote Oregon State Parks superintendent David Talbot to a legislator in 1973, it was "highly unlikely that the Cape itself would be developed for some other use. . . . It seemed obvious that nobody in his right mind would build any type of structure on the Cape."[40] Maybe not. But Norma's view was that Oregon State Parks should enlarge its mission beyond developing campgrounds; it should direct its efforts toward preserving natural areas.[41] She was supported in this view by the environmental group Oregon Shores Conservation Coalition, which strongly favored purchasing the entire site.

Soon after the Highway Commission gave the property a pass, Portland General Electric (PGE) announced that it had acquired an option to buy it.[42] The company had the idea of building an ocean-cooled nuclear power plant on an upland site near the cape. In February, legislators asked the Highway Commission to reconsider. A subcommittee of the Joint Ways and Means Committee recommended that the state buy Cape Kiwanda and the surrounding area for use as a state park. There was talk of another bill to prevent PGE from locating a nuclear power plant on the site, but that came to nothing.[43] The subcommittee's recommendation was taken up in the House Environment and Land Use Committee, of which Norma was a member.[44] Committee chairman Nancie Fadeley later told the *Capital Journal* that she had received more mail favoring state acquisition of the rugged cape than on any other environmental topic.[45]

Republican representative Paul Hanneman of Cloverdale, a coastal town south of Cape Kiwanda, was floating a different idea: the state should hold out for a donation. He said "some possible owners" might be inclined to make a gift of the cape, and added that he supported private development of the inland areas. It seemed clear that by "some possible owners" he meant PGE. PGE officials obligingly said they would "probably make it [the cape] available to the public one way or another."[46] Hanneman's idea struck a chord with some. The *La Grande Observer* editorialized that to buy the land now would be "a waste of money." Better to let PGE build its power plant and donate the cape itself, which was useless for development. "The public can have the cape, and the half million dollars or more it would cost, too, if the legislature lets well enough alone."[47]

Norma's view was that any such donation would be "a gift horse we should look straight in the mouth."[48] She said she would introduce a bill to prohibit a utility from making such a donation unless it comes out of the company's profits. In a tart reply to the *Observer* editorial, she wrote, "I can't see why ratepayers should buy Cape Kiwanda for the rest of the state."[49] In May, PGE decided it would not buy the cape property after all. The announcement took some wind out of the legislature's sails, said the *Capital Journal*. Why the big hurry now? "The utility's decision may have killed chances for legislative approval for acquisition," because legislators on the Ways and Means Committee "saw no need now for the state to be concerned because the cape cannot be developed."[50]

Dismayed environmental advocates passionately disagreed. There was nothing to stop commercial development, they said. It was more important than ever to secure the cape in public hands.[51] The noted nature photographer Ray Atkeson called Kiwanda "the most photogenic coastal area in America." He pointed out that its natural features were no more dangerous than, say, those at Mount Hood, and that proper fencing and posted signs could go far to reduce hazard to the public. "If officials of Oregon fail to preserve Kiwanda for public enjoyment it will be a failure long remembered."[52]

In late May, Norma introduced House Joint Resolution 21, directing the Oregon Highway Commission to enter into negotiations with owner McPhillips. "Her troubles began even before the debate opened," wrote Don Jepsen of the *Oregon Journal*. Representative Hanneman had distributed a letter to members pointing up the differences between Norma's proposal and his own. Instead of fighting for her own proposal, Norma offered to substitute Hanneman's and send her own bill back to committee. "I'm not hung up on sponsorship," she said. "I just want to insure that the cape is preserved." But House speaker Dick Eymann ruled her move out of order. "Mrs. Paulus gamely but vainly tried to save HJR 21 in her closing arguments," Jepsen wrote. She pointed out that the Highway Division didn't have to buy the whole parcel—it could save money by buying the cape itself and negotiate easements for other areas, and "said the acquisition had become the leading environmental issue in Oregon." The measure went down thirty-four to twenty-three.[53] The bill went back to a committee to be reworked.[54]

The defeat of HJR 21 energized Governor McCall. He prodded McPhillips to sweeten the deal, and McPhillips did. In negotiations with Highway Commission chairman Glenn Jackson, McPhillips offered the cape and two miles of oceanfront property for $792,000. It was more than the $488,000 he'd been asking when negotiations had foundered the previous summer, but far less than the $1.75 million he'd initially wanted for the whole parcel.[55] McPhillips offered to split off 127 acres, including the cape, plus a mile of beachfront to the north of the cape—and said he'd throw in an additional mile of beachfront for free.[56] The total beach frontage alone was worth about $1.5 million.[57]

In the end, no legislation was needed. The Highway Division gave in and bought the cape, using mostly federal funds. While environmental groups were displeased that the state had not acquired the whole 302-acre tract,[58] the outcome was widely viewed as "a welcome compromise,"[59] wrote the *Oregon Journal*. "We did get our state park," Norma said later, although "not without a lot of blood let. . . . But so far nobody's fallen off and killed themselves."

FORGING AHEAD

Even as a member of the minority party in 1973, Norma was growing in political savvy and confidence. She forged ahead with her environmental agenda. It was in this session that she worked with colleagues of both parties to create Oregon's far-reaching land-use planning system (covered in chapter 4). She also promoted some smaller initiatives, like keeping snowmobiles out of Oregon's backcountry. She cosponsored two bills (HB 2282 and HB 2969), one to limit, and the other to ban, the use of off-road vehicles on public lands. When it came to issues she cared about, Norma liked to investigate things personally. So one winter Sunday in 1973, she, Bill, and the two children took a ride out of Dutchman Flat into the Three Sisters area in Central Oregon with some snowmobile enthusiasts.

One of the tour leaders was a man named Pegleg Johnson, an amputee who cherished off-roading because it enabled him to get out into the woods. Perhaps hoping to convince Norma and her family of the wholesomeness of motorized backcountry travel, he invited Norma and Liz to ride in his snowmobile. Fritz rode with another member of the group. "And my dad got stuck driving his own vehicle," remembered Liz, who was eleven years old at the time. Bill ran his machine into a tree and dislocated his shoulder, an injury that exacerbated his chronic shoulder troubles.

Afterward Norma told her House colleagues that the family had enjoyed themselves, despite Bill's injury. "I must say we had a really good time. The people who took us out were really wonderful hosts." Nevertheless, she still believed the noise and stink of off-road vehicles assaulted both the natural environment and the serenity of skiers and others who managed to get themselves out into nature without internal combustion engines. She objected to snowmobiles' propensity to swoop into areas "where man has never been before, and upset the balance of nature."

The off-road-access issue proved to be a nasty fight with much public outcry. Late one night, in the middle of the controversy, the phone rang at the Paulus home. Bill answered. An angry, gravelly voice said, "Whenever I hear the name Norma Paulus, I want to puke." Without missing a beat, Bill replied, "Norma Paulus. Norma Paulus. Norma Paulus." The caller hung up. Norma said later, "I got thousands of letters opposing what I was trying to do—control off-road vehicles because they were tearing up the dunes, they were tearing up the area above Pacific City and tearing up Cape Kiwanda, tearing up the mountain passes."

Norma understood that Oregon's livability was at risk not only from industrial polluters but from Oregonians who were mindlessly loving their state to death. "It's you and me," she said. "With hundreds of thousands of us going out into the woods or to the beach each weekend, pretty soon there will be nothing for us to go out there for."[60]

Norma addressing the chamber in the Oregon House of Representatives. Gerry Lewin, courtesy of the *Statesman Journal*. Willamette Heritage Center, 2016.023.0041.012.

Chapter 4
Land-Use Pioneer

> Until recently, in Oregon, we were a strong middle-class society.
> We had very few rich people, we had very few poor people. Most
> people owned their own homes, which was a stabilizing force.
> And there was the fact that everybody's paycheck in one way
> or another came from timber, and workers had good wages.
> The average person thought the beach belonged to him, that
> Mount Hood belonged to him. It was part of our heritage, and
> everybody understood the need to protect it.
>
> —Norma Paulus

Like many Oregonians in the early 1970s, Norma tended to think about the condition of Oregon's farmlands, forests, rivers, and beaches under the practical heading of "livability." Norma and Bill took their children hiking and skiing and sailing and to the beach.[1] They knew an unspoiled natural environment was a precious asset. "We started taking a real interest in environmental and land-use issues after we were married and started having children," she said.[2] She understood that the concept of "livability" had both environmental and economic dimensions. Unbridled development certainly harmed Oregon's scenic beauty, but it was also bad for the economy. Farmlands represented a vital economic sector. Oregon's population had grown by 18 percent during the 1960s and another 26 percent during the 1970s.[3] Most of the growth was concentrated in the Willamette Valley, with more than half in the Portland area, and many newcomers had been attracted by Oregon's fabled landscapes.

Like many Oregonians, Norma was dismayed that Oregon was being eroded by untrammeled development. Subdivisions were encroaching onto prime farmlands, beaches were being overshadowed by high-rise condominiums and hotels, and scenic vistas were marred by billboards and strip malls. This trend found a vocal critic in Governor Tom McCall. McCall's own Republican Party had declined to support him in his first campaign for governor in 1966,[4] but his platform of "livability" had resonated with the voters and swept him into office. In the colorful language for which he was well known, he told the

Oregon Senate in 1969: "The steady scatteration of unimaginative, mislocated urban development is introducing little cancerous cells of unmentionable ugliness into our rural landscape whose cumulative effect threatens to turn this state of scenic excitement into a land of ascetic boredom."[5]

McCall was convinced that a statewide planning and regulatory framework was needed to rein in development and channel it into areas where it could complement Oregon's scenic beauty and rural economic well-being. This was a governor who in 1971 famously told a national television audience, "Come visit us again and again. This is a state of excitement. But for heaven's sake, don't come here to live."[6] The remark triggered a backlash from the business community, but McCall was unrepentant. "We don't have a 'no growth' policy," he said later. "We have a wise growth policy."[7] And, "We need growth, but not the chain-letter type that leaves future generations with an empty mailbox."[8]

McCall's views were especially controversial among real estate interests, large timber corporations, local governments eager to attract economic development, and farmers reluctant to limit their opportunities to subdivide their land. Many citizens likewise were dubious about the heavy hand of government and disagreed with the governor's penchant for centralized land-use planning. Nevertheless, McCall's exhortations tapped into a broad current of worry that the state's prime farmlands were being scraped of their topsoil and planted with houses and shopping centers. Most Oregonians realized that they were at risk of losing these precious lands, especially the rich, high-producing acres in the Willamette Valley, if nothing were done to protect them.

EARLY EFFORTS

Norma had got her first taste of land-use planning in 1969, when McCall appointed her to the Marion-Polk Boundary Commission. It was her first experience in public office.[9] The boundary commission was charged with overseeing growth within and around Salem. It encompassed two counties, as the city straddles the Willamette River, with Marion County on the right bank and Polk County on the left. The commission was one of several efforts in the late 1960s and early 1970s to use coalitions of local governments[10] and city boundary restrictions[11] to manage urban growth.

As a new commission member, Norma found herself working with some formidable players in the coalescing effort to develop the comprehensive land-use planning system that came to fruition in Senate Bill 100 in 1973. A key player was Wesley Kvarsten, planning director for the City of Salem and for both Marion and Polk Counties, and a strong advocate of mandatory limits on

growth. Another heavy hitter was L. B. Day, a union official and Salem legislator who would go on to become the first director of the Land Conservation
and Development Commission, the state agency charged with developing
statewide planning goals and overseeing the counties' planning and zoning.

Oregon had been working toward some form of planning to preserve
farmlands since the 1940s.[12] In the early 1960s, the legislature had enabled
counties to zone farmlands for exclusive farm use and to offer their owners
tax breaks for continuing to farm those lands. The zoning had to be part of
a countywide land-use plan, however, and most counties lacked the capacity
or the will to take on comprehensive planning. By October 1962 only two
counties, Polk and Washington, had created exclusive farm-use zones under
the law.[13]

In 1967, two years before Norma was named to the boundary commission, L. B. Day, then a House member from Marion County, introduced a bill
that proposed another approach to preserving the county's prime farmlands.
Day was secretary-treasurer of the Teamsters Union local representing Marion
County's cannery workers. He knew that farmlands had to keep producing
crops in order for his members to stay employed. His bill proposed a system
of voluntary zoning, coupled with payments to farmers to keep their lands in
production and options for counties to buy up development rights.[14] Norma
and Day were acquainted. They had met in the mid-1960s, when, as a new
lawyer and young mother raising two bright children, Norma was at the
capitol lobbying for educational programs for talented and gifted students. At
the time it was unlikely that either of them guessed how influential the other
would become.

Norma appreciated Day's blunt, cut-to-the-chase manner, which was to
become legendary in how he shepherded—some say bullied—the land-use
system through its first vulnerable years. "He was a very strong ally," Norma
said. "He was environmentally concerned. And the way he did business was,
'This is the right thing to do; this is what the statute says, and if you don't do
it and you don't understand how to do it, then you ought to get out of the way
and let somebody else do it.' He assessed the problem very quickly and was
always well grounded in legal standing for his positions. He was a real mover
and doer and shaker."[15]

It was Day, incidentally, who would soon open the way for Norma's first
legislative campaign. He resigned his Marion County Position 4 House seat in
1970 to become an aide to Walter Hickel, President Richard Nixon's interior
secretary.[16] That was the seat that Norma sought and won in 1970.[17]

Day's bill did not pass, but the House set up an interim committee to study the problem and develop legislation for the 1969 session.[18] This committee's work resulted in a suite of bills introduced in 1969. The most important was Senate Bill 10, which required all thirty-six Oregon counties to develop land-use plans that included the zoning of all lands within county boundaries. Planning was to be guided by a comprehensive set of environmental and economic goals.[19]

Counties were given until January of 1972 to complete their plans and zones. Some counties tackled this task soon after the law was enacted. Others struggled with lack of funds and planning expertise.[20] Local officials faced hostile constituents and, sometimes, recall elections.[21] In 1970, opponents mounted an initiative petition to overturn SB 10.[22] The initiative was defeated, but it was becoming clear to planning advocates that SB 10 was not going to be enough.

NORMA'S IRON RING

By the time Norma showed up for her first Marion-Polk Boundary Commission meeting, statewide interest in comprehensive land-use planning had grown to a groundswell, with the vigorous urging of Governor McCall, who saw himself as Oregon's chief planner.[23] Norma now had a front-row seat. She was aware of the controversy over SB 10, which lawmakers were debating that year, and dismissed most critics as misguided and ignorant, and, sometimes, bigoted. "They likened the McCall plan to a very subversive act," she said.[24]

> They said it was almost as bad as Communism.[25] [They claimed] Tom McCall had gotten his orders from this Room 213 on the fifth floor of a building in Chicago, and then they'd go from Chicago to the United Nations. And then behind the United Nations were the international bankers. And then if you followed them that far they'd allow as how the international bankers were mostly Jews.[26]

She found it hard to believe people actually said things like that. "But being a member of this commission that was pulling down the hammer on [urban growth], that's what I was hearing." These adversaries, she says, were particularly suspicious of regional governmental coalitions—like her boundary commission. "They said if you take away the county government, before long it would be world government, and that was a very bad thing. It was all nonsense, but they were serious."[27]

Cooperation among local and state governments was, of course, an essential component of Oregon's pioneering land-use planning system. Norma

worked with pioneering land-use planner Wes Kvarsten, who later, as executive director of the Mid-Willamette Valley Council of Governments,[28] pulled
the City of Salem and Marion and Polk Counties together in 1973–1974 to
implement the first urban growth boundary in Oregon.

Naturally, the idea of an urban growth boundary—this one was sometimes dubbed "Kvarsten's Corset"[29]— met with resistance. "They also called
it 'Norma's Iron Ring,'" she remembered with a smile. But she had maintained
since her first day on the commission that a measure like this was needed to
save Marion County "from becoming another Los Angeles County."[30] "I don't
remember that we had any strong divisions as a commission on this," Norma
recalled later. "I think we were pretty much unanimous. The farmers, of course,
saw this as a forerunner to our real land-use planning, which had its beginnings
in farm protection, agricultural law protection."[31]

Some farmers, she told a reporter in 1970, didn't want to be "saved from
urban growth"—it was more profitable for them to subdivide their land than
to grow crops on it. But it would be better, Norma said, if everyone paid more
for food so that farming could be more profitable: "The housewife doesn't care
if hairdos go up a dollar, but she kicks if a can of beans goes up a penny."[32]

Serving on the boundary commission "was a very satisfying experience.
It was the first time that I was really involved in collaborative policy-making
that was sanctioned by government or was part of a government. It was a very
positive experience for me."[33]

THE 1971 SESSION: TWO FRESHMEN

By the time Norma entered the legislature in 1971, she was ready to plunge into
the intense work of crafting comprehensive land-use legislation that had a chance
of passing. The effort would not succeed in that session, but several important
threads were coming together to produce a momentous new law in 1973.

First, the governor and his staff were mobilizing state and local government agencies to do something about urban sprawl in the Willamette Valley.
An intergovernmental task force called Project Foresight developed two contrasting scenarios for growth until the year 2000: continue growing without
any restrictions, or encourage concentration of growth within city limits to
preserve farmland. According to Brent Walth's 1994 biography of Tom Mc-
Call, *Fire at Eden's Gate*,

The project panel produced two scenarios of four decades of future
growth. One portrayed a Willamette Valley unshielded from the

blast of population and development, a valley clogged with traffic, stripped of farmland and hemmed in by housing tracts. The second showed a well-planned valley, one in which the state had carefully directed four decades of growth. Land was set aside for development, other land stood free for forestry and farming, and highways and mass transit worked together.[34]

A proposal for an upscale residential development south of the Willamette River near Wilsonville presented an intriguing case study. The new Charbonneau project was the specter of what planning advocates were trying to avoid. Charbonneau's developers, a thrift company called Benj. Franklin Savings and Loan,[35] had followed all the rules and produced a blueprint for a high-quality, attractive neighborhood—one that would gobble up 477 acres of prime farmland five miles outside the Portland metro boundary.[36] Not surprisingly, Project Foresight's findings gained more traction in the Portland area than in Oregon's rural counties. A 1972 editorial from Portland's KATU television station lamented that "local governments simply have not exhibited the backbone necessary to reject a proposal that may have short-run economic advantages but also entail long-range ecological destruction."

> The future of the Willamette Valley must not be left in the hands of capricious local officials, else the tragedy of Project Foresight's first alternative might soon be upon us; a nightmare alley between Portland and Eugene. But that decision can only be made by the legislature, whose individual members are responsible to local constituencies and may find support of statewide zoning politically suicidal.[37]

Aware of the depth of opposition to a growth boundary, Governor McCall was stumping the state,[38] gathering key opinion leaders behind the idea of statewide planning. Prominent supporters of new zoning laws included Glenn Jackson, the CEO of Pacific Power & Light and the citizen chairman of the Oregon Highway Commission.[39] Jackson was a respected and powerful figure in the business community, reckoned by some to be the most influential business and civic leader in Oregon.[40] When Jackson agreed to chair a major Portland land-use conference organized by the governor in November of 1972, his gesture of support brought other business leaders on board.[41]

McCall and his staff were also mobilizing and inspiring environmental activists and organizations like the Oregon Environmental Council, Oregon Shores Conservation Coalition, and Oregon Student Public Interest Research Group (OSPIRG). In 1974, with McCall's support, OSPIRG's staff attorney Henry Richmond III would go on to start the land-use protection group 1000 Friends of Oregon.

THE FIRST TRY

While the governor and his staff were at work building support, the 1971 legislature created the Oregon Coastal Conservation and Development Commission and charged it with developing a management plan for Oregon's coast.[42] There was no funding for the new mandate, however, which made it difficult for the commission even to inventory the resources that needed management. The OCCDC's efforts bogged down in procedural disputes, as well as substantive disagreements between environmental advocates and pro-development players, such as port commissioners and real estate interests, about the OCCDC's scope and mission.[43]

Toward the end of the 1971 session, Norma's fellow freshman legislator, Senator Hector Macpherson, started working with environmental groups and the governor's office to improve on SB 10. Macpherson, a Linn County dairy farmer and a thoughtful man (one writer described him as "rawboned and somewhat cerebral"[44]) was concerned that the counties were not moving forward fast enough with their plans and zones under the 1969 law.

Macpherson had been elected to the legislature after serving on the Linn County Planning Commission. He was convinced that Oregon needed a strong statewide plan for future growth, or its citizens would face "a land defiled and unsightly, a monument to man's greed and shortsightedness."[45] Macpherson did not trust his fellow farmers to resist the allure of developers' dollars: "Scratch a farmer," he once said, "and you'll find a subdivider."[46] Some of the counties, he allowed, were doing a fairly good job with SB 10, but "others were doing a lousy job. It was time to get some statewide standards set up to make a more credible job of the planning process."[47]

Early in the 1971 session, Macpherson had pressed Senate leaders to form an interim study committee on land-use issues. When that proved unsuccessful, he approached McCall and his staff and persuaded them to call together an informal policy committee with himself as a member. The task of this group was to work between legislative sessions to come up with improvements to SB 10.[48] The committee included representatives from two important environmental groups, the Oregon Environmental Council and the Oregon Shores Conservation Coalition, as well as the planning director for Lane County and representatives of industry, farming, and business groups.

After many hours of study and discussion, Macpherson's group hammered out the initial version of what became Senate Bill 100. It was a complex, far-reaching piece of legislation that called for regional governmental councils to adopt plans and zones and gave the state ultimate authority over "areas of critical state concern." It would create a new state agency to establish statewide planning goals, ensure that county plans conformed to them, and set guidelines for local governments as they prepared and carried out their planning.[49] With high hopes, Macpherson and his group awaited the opening of the 1973 legislative session.

"GREENWAY" COMPROMISE

Governor McCall opened the 1973 legislature with a speech vigorously exhorting lawmakers to pass land-use legislation. Norma Paulus sat in the audience, ready to start her second term. In characteristic vivid prose, the governor told the assembled legislators,

> There is a shameless threat to our environment and to the whole quality of life—unfettered despoiling of the land. Sagebrush subdivisions, coastal condomania and the ravenous rampage of suburbia in the Willamette Valley all threaten to mock Oregon's status as the environmental model for the nation. . . . The interests of Oregon for today and in the future must be protected from the grasping wastrels of the land.[50]

As the Senate began grappling with the legislation that Hector Macpherson's group had been working on between sessions, Norma plunged into the land-use debate in the House, working to craft a bill to protect the lands along the Willamette River. Advising her in this effort was L. B. Day, then working as McCall's environmental aide.[51]

It was a delicate task, one that required the respectful cultivation of the people who owned the land along the river. Many of these farmer-landowners were dubious about land-use planning in general—they worried that a statewide system would take away their right to manage their own land as they saw fit. And in particular, they were highly suspicious of the idea of a "Willamette Greenway," McCall's vision of a 185-mile ribbon of public parkland between

Eugene and Portland, where people could hike and ride their bicycles and have easy access to the river. For his Greenway to become reality, the state would have to acquire the land, and this was a major sticking point.

Glenn Jackson, chair of the Highway Commission, was a strong supporter of the public Greenway. In the previous year, Highway Division agents had traveled up and down the valley to talk to riverfront landowners about selling.[52] This created an uproar among the farmers, notably George and Liz VanLeeuwen, who farmed a pretty spot above the river between Eugene and Corvallis known as Irish Bend. Knowing the state had power to condemn private lands for public uses, the VanLeeuwens and many of their neighbors felt strong-armed. In some cases the Highway Division actually did initiate condemnation proceedings.[53] The landowners got together and formed a lobbying group called the Willamette River Frontage Owners Association.[54]

Norma was already working with L. B. Day and fellow Willamette Valley legislators, as well as farmers and state parks officials, trying to find a way to preserve the unspoiled character of the Willamette's riverbanks without trampling on landowners' rights. If land-use planning were ever to become a reality in Oregon, she knew, "we had to bring the agricultural community totally on board. They wanted to protect farmland, but didn't want someone coming out of Portland telling them how to do it."[55]

In May of 1973, members of the House Environment and Land Use Committee took a boat ride up the river. At the tiller was George VanLeeuwen. They cruised from Harrisburg to Corvallis, viewing riverbanks that McCall wanted as part of his Greenway. They saw a stretch of shoreline that had been recently denuded of trees and shrubs. The landowner had reportedly chainsawed the vegetation down—destroying a heron's nest in the process—in order to turn the riparian woods into cleared farmland, so he could get a higher price if and when the state acquired it for the Greenway.[56]

VanLeeuwen told the lawmakers that most farmers don't treat their land this way: "It's unnecessary and undesirable to strip right down to the water's edge." But, he added, "This didn't happen until they got their pants scared off them" by the Highway Division. The following month, June of 1973, Norma sponsored compromise legislation in the form of House Bill 2497, also known as the Willamette River Greenway Act. Though the bill had "Greenway" in the title, it differed markedly from McCall's vision. It protected farmland along the river from urbanized and recreational development, but also prevented the Highway Division from condemning river frontage for parks unless the land was turned to other uses.

"We don't need wholesale condemnation to preserve the integrity of the Willamette River," Norma told the *Capital Journal*.[57] "It makes more sense to have farmlands along the river than picnic benches." In her view, HB 2497 fulfilled the spirit of land-use planning and farmland conservation by preserving the economic and ecological values of the land while respecting property rights.[58] The bill passed fifty-eight to one.[59]

By this time Norma was a rising star in the progressive, McCall-inflected strand of the Republican Party.[60] Her and Day's skillful handling of what could have been a major obstacle in the land-use planning program had pushed her to the forefront. Colleagues began to speculate on the political future of this bright and ambitious young woman. As Charles K. Johnson relates in his biography of Governor Bob Straub, *Standing at the Water's Edge*, "After the vote was over, then state representative Stafford Hansell, a sage political observer, walked up to Rep. Paulus on the floor of the House chamber and shook her hand. 'Congratulations, Norma,' Hansell said. 'You've just gotten yourself elected Secretary of State.'"[61] It would take a couple more years, but Hansell's words proved prophetic.

MEANWHILE, BACK IN THE SENATE

SB 100 still faced major opposition. McCall's vision of statewide control did not sit well with many senators—notably the conservative Democratic president, Jason Boe.[62] But it had one highly influential advocate in Portland Democrat Ted Hallock, who was friends with the Republican governor. Like McCall, Hallock had a background in broadcast journalism, and he was almost as colorful and profane.[63]

While Norma and Day were working on Greenway legislation in the House, Hallock was holding hearings on the version of SB 100 that Hector Macpherson and his group had drafted. The hearings took place in the Environment and Land Use Committee, which Hallock chaired.[64] Macpherson also sat on that committee, but he and Hallock were in the minority in favoring land-use planning. Most other members were skeptical or actively opposed. Hallock's hearings attracted many parties with a wide range of interests and opinions. There was much wrangling over certain provisions of the bill, especially those concerning how much power the state would wield over local resources and where the plan's management responsibilities would reside. After multiple hearings, it became clear that the SB 100 as written could not pass.[65]

Fearing he was about to lose the whole thing, Hallock, with McCall's support, called a special committee of lobbyists and land-use advocates to write a compromise bill[66] and appointed the pugnacious L. B. Day to chair it. With his labor, legislative, and environmental credentials and his forthright persuasive skills, Day was considered a good choice.[67] As Hallock put it, "He was a doer, a head-knocker."[68] Day summoned the key opponents of SB 100 to join the committee. These included representatives of the League of Oregon Cities, Oregon Home Builders Association, and Associated Oregon Industries. Then, according to one participant, he gathered everybody in a room and harangued them until they came around. "He was loud, aggressive, belligerent, threatening," recalled Fred Van Natta, lobbyist for the Home Builders Association. "By the time he's done with you, you figured, 'Well, I better ask for the bare minimum.' And that's what we got."[69]

Out of Day's committee came a further revision of SB 100 that eliminated two of its most controversial provisions: state control over "areas of critical state concern," and location of management authority in regional councils of government. Land-use planning would instead be managed by the thirty-six counties, guided by statewide goals to be developed by a new agency, the Land Conservation and Development Commission.[70]

ON BOARD

The compromise on SB 100 had brought many former opponents on board,[71] although some environmentalists were dismayed that so many concessions had been made.[72] Hallock brought the revised SB 100 to the full Senate, where it passed eighteen to ten. McCall, Hallock, and Day were cautiously optimistic that the bill would also pass in the House, which was controlled by Democrats. However, they feared that if there were any further debate, the delicate compromise forged in Day's committee would unravel.

The bill was assigned to the House Environment and Land Use Committee, chaired by Nancie Fadeley, a strong supporter of land-use planning.[73] The eleven-member committee had five women members, including Norma.[74] As Fadeley recalled later, a concern for the environment was then regarded as "sort of a softy," meaning a woman's issue. "Men did things like economic development, taxes, Ways and Means," said Fadeley. "They really didn't consider [environmental] issues substantive or important. So they were willing to leave the environment to us."[75] Hallock sternly charged the committee to approve the bill and deliver it to the House floor exactly as written. "I told them . . . not to change a fucking period," he said.[76] The committee approved SB 100 without changing an iota of text or punctuation, and sent it to the full House, where it passed easily.[77] On May 29, 1973,

McCall signed it, and the Oregon Land Conservation and Development Act was law.[78]

SB 100 created a new state agency, the Department of Land Conservation and Development (DLCD), along with a citizen commission, the Land Conservation and Development Commission (LCDC) to direct the agency's activities.[79] McCall appointed L. B. Day as LCDC's first chairman. A subsequent bill, Senate Bill 101, strengthened statewide protections for farmland against urban sprawl.[80] Cities and counties were now required to develop comprehensive land-use plans. LCDC's first task was to develop statewide goals to guide their planning. In 1975 the commission adopted fourteen statewide planning goals addressing farmland, forestland, air and water quality, recreational sites, areas of natural hazard, transportation, energy resources, public facilities and services—every resource that a city or county was required to manage and conserve.

Two years later, Norma's compromise Greenway bill, HB 2497, became part of the overall land-use system when LCDC folded its principles into an additional planning goal, Goal 15, which reads, "To protect, conserve, enhance and maintain the natural, scenic, historical, agricultural, economic and recreational qualities of lands along the Willamette River as the Willamette River Greenway."[81] In 1976 LCDC adopted the final three planning goals, Goals 16 through 19, to guide planning of coastal resources. Those goals took effect in 1977.[82]

STRAUB PUSHES FOR A GREENWAY PARK

After riling up the farmers in 1972 with perceived threats of condemnation, McCall had backed off a little. Over the next couple of years his administration pressed on with offers to purchase riverfront land, but turned up only two willing sellers out of the six hundred-some owners contacted.[83] But the idea of a riverfront park was not dead yet. The year 1975 began with a new legislative session and a new governor, Bob Straub. As he departed the governor's office, McCall had warned Straub not to push things with the farmers.[84] But Straub had long cherished the vision of a green playground along the Willamette River. SB 100 didn't go far enough for him, and he set out to do what even Tom McCall and Glenn Jackson couldn't do: turn the Greenway into a public park.

The Willamette Valley farmers again had Norma on their side.[85] "So many farmers were terrified of Straub's Greenway idea," said Norma. "I had already carried a lot of water for Governor McCall on land-use planning, and I wanted to find a way to help the farmers that also preserved the riverbanks as they were."[86] The farmers also had L. B. Day, who by now was running the Land Conservation and Development Commission. Day "furiously defended his agency's turf"[87] against the governor's administration, and especially Glenn Jackson's Highway Division. He and Norma canvassed the valley, speaking at farmers' rallies organized by the VanLeeuwens and their supporters.

A bill to restore the power of eminent domain for Willamette River parkland—a key piece of Straub's plan—was introduced in the House in 1975. The bill was assigned to Nancie Fadeley's House Environment and Land Use Committee, the same committee that had approved the revised SB 100 in 1973 with no change. Straub's bill never made it onto the House floor.[88] The economic and ecological values of the Willamette shore remain protected under Goal 15, as part of the overall land-use planning system, but not as a public park. While some riverfront parks were created later (most of them in urban areas), the rural riverbanks between Eugene and Portland are still mostly privately owned working farmland, thanks to Norma's Greenway compromise.[89]

Oregon's land-use planning system has survived mostly intact after challenges in 1976, 1978, 1982, 2000, and 2004.[90] It may seem remarkable that so many different interests could come together to create something so comprehensive, complicated, and enduring—especially when it required tackling deeply divisive issues like government regulation and property rights. Yet "the people stood up on their hind feet in this state," Norma said, "and said no, no, no, we want land-use planning."[91] She explains it in this way: Oregon's land-use system arose at a unique historical moment, an intersection of compelling circumstances and forceful personalities—Tom McCall's chief among them. "You have to understand that the average Oregonian loved Tom McCall," she said. "People drove 55 [miles per hour] because he asked them to. People went odd and even overnight [referring to McCall's dictum during the 1973 oil crisis that drivers buy gas on odd or even dates according to their license-plate numbers] because he asked them to."

Besides, she said, Oregon could afford to be forward-looking in those days. "Oregon felt really good about itself. The economy was doing pretty well then." Because of this stability and sense of community, Oregonians felt a sense of ownership of their state's natural beauty. "The average person thought that the beach belonged to him, that Mount Hood belonged to him. There was a very strong push from all walks of life and all four corners for protection of our environment."

ERA rally on Oregon Capitol steps, June 30, 1981. Ron Cooper. Family archives.

Chapter 5
A Journey to Feminism

> I know I am a person. You know I am a person. And it is about
> time the United States Supreme Court knew it.
>
> —Norma Paulus

In the close-knit town where she grew up, Norma Jean Petersen was exceptional, and she was treated that way by parents, teachers, and peers. As a result, she seldom doubted her own abilities. She was not cocky, but she was confident. Her energy and drive had helped her excel in her studies, be a leader in school, overcome a bout with polio, secure a plum job in Oregon's highest court at age twenty-three, and put herself through law school without getting a bachelor's degree first. She'd been taught to excel on her own merits, and she'd pretty much done that all her life.

When she moved from Burns to Salem, she'd traded one supportive community for another. She'd had an exceptional champion and mentor in her boss, Chief Justice Earl Latourette, who had recognized her aptitude and encouraged her to go to law school. It was the judge who drew her attention to the statute that permitted special students to be admitted to law school even if they didn't have undergraduate degrees. After graduation she set up a practice in appellate law, which gave her some control over her work schedule and helped her harmonize her professional life with marriage and motherhood. She felt on an equal footing with her professional colleagues. And she was married to a secure, self-confident man who appreciated her talents and accomplishments.

Norma was accustomed to seeing herself first as an individual with more-than-average energy and talent, and only secondarily as a member of a socially defined class called "women." So when she started her political career in the late 1960s, as the second wave of feminism was cresting the reefs of American culture, she kept her distance at first. It wasn't that she clung to old, restrictive views about a woman's place. On the contrary, her own life demonstrated what a woman could do if she applied brains, passion, and energy to any endeavor to which her heart called her—whether in the home or in the House.

But she had suffered only lightly the sting of discrimination, which may be why the feminists' complaints of pervasive sexism, their exhortations to solidarity, and their more attention-getting demonstrations left her cold. "If you had asked me in 1970 what I thought about *The Feminine Mystique* [Betty Friedan's 1963 book, credited with galvanizing the feminist movement's second wave]," she recalled, "I would have said, 'I don't have time to read frivolous things.' Because I never felt that I had been discriminated against."[1]

When she ran for office, her bubble burst. Nothing in her experience had prepared her for the blatant sexism she encountered on the campaign trail. "It just hit me square in the face," she said. "It was staggering to me that the only thing keeping me back from getting people's votes was that I was a woman. It turned me inside out overnight."[2]

THE RIGHT TIME

When Norma joined the legislature in 1971, women's issues were rising to the top of the legislative agenda. Lawmakers were targeting laws that discriminated against women in the workplace, home, divorce courts, public accommodations, insurance benefits, marital-property and inheritance matters, and other areas of life. They were passionately debating proposals for legal abortion, publicly funded day care, and freely available birth control information.[3]

By 1973, in Norma's second session, there were more women lawmakers in Oregon than ever before. She was one of eight women in the House; the two women in the Senate were the veteran legislator Betty Roberts and her colleague Betty Browne.[4] The women formed a caucus across chambers and across the partisan aisle, pledging to work together to pass legislation redressing unfairness in the law and advance the empowerment of women. "We just came alive that session," said Norma. "We made a list of all the women's issues, and a list as long as your arm of all the statutes that discriminated against women."[5]

Of the many items on the caucus's to-do list, one seemed to wrap them all together: ratifying the Equal Rights Amendment. The ERA was a proposed amendment to the US Constitution that would forbid discrimination on the basis of sex; it was then making its ratification rounds through state legislatures. The time seemed ripe for Oregon to ratify the ERA. The president of the Senate, Jason Boe, and speaker of the House, Dick Eymann, were both ERA supporters.[6] The Democrats were in the majority in both houses for the first time in eighteen years, and many of the Republicans were, like Paulus, progressive in their views.

Moreover, Oregon had a visionary Republican governor in Tom McCall, who had opened the 1973 session with a ringing call: "I urge you to ratify this Amendment as your first order of business in this session—and as a continuation of our mutual respect for human rights."[7] Even so, Norma and the rest of the caucus knew that ERA opponents were sowing a thicket of arguments, some reasoned and thoughtful, most simply scare tactics. A vote for ratification would require canny strategy and forceful persuasion.

Soon after opening day 1973, Norma paid a visit to her friend Betty Roberts in her Senate office. Norma had admired Roberts ever since seeing her interviewed on television when she was a new mother at home with baby Elizabeth. In that interview, Roberts, then in the House, was talking about her plans for funding public kindergartens and her support of legalized abortion.[8] Now they were colleagues.

"Betty," said Norma, "the women in the House think we need to form a women's caucus to talk about getting the ERA passed. Since you're the senior woman in the Senate I think you should call and chair the meeting."[9] Roberts called the meeting, and all the women legislators came. From the House came Republicans Norma Paulus, Mary Rieke, and Mary Burrows and Democrats Nancie Fadeley, Grace Peck, Mary Wendy Roberts, Peg Dereli, Pat Whiting, and Vera Katz; from the Senate, Democrats Roberts and Browne.[10] The women called themselves the Equal Rights Alliance—the name gaining strength from the familiar acronym. They worked together extraordinarily well. Norma said: "I think most women in the legislature were so used to juggling things, they didn't care much about the credit. It wasn't a power trip. It was a way to get things done, and have an influence. They'd walk into a meeting and say, 'I know why I'm here, I know what the issue is, just tell me what my part is.'"[11]

When Norma and Nancie Fadeley approached Speaker Eymann for support, he proved a key ally. "We explained our strategy to him. We told him, 'We've got all these laws that discriminate against women. We know how to draft the bills we need, and we're drafting them. We've got women gathered inside the legislature. We know the climate is right. We know we can pass these bills. What we need is a committee we can get them out of.'" "Let me think about it," Eymann said. A few days later he announced that he'd formed a new committee, the House Environment and Land Use Committee, to be chaired by Nancie Fadeley. Norma and three other women would sit on the eleven-member committee.

The Environment and Land Use Committee would become the birthplace for most of the significant women's-issue legislation passed in the 1973 session.[12] "I've given speeches for 25 years praising Eymann for doing that," Norma said.[13]

SCARE TACTICS

The text of the Equal Rights Amendment was stately and simple: "Equality of rights under the law shall not be denied or abridged by the United States or by any State on account of sex." By the time the 1973 session opened, twenty-two states had ratified the ERA. Paulus, Roberts, and the rest of the Equal Rights Alliance were determined to make Oregon the twenty-third.

Their efforts were energized by activist and lobbyist Gretchen Kafoury, whose husband, Stephen, served in the House as a Democrat from Multnomah County. Gretchen Kafoury had made headlines in 1971 when she led demonstrations outside the meeting place of the Portland City Club (whose motto was "Conscience of the City"), after its all-male membership voted twice to deny membership to women.[14] Kafoury was an early inspiration for Norma. "After the 1971 legislative session I got a flyer from her asking me to come to a meeting. I'd never met her, but I went to the meeting. It was in the Meier & Frank tea room, a very raggle-taggy group, but it was the first time I'd ever heard some of these discrimination issues discussed among a group of women. And I came to adore Gretchen and felt very loyal to her. Even though I never served with her,[15] I felt like sort of her Republican counterpart in the legislature."[16]

Kafoury was awed by Paulus. "She was so damn classy, this tall classy woman, kind of intimidating for me," she said. "But all these kinds of things, physical characteristics, roots, backgrounds—all these melted away because we were united in this common cause."[17] The women became fast friends.

Three different ratification bills were introduced, two in the House and one in the Senate. The women's caucus had planned to work for passage of the Senate bill, but it happened that the first scheduled hearing was on one of the House bills. It was held in the State and Federal Affairs Committee, chaired by majority leader Les AuCoin. AuCoin was a Democrat and an ERA supporter.[18] The hearing, held in late January of 1973, attracted an overflow audience. The main witness in favor of the amendment was Carol Hewitt, a lawyer who represented the American Civil Liberties Union's position on women's issues. Others who spoke in favor of the bill were representatives Roger Martin and Nancie Fadeley, labor commissioner Norman Nilsen, and Kathleen Nachtigal, a lawyer who chaired the state Wage and Hour Commission. Their testimony mostly concerned the practical, workplace benefits of the amendment: it

OREGON LEGISLATIVE ASSEMBLY—1973 REGULAR SESSION

Enrolled
Senate Joint Resolution 4

Sponsored by Senators BROWNE, ROBERTS, Representatives FADELEY, DERELI, KATZ, PAULUS, RIEKE, ROBERTS, WHITING

Whereas the Ninety-second Congress of the United States of America, at its second session begun and held at the City of Washington on January 18, 1972, by a constitutional majority of two-thirds vote in both houses adopted a Joint Resolution proposing an amendment to the Constitution of the United States, as follows:

"ARTICLE—

"Section 1. Equality of rights under the law shall not be denied or abridged by the United States or by any State on account of sex.

"Sec. 2. The Congress shall have the power to enforce, by appropriate legislation, the provisions of this article.

"Sec. 3. This amendment shall take effect two years after the date of ratification."; and

Whereas the proposed amendment shall be valid to all intents and purposes as part of the Constitution of the United States when ratified by the legislatures of three-fourths of the several states within seven years from the date of its submission by the Congress; now, therefore,

Be It Resolved by the Legislative Assembly of the State of Oregon:

(1) The proposed amendment to the Constitution of the United States relating to equal rights for men and women, as set forth in this resolution, hereby is ratified.

(2) The Secretary of State shall send certified copies of this resolution to the Administrator of General Services of the United States, to the presiding officer of the United States Senate and to the Speaker of the House of Representatives of the United States.

———◇———

Senate Joint Resolution 4 for the Equal Rights Amendment signed by its sponsors, all of whom are women. Norma Paulus Papers, Willamette University Archives and Special Collections_Personal Clippings Scrapbook 1972–73_014a.

would require equal pay for women doing the same jobs as men and would forbid sex discrimination in hiring and firing.[19]

The opposition came forward in the form of groups with names like Preservation of Womanhood ("whose state chairman was a man," noted Betty

Roberts), the Movement to Restore Decency, and Parents for the Preservation of the Family. Representatives of these organizations rose to declare that if the ERA became part of the Constitution, society would crumble into decay. One woman said, apparently without irony, "We women have so much to lose if we are granted equality." Others said the amendment would force schoolchildren to share bathroom and shower facilities, would do away with fathers' obligation to support their children, would erase any distinction between the sexes, and would destroy the American family.

The "share toilets" tactic powerfully irritated Norma. "We were trying to help people understand the basic constitutional issues of the Equal Rights Amendment," she said, "and the naysayers would always come up with this nonsense that we'd all have to use the same public toilet." Some of the women referred to this persistent red herring as "potty politics." The well-known and highly regarded Salem teacher Mary Eyre—one of Norma's early mentors—testified and offered this rebuttal: "I don't know about you, but I have a toilet in my house and it's unisex. It's unisex today, it was unisex yesterday, it was unisex when it was put in there. Some of you won't remember this, but I used to ride trains all the time as a little girl, and the toilets were unisex."[20]

Representative Roger Martin, a Republican from Lake Oswego and an ERA supporter, polled the four major oil companies that did business in Oregon. He reported that all of them planned to keep providing separate facilities as long as the public wanted them—although one respondent pointed out that many of the rural filling stations already had only one toilet, and it had been that way for a long time.[21] Another scare story was that, if the ERA became law, women would be drafted and have to fight alongside men. Betty Roberts pointed out that Congress already had the power to draft women. Moreover, for women already in the military—and men, too—the duties assigned were typically based on skills and capabilities, as opposed to sex.

Norma agreed with Roberts's assessment. "Military service does and should depend on the strength and agility and talent and experience and training of the individual," she said. "There are many men serving in the Armed Forces who never get out from behind the desk. Or they're drivers, or they do any number of non-combat jobs. The ERA opponents were just throwing all these other things in to keep us from having a thorough discussion of the Constitution."[22]

After that hearing, the ERA supporters had an idea of what they were up against. Betty Roberts wrote, "We knew advocates in other states had been running into last-minute, mostly irrational opposition. In California, state senators favoring the ERA were sent dead mice—the message apparently being that if they supported the ERA they were mice, not men. In another state, legislators received bullets for their wives." Paulus, Roberts, and the other ERA supporters knew they had to press hard with their logic, patiently reiterating the compelling reasons for passage. They marshaled their arguments for the hearing on the Senate bill, set for less than a week after the hearing.

In the Senate bill hearing, Carol Hewitt again laid out the case. The Fourteenth Amendment, she said, guaranteed protection against racial discrimination, but nothing in the Constitution forbade discrimination on the basis of sex. Indeed, the US Supreme Court had ruled that the protections in the Fourteenth Amendment applied only to racial discrimination—meaning the amendment's protections did not extend to people who experienced other kinds of discrimination. Yet it was clear, Hewitt argued, that women were experiencing discrimination every day, in the workplace, in public accommodations like hotels and restaurants, in financial practices, and in marriage, divorce, and inheritance laws. Federal protection was needed for women, just as it was needed for African Americans and other minorities. Other speakers provided details of the kinds of inequities women faced. It was a long, sorry list. Women could legally be paid less than men for the same work, were restricted from holding certain jobs, turned away from restaurants and hotels, and denied admission to some schools. They were treated unfairly in insurance and credit matters. They couldn't keep their birth names when they married.

The opponents showed up at this hearing with more of the same fearful and mostly irrational rhetoric. Nevertheless, the bill was voted out of committee and went to the Senate floor, where it passed by a generous majority: twenty-three to six. A week later the bill received its final hearing in the House. Here was the final hurdle: here was where Oregon would ratify the amendment, or not. Representatives Nancie Fadeley, Vera Katz, Mary Rieke, and Norma Paulus spoke passionately in favor of the bill. They were joined by several male legislators, both Democratic and Republican.

When Norma got up to speak, she characteristically cut to the heart of the matter, stressing the vital distinction between social custom and legal fairness. People were entitled to their various opinions on women's place in society, she said. But the law ought to treat everybody equally:

> I believe I can separate the Equal Rights Amendment from the Women's Movement for those of you who feel uncomfortable about certain aspects of the Women's Movement. . . . The Women's Movement purports to change attitudes—I support that

movement, wholeheartedly. It seeks to change the attitudes, social attitudes between men and women. But that's not what the Equal Rights Amendment does. The Equal Rights Amendment seeks to change the government's attitude toward women. Today, I don't care what you men really think of me or what your attitude toward me is, but I do care what the government thinks of me and what its attitude is toward me.[23]

Her speech was informal, even lighthearted, but compelling. She pointed out her legislative colleague Bob Elliott and noted that the US Supreme Court had always recognized the rights—the "personhood"—of him and all white men. But when it came to recognizing the personhood of men of color—and here she pointed at Representative Bill McCoy, the House's sole African American member—the court had dragged its feet until it "smelled the smoke from the courthouse burning." Now it was time to extend the same recognition to women. "I know I am a person," Norma told the assembled legislators. "You know I am a person. And it is about time the United States Supreme Court knew it."

Recalling the speech later, Norma said, "Before I started to speak, I leaned over and asked them if they'd mind if I mentioned them in the speech, and they said they wouldn't. So I used Bob Elliott, who was sitting right in

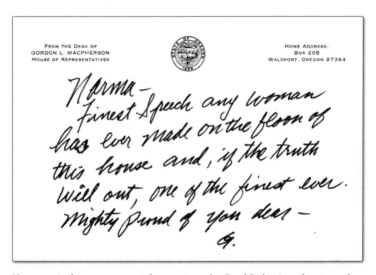

Norma received numerous congratulatory notes on her Equal Rights Amendment speech to the legislature, like this one from State Representative Gordon Macpherson. Norma Paulus Papers, Willamette University Archives and Special Collections_Personal Clippings Scrapbook 1972–73_015b.

At the 1973 signing of the Equal Rights Amendment resolution with Governor McCall were *(L-R)* Senate President Jason Boe, House Speaker Richard Eymann, Secretary of State Clay Myers, Representative Nancie Fadeley, Representative Norma Paulus, and Representative Grace Peck. A personal note on the photo reads, "Warm thanks, Norma, for championing equal rights, from Gov. Tom McCall." Photographer unknown. Family archives.

front of me, a very handsome man with a shock of gray hair, just a beautiful human being. And I used Bill McCoy, who was the first black man to serve in the legislature."[24]

> I used them to convey the idea that Bob was white, male, privileged—a very fine man and a very fine legislator, but nevertheless a member of that class of people that we call the power structure. I said that my colleague from Washington County, Bob Elliott, has always been viewed as a "person" under the Constitution, because he is white and he is male. And it's only been within my lifetime that the Supreme Court has said that "person" also means Bill McCoy. And I said that the reason we're here today is to say that "person" means not only Bob Elliott and Bill McCoy, but Norma Paulus and all the other women. And I said, that's what this Equal Rights Amendment does, and that's all it does. And then we passed it, overwhelmingly.[25]

Governor McCall signed the bill into law, and Secretary of State Clay Myers sent Oregon's ratification to the US Congress.[26]

In April of 1973, speaking at the Business and Professional Women's annual banquet for senior high school girls, Norma described herself as "a firm believer in 'Women's Lib,'" according to a newspaper account of the speech. "But she feels the correct definition is 'freedom of choice,' and that everyone should have the opportunity to exercise their rights of choice, responsibility for one's self, and equality."[27]

In the end the ERA failed to gain the required number of state ratifications to become law. Yet for Norma, the unified campaign to pass the ERA in Oregon helped her better understand the deep patterns of discrimination woven through the fabric of law and culture. "It's hard for people to realize now, so many years later," she said. "It seems like yesterday to me! But people today don't realize that there were so many laws that openly and blatantly discriminated against women."

If she had been a reluctant feminist before, she was a committed one now. "This movement just came alive. It was exciting to be a part of it, because it was everyone—we were women in agriculture, women working to change inheritance taxes, working on labor issues, credit issues, on everything. We were this great coalition of women of all shapes and sizes from all over the state, of different educational levels and persuasions. It was just like being on fire."[28]

MORE WORK IN 1975

Another high priority for the women's caucus was to reform the inheritance laws. Norma remembered stories she'd heard as a child about farm wives who had suffered financially when their husbands died. She remembered one widow who was forced to pay inheritance tax on everything in the estate. "It included a silver service that she had received from her mother," Norma said. "The wife had brought it into the marriage, and it was worth several thousand dollars, and she couldn't prove her mother had given it to her, so the law assumed that her husband owned it and she inherited it and she had to pay taxes on it."[29] Farm wives, she said, typically worked right alongside their husbands, in full partnership, to build and run the farm. "But if the husband dies first, the law assumed the wife inherited the whole estate and so had to pay inheritance tax on the whole thing. None of her contributions over the years counted." The law, she said, didn't treat men the same way.

Norma and Mary Rieke, her Republican colleague in the House, enlisted the support of the women's caucus in 1975 on a bill to reduce inheritance taxes on widows. They had brought a similar bill before the 1973 legislature, but it had failed to pass. They came back in 1975 with an approach that was more palatable to opponents who were concerned about the potential loss of tax revenue.[30] The women had done their homework thoroughly. They had researched the bill's legal precedents, fiscal implications, and social consequences, and they had secured the necessary support from like-minded colleagues. "We had all our votes lined up," Norma said. "Mary Rieke was carrying it on the floor of the House. She wasn't as relaxed about carrying bills as some of us. But she got up, went through all the charts, gave all the explanations, talked about how we almost got it passed last session. And we knew we had the votes."

Norma remembers Rieke[31] as a reserved person, a model of decorum, not given to flamboyance or public outbursts. "She was very traditional, conservative—a wonderful lady," Norma said. "She'd put a lot of her heart and soul into this issue. It was as big a matter to all of us as it was to her, but it had been a commitment of hers for a long time."

Rieke finished her presentation and sat down. Everything seemed set for a "yes" vote. Then Wally Priestley, a Democrat from Portland and a member of the revenue committee, stood up to speak. Norma and Rieke exchanged glances. What now? Everybody was supposed to be on board with this bill, or at least resigned to its passage. Priestley had a reputation as an odd duck, a dreamy-eyed idealist who roomed at the YMCA and sometimes slept overnight on a capitol sofa. He'd been known to set off the fire alarm by bringing his own toaster to make toast in the capitol lounge. He was a hopeless political romantic, in Norma's view. "Such a gentle person, and he would persist with these socialist ideas no matter where he was. His arguments were always interminable, and always in this gentle voice."[32]

Priestley got to his feet and took the microphone. "Members," he said, "I move to reconsider." This would have delayed the vote and possibly killed the bill. Mary Rieke leaped out of her chair and yelled, "Wally Priestley, you prick!" She froze, horrified at her outburst. Then, said Norma, "she grasped her chest and got pale and fell into her chair, and then she and the chair went ass over teakettle." Speaker Dick Eymann quickly gaveled the House into recess. Someone helped the distraught Rieke to her feet.[33] Norma took her by the arm and gathered the rest of the women's caucus around. "And they all gave her a standing ovation," said Norma.

CHANGING LAWS, CHANGING ATTITUDES

By end of the 1975 session, Norma was fully on board with a feminist agenda. She continued to champion legal protection for a woman's freedom of choice in every aspect of life, including her reproductive life. She applauded a decision by the US Supreme Court that challenged inequities in Social Security law because they discriminated against women.[34] She expressed disappointment that the 1975 session did not make enough progress on women's issues, and criticized House speaker Phil Lang for being less friendly toward women's issues than the previous speaker, Dick Eymann.[35] In a March speech to a statewide women's conference at Marylhurst College, she said, "I don't believe women are going to have economic power until they have political power. You're not going to have political power until you start electing men and women with a feminist viewpoint."

When school districts complained of the expense of granting girls equal access to athletic programs, as the federal Title IX law required, Norma told them that a lawsuit would be even more expensive. Schools that nurtured their girls' sports teams and gave them more money and status were applauded by Norma. "Public sentiment may be for the status quo," she warned, "but the law is on our side."[36] Yet she also preached personal responsibility. All the legal protections in the world, she maintained, were of no avail if women didn't step forward and take charge of their lives. In speech after speech, she exhorted women to use the power they had, starting at home.

> I would look out into the audience and say, "You're here because you want to know how you could change your life."[37] And I'd say, "Listen. If you are working all day and you're doing the laundry and you're driving the kids to lessons and you're driving them to football practice and you're coming home and emptying the dishwasher and the dryer—if you've got a dishwasher and a dryer—and your husband comes home from work, picks up the newspaper, grabs a can of beer and sits down in front of the television set . . . " Well then, I said, "You are really stupid!" And that's just what I'd tell them.

"And they'd look at me like this"—here she screwed her face into a dumbfounded expression. "And I'd say, 'No one can do that! You cannot work full-time and do full work at home. You just can't do it.'"[38]

PASSING THE ERA—AGAIN

As it turned out, the ERA's opponents weren't quite done. A Republican legislator from Portland, Drew Davis, introduced a bill in the 1977 session to overturn Oregon's 1973 ERA ratification. Davis was allied with the Eagle

Governor Bob Straub signing the second passage of the Oregon ERA Amendment in 1977 with Norma and others looking on. Photographer unknown. Family archives.

Forum, a conservative organization founded by the antifeminist activist Phyllis Schlafly.[39] The Eagle Forum was a small presence in Oregon politics—"It hadn't yet been trained by [televangelist] Pat Robertson to organize through the evangelical churches," said Norma[40]—but it was a harbinger of the religiously motivated conservative politics that would come to dominate the Republican Party in the next few years.[41]

Schlafly had stumped the nation campaigning against the ERA. She warned that it would violate the "special respect" for women that she claimed had been practiced since "the Christian age of chivalry," and that was modeled on "the honor and respect paid to Mary, the mother of Christ."[42] She had not visited Oregon, but when it was rumored she would come, Norma said, "we joked about sending her a telegram [saying] we were going to set her hair on fire."[43]

From the secretary of state's office, Norma watched with mounting concern as Davis introduced the bill to rescind the 1973 ratification. "I went to Nancie Fadeley and I said, 'What is this? Who is this crazy guy and what is he doing?'" Fadeley assured Norma, "We'll take care of it."[44] When the bill was introduced, Speaker Lang referred it to the Special Committee on Equal

Norma at the National Women's Political Caucus with Marian Milligan (*at left*) and two unknown women, Cincinnati, Ohio, 1979. OSA Norma Paulus Photos, 6/19, "National Women's Political Caucus, Cincinnati 1979."

Rights. This was a surprise to everyone, wrote Betty Roberts, "because at that point there was no such committee." As the House was adjourning for the day, Lang announced the formation of the Special Committee on Equal Rights, with himself as chairman and Nancie Fadeley as vice chairman.[45]

The new committee met forthwith. Fadeley amended Davis's bill by removing the word "rescind" and replacing it with "reaffirm." The amended bill was approved by the committee and introduced on the House floor. In a surprising flip-flop, Davis voted "yes" on Fadeley's amendment. He said he'd introduced the repeal bill only to give the people a chance to be heard.[46] The amended bill was passed by the House and subsequently by the Senate. "So I think we're the only state in the nation that ratified the ERA twice," Norma said.[47]

In October of that year, as the national ratification process continued, Norma spoke to a Eugene luncheon meeting of the League of Women Voters, which strongly supported the ERA. She told the audience of about two hundred men and women to stop apologizing for their opinions and to advance their cause "like a mission." Yet, candid as always, Norma acknowledged that changing people's attitudes would be harder than changing the law.[48] What's more, she said, the attitudes of women themselves could be surprisingly hard to change: "Those of us who had succeeded in the male-dominated professions didn't want more women in them, because that would destroy our uniqueness and newsworthiness." Sometimes, she conceded, "I was guilty of that myself."

But the irrational fear that the ERA would break up American families, she said, was a delusion. On the contrary, "the ERA will save the family."[49] Social pressures to marry and have children were leaving women adrift in middle age with nothing meaningful or productive to do. "The American family is disintegrating, becoming a national joke, and the women's movement and ERA are not a cause of that destruction; they are a result of it."

Norma at microphone, September 1975. Dana Olson/*The Oregonian*.

Chapter 6
Sunshine in Government

> I believe everyone has an obligation to contribute something to
> the state or community—serving in public office, licking stamps,
> giving money or informing himself about the issues. The fewer
> people who assume that obligation, the less the system works.
>
> —Norma Paulus

On June 17, 1972, not long after Norma finished up her freshman session,
burglars broke into an office complex called Watergate in Washington, DC.
Their target was the headquarters of the Democratic National Committee.
Discovery of the break-in and the ensuing cover-up by the Nixon White
House unraveled a conspiracy that reached into the Oval Office. The Watergate scandal brought down a presidency and shattered the faith of American
citizens in their government, a trust already eroded by the seemingly endless
conflict in Vietnam.

In 1973, near the beginning of her second session, Norma became acquainted with another rising star in the Republican Party. Dave Frohnmayer
was a lawyer from Eugene who had worked in Washington as a speechwriter
and policy adviser for a top Nixon aide, Robert Finch.[1] Frohnmayer had come
back to Oregon in 1971. He wasn't a fan of Nixon, and while the administration's "dirty tricks" hadn't yet hit the headlines, Frohnmayer was dismayed at
his party's rightward swing on some important policy issues. Together with a
cadre of moderate Lane County Republicans, he formed the Rubicon Society.
"It was a self-conscious allusion to Caesar's crossing of the Rubicon," he said.
"We were at a point of no return."[2]

As the 1973 session opened, Frohnmayer and like-minded colleagues
were establishing the Oregon chapter of Common Cause, a nationwide citizen's advocacy group started in 1970 to push for more transparency in government. (Its founder, activist and clean-government advocate John Gardner,
landed on President Nixon's infamous "enemies list" after the organization

sued the president's reelection committee in the early 1970s for violating campaign finance law.)

Frohnmayer and others in Oregon Common Cause drafted model legislation to require public bodies to conduct open meetings and maintain open public records and to require officials to disclose potential conflicts of interest. They also worked out a campaign finance reform proposal that Frohnmayer believed would not violate constitutional guarantees of free speech.

In 1973 they took their work to a joint House-Senate committee that was working on laws governing open meetings and open records. Norma served on that committee along with her friend and mentor Wally Carson. By this time the headlines and airwaves were awash with the Watergate scandal. "And there was so much dissatisfaction with government, and people's perception of government was so negative," Norma said, "that we knew we had to make our government more open to public scrutiny and public participation."[3]

Norma had had an unpleasant personal encounter with government secrecy during her freshman session, when members of one of the committees on which she served—all of them male, of course—retreated into the men's room and continued discussing business there. Furious at being excluded, Norma marched into a nearby press room and collared a reporter, Clarence Zaitz, and informed him that there was a secret meeting going on the men's room. Zaitz went in to investigate, and presumably the meeting was hastily adjourned. Secrecy had never been Norma's way. "With the exception of things like personnel records, everything the government does should be open to the public—records, meetings, emails, everything," she said. "That experience I had as a freshman made me realize we had to do something."[4]

In the 1973 session, Norma, Carson, and the other members of the joint committee worked closely with Frohnmayer and Oregon Common Cause, meeting every Monday night for several months[5] to hammer out Oregon's pioneering laws governing public meetings and public records.[6] The legislation required a constitutional amendment, which Norma helped draft. The sunshine laws, passed in both houses of the legislature, were approved by the voters and remain in place today.[7]

The open meetings law requires that the deliberations of public bodies and their advisory committees be open to the public, with reasonable advance notice of meeting time, place, and agenda. The law spells out exceptions such as labor negotiations and discussions of personnel performance, but it makes it clear that openness is the default for conducting government business. The open records law, similarly, requires that citizens be given access to records of all activities of elected officials and public bodies, with certain spelled-out exceptions.[8] The campaign finance portion of the package was passed by the legislature but later declared unconstitutional.[9] To date Oregon has not set any limits on campaign contributions and has no public finance system to help fund election campaigns.[10]

Norma was not in favor of public campaign financing in 1973, but since then she's reluctantly come around to supporting it. "We've tried everything else, and nothing has worked," she said. "I'm willing to try just about anything to get a handle on campaign finance."

A NEW HIGHWAY BUILDING?

Toward the end of Norma's freshman term, the Highway Commission had announced plans to build a new headquarters near the Salem airport,[11] several miles away from downtown Salem. Like most state agencies then, the transportation department was headquartered in the capitol neighborhood. The Oregon Capitol sits in a T-shaped park just east of downtown Salem. The Capitol Mall and surrounding neighborhood are managed by a state agency called the Capitol Planning Commission. The commission was created by the legislature in 1949 with the goal of preserving the beauty of the historic neighborhood—then bounded north and south by Center and State Streets and east and west by Twelfth and Cottage Streets—and protecting it from commercial encroachment.[12] In 1958 the commission unveiled a long-range master plan for the Capitol Mall, which by then included the five-block stretch northward to D Street. The 1958 plan and subsequent revisions governed construction and remodeling of state buildings within the mall. Over the years the commission acquired nearly all the private property within the mall neighborhood.[13]

Because Salem is the seat of state government, public buildings make up a large fraction of the city's built environment. Consequently, issues concerning state properties tended to loom large in city planning conversations. Having served on the Marion-Polk Boundary Commission, Norma was interested in land-use issues in and around Salem. As a freshman legislator in 1971, she'd been surprised to learn that Salem-area lawmakers like her were restricted in their influence on state decisions about their hometown. Of the Capitol Planning Commission's (then) six members, only two were elected—the Senate president and the speaker of the House—and they served only in an advisory, nonvoting role.

That a small handful of mostly unelected people could make important long-range decisions violated all Norma's convictions about representative government. The fact that the commission's role was mostly advisory didn't change her opinion. She did not agree with many of the Capitol Planning Commission's policies; she was not in favor, for instance, of treating Summer Street, a thoroughfare through one of Salem's most graceful older neighborhoods, as a scenic avenue of approach to the north face of the capitol. More to the point, she didn't like the commission's heavy hand in acquiring private properties for future preservation or development. "We had sacrificed Salem's best residential district to the state Capitol," she said. "It destroyed the neighborhood when the state condemned the properties, and they're still sitting there and nobody can own them. [The state] can rent or lease them, is all. It was a very major mistake for them to do that. It was done in an untoward manner."[14]

Even so, Norma recognized that the state's business ought to be conducted with due process. While she may have faulted some of its decisions, the commission did have a legitimate mandate to manage the siting of state buildings, and its policy was to cluster them around the capitol. So when the Highway Division announced its plans to move out of the neighborhood, Norma suspected powerful hands pulling strings behind the scenes.

Oregon's transportation policy is set by a citizens' commission appointed by the governor. The chairman of the Highway Commission (it was renamed the Transportation Commission in 1973) was Glenn Jackson, a businessman with strong ties to the biggest Oregon industries.[16] He had sat on the Highway Commission since 1959 and would serve until 1979. His tenure was a time of major expansion of the state's transportation systems.[17]

Jackson was also a rancher, land developer, newspaper publisher, and World War II veteran. By most accounts he was an unassuming and widely respected man, renowned for his ability to broker deals between opposing interests.[18] By all accounts he wielded enormous behind-the-scenes influence in the development of Oregon's transportation and parks infrastructure. As Highway Commission chairman, he had a lot to say about the spending of the Highway Division's budget.

At that time the Highway Division occupied a graceful 1951 neoclassical building within the Capitol Mall, but agency officials had deemed it "outmoded."[19] The Highway Commission had considered and rejected two other properties along the mall. It favored a new building in east Salem, on a site near the Highway Division's materials lab, where there was plenty of free parking. Everything seemed like a go. The 1971 legislature had approved the funds, and the Joint Ways and Means Committee had added a budget note specifying that the building would be situated on land near the Santiam Highway (US 20)[20]—a tacit endorsement of the Highway Commission's desire for the east Salem location.

Norma saw the move as an end run around established procedure. Further, she was convinced that Jackson's outsized role in Oregon's affairs tarnished the ideal of open and transparent government. Norma speculated that Jackson, who had enterprises based in Medford, might favor the airport location because it would be personally convenient for him. "Then he could just hop right on [an airplane and] walk to his office."[21] Further, she said, "What they wanted to do was use [highway] trust fund money to build the new building, and then use the old highway building—which was also built by the trust fund, I assume—for something else. It was not a good way to do the government's business."[22]

Highway projects in Oregon were (and still are) financed from a dedicated highway trust account[23] funded mostly by gasoline taxes. Norma was convinced that the highway fund—one of the state's largest pots of money—was not subject to the same strict legislative oversight as the budgets of other state agencies. In fact, she'd recently testified before the House Transportation Committee in favor of a constitutional amendment to free up some of the highway fund for other uses. She called the highway fund "the biggest sacred cow in state government," and told the committee that the Highway Commission should have to "stand in line like other agencies" to get its share of operating funds.[24] She added: "When [Jackson] sat on top of the state Highway Commission and pretty much controlled it . . ., that was a very, very large budget with all kinds of priorities, and it affected more Oregonians . . . than any other agency."

Norma had no personal quarrel with Jackson, but she would feel the same way, she said, about anyone in his position: "You could extend a lot of favors if you were disposed to operate that way." In fact, she remarked, it was a good thing he was honest, "because he had a great deal of power [with] little or no legislative oversight."[25] She could see that the Capitol Planning Commission, as it was then constituted, was no match for this kind of power. Early in 1973, at the beginning of her second term, she and like-minded legislators developed House Bill 2667, which would give the commission authority over all building, remodeling, and siting of state agency buildings anywhere in Marion and Polk Counties—not only on the Capitol Mall. The bill would also shift money from the General Services and Executive Department budgets to the commission, so it could hire a staff to support its work.

In selling the idea to her House colleagues, Norma said such a law "will bring some order to planning" in the capitol area without requiring additional state funding.[26] Even before it passed, the bill had the effect Norma wanted. Political reporter Charles E. Beggs reported that HB 2667—"the result of several years of bickering between the commission, local officials and state planners in the Executive and General Services Departments"—promised to head off the move to locate a new highway building in east Salem.[27] After several weeks of discussion and revision, HB 2667 passed both House and Senate. It was signed by Governor McCall in June, with an emergency clause dictating that it would take effect immediately.

The law effectively killed plans for a new highway building. "It's possible the commission could approve an East Salem site," wrote Don Jepsen of the *Oregon Journal*, "but not likely. One thing seems certain—Ways and Means may have the power of the purse in releasing funds for the new building, but it neatly had any authority on siting severed with a stroke of McCall's pen."[28]

The Capitol Planning Commission's new powers pleased Salem city officials, who had worried about the difficulties of managing the sprawl of state office buildings all over town. "The City of Salem has gone a long way toward encouraging the legislature to continue developing the Capitol Mall," the *Oregon Statesman* editorialized, "instead of fractionating state government by starting an East Salem state government office complex."[29]

LURING THE TOURISTS

A few months later, another move from the Transportation Commission raised Norma's hackles again. After the 1973 session, Glenn Jackson persuaded the Legislative Emergency Board, the committee of fifteen legislators that oversaw budget matters between legislative sessions, to transfer $200,000 out of the highway maintenance budget and use it to buy advertising to encourage out-of-state travelers to visit Oregon.[30]

Norma, her Senate colleague Wally Carson, and several other legislators were angered by the high-handedness of both Jackson and the E-board (as it was known in shorthand). "The legislature openly and cleanly fought the battle and won twice against the tourist advertising budget," Norma said. "And then Glenn Jackson, the most powerful politician in the state, waltzed in and in a five-minute time span changed all that around."[31] Paulus and Carson began developing legislation for the 1975 session that they hoped would rein in the power of both the E-board and Jackson. One of their proposals would limit the service of any Transportation Commission chairman to two terms. It would also bar principal stockholders of any state-regulated utility from serving on the commission at all. This proposal was clearly aimed at Jackson, who chaired the executive committee of Pacific Power & Light Company. If it passed, it would retroactively unseat him.

That idea was the first of a package of far-reaching reforms developed by Paulus and Carson. They also wanted to shift the legislature from a biennial to an annual body. They wanted to give the legislature power to call itself into session—an idea the voters had rejected in the May primary, leaving in place the governor's sole authority to call the legislature together. They wanted to remove the state tourism budget from the dedicated gasoline-tax highway fund. These three proposals would require amending the state constitution. Finally, they wanted to abolish the Legislative Emergency Board altogether, replacing it with a federal grant commission whose sole job would be to oversee state use of federal funds.[32] Suspecting all this might be too much for the legislature to swallow at once, Paulus and Carson proposed a series of interim steps that would drastically reduce the power of the Emergency Board. They argued that these reforms were needed in order to shift power away from the executive branch and back into the legislative branch—the people's branch—where it belonged.

Norma regarded the E-board as an artifact of a more leisurely, less complicated era, when citizen-legislators could ride into Salem for three months, take care of all the state's business, and go back to their farms or shops. Times had changed—the state's business was now pressing enough, she argued, to require legislators to meet yearly. Annual legislative sessions would reduce the need for a select cadre of legislators to mind the store for the better part of two years while the legislature was out of session. They would also enable legislators to respond to constituents' needs "more quickly and more expertly in a calmer manner."[33]

To those who feared that annual sessions would lead to a permanent professional class of legislators, she responded, "The kind of people you get now to serve in the legislature are 'kept women' like myself and young men without families who don't have the day-to-day life experience to serve in the legislature." Businessmen and others with a full professional life, she said, couldn't afford three months or more away from their jobs every two years. Annual sessions would lessen the burden and encourage greater numbers of qualified candidates.

How did all this fly with the legislature? The Carson-Paulus proposals "didn't even get serious hearings," Norma said ruefully, much later. "But they caused a lot of comment."[34]

TOURISM ADS, NO. 2

Apparently undaunted by the Jackson tourist-ad controversy, the Department of Transportation came to the legislature in 1975 and announced another ad campaign. The ads would be funded by the $200,000 Emergency Board appropriation that had been approved the previous year.

By this time Norma, serving her third term, had hit her stride as a seasoned legislator, and she was outraged. In a January speech in the House, she flourished a tearsheet for an ad scheduled to run in the February issue of *Sunset*, a California-published lifestyle magazine. The ad was titled, "An Invitation from a California Man," and featured a testimonial from a visit to Oregon.[35] The space for the ad cost $23,000, said a Department of Transportation spokesman; the design work, done by Portland agency Cole and Weber, cost additional money.[36]

"We're paying $200,000 for blather like this," Norma said. She was even more incensed at a promotional letter from *Sunset*'s executives to Oregon legislators and public officials, describing Oregon's ideal advertising campaign to target the wealthy leisure class. Cultivating affluent travelers, the letter said, would prove "highly profitable for Oregon and with light environmental impact." Norma charged that it was "outrageous" that ads portraying Oregon as a "rich man's paradise" were paid for by Oregonians' gasoline taxes. It was nothing but a blatant appeal to rich people.

And what was wrong with that? countered Gary Sund, a spokesman for the Department of Transportation. "It is the policy of our travel information section to promote Oregon to those who are more affluent and can predictably expect to stay longer and spend more money in the state," he said. "More out-of-state tourists . . . add up to more Oregon jobs." There was no point, he added, in pitching Oregon to lower-income folks: "Oregonians have expressed their dismay with campground availability, so we do not promote Oregon camping to out-of-staters."[37]

Given Norma's support of small business and environmentally friendly economic growth, her fury at the tourist ads may seem surprising. Perhaps what riled her was the casual assumption that rich visitors were desirable and poor ones were not. Maybe the division of citizens into hotel guests (from California) and campers (from Oregon) touched something in her working-class soul. What disturbed her more, though, was seeing taxpayers' money spent at the behest of an unelected commission, and over the wishes of a legislature that had already voted down tourist advertising.[38] Her point was not that Oregon did or didn't need rich tourists. It was that the people's elected

Norma reflecting on her successful legislative career from her home in Salem, Oregon. Gerry Lewin, courtesy of the *Statesman Journal*. Willamette Heritage Center, 2016.023.0041.001.

representatives ought to be making that decision, not a state agency or an appointed commission.[39]

Here again she was demonstrating her faith in transparent, open, and truly representative government. She believed that empowered citizens would do the right thing for themselves and for society. She once told political commentator Paul Harvey, "I believe everyone has an obligation to contribute something to the state or community—serving in public office, licking stamps, giving money or informing himself about the issues. The fewer people who assume that obligation, the less the system works."[40] A citizen's first duty, she believed, was to vote. In another of Norma's key accomplishments in the 1975 session, she worked hard to amend Oregon voter law to make it easier to register. She was by then vice-chair of the House Elections Committee,[41] and her convictions carried some clout. The revisions permitted a would-be voter to register in person on election day, eliminating the former thirty-day cutoff period. They also made it possible to send a voter-registration form in by mail, rather than deliver it in person.

Her passion for making voting easier and more convenient for citizens was Norma's first step toward Oregon's pioneering vote-by-mail system. In 1981, in her second term as secretary of state, she would work with the legislature to try the vote-by-mail concept in certain local elections. In 1998 Oregon voters would overwhelmingly approve vote by mail for all elections.[42]

MINDING THE BOOKS

In February of 1975, a financial audit of all Oregon's state agencies found widespread irregularities. Auditors commissioned by Secretary of State Clay Myers found that more than fifty state agencies were plagued by serious accounting flaws, unauthorized expenditures, leaks from cash accounts, and in some cases deliberate thwarting of legislative spending controls. In two agencies—the Executive Department and the Department of Revenue—the books were in such terrible shape that the auditor couldn't determine anything about the financial condition of the agency. The revenue department in particular was criticized for loose handling of cash receipts and undelivered refund checks—problems that had been spotlighted in earlier audits "without major improvements." The legislature, too, was faulted for questionable spending policies, including unauthorized legislator expenses and staff bonus and vacation pay.[43]

Norma's reaction to these disclosures was not precisely shock. She was not so naïve as to think everyone in government was cash-register-honest all the time. But the audit's findings reinforced her conviction that the best recipe for honesty was transparency. "I was convinced we had an honest state government," she said, "but there was no accountability, because there simply wasn't a system that would allow it."

Perhaps she had an inkling that she might soon be in a position to do something about that. By the end of 1975 she had become thoroughly familiar with her job. She had earned a reputation as the go-to person for citizens experiencing difficulties with state agencies. "Other legislators would call me and say, 'My constituent has a problem with the revenue, or natural resources [agencies].'"[44] She felt she understood state government inside and out. She was also gaining a broader public audience, owing both to her high profile as a legislator and her effectiveness at getting the lawmaking job done. Did she want more of the same? Or did she want something different? She pondered the question and made up her mind. "Having worked every day, every hour for six years in the legislative arena," she said, "I knew I wanted to move up."[45]

As a minority member, she could not realistically aspire to be speaker of the House. She considered a run for the Senate, but another prize glittered beyond it: the secretary of state's office. The current secretary of state, Clay Myers, was retiring after two terms, prevented by law from seeking a third. "It occurred to me," she said, "that there was a better way to spend my life."[46] In October of 1975, Norma announced that she was "98 percent sure" she would run for Myers's seat.[47] If she won, she would be the first woman secretary of state—and the first woman elected to statewide office—in Oregon's history.[48]

for Secretary of State

Norma Paulus Committee, 1645 Liberty S.E., P. O. Box 426, Salem, Oregon 97308 4 5 76

Secretary of state campaign pamphlet, April 1976. Norma Paulus Papers, Willamette University Archives and Special Collections_1976 Campaign for Secretary of State Scrapbook 007.

Chapter 7
An Historic Election

When I went into the legislature my party was in power. By the
time I had served six years there—and I think by an impartial
analysis was regarded as a very effective legislator—I looked
at the situation very coldly and thought, "There is no way I
am ever going to be Speaker of the House. There is no way I
am ever going to be President of the Senate. So what shall I do
now?" And I thought, "Well now I'll run for the next office, the
highest office that is available," and that was the Secretary of
State's position.

—Norma Paulus

In 1976, with nearly three terms as a legislator behind her, Norma Paulus knew
it was time to make a move. She had invested six years of her life in politics,
more than enough time to convince herself she was good at it. She wanted to
spend what she called her "most productive years" in the political arena.

Staying in the legislature wouldn't achieve that goal. With the Democrats controlling both houses, she knew she would never make speaker of the
House or president of the Senate. "It's one thing to stay in the legislature if
your party is in power and you have a significant role in the policymaking,"
she said. "But if you find that you're not in power, you're always going to be
relegated to a secondary role. And if you're viewed as a real comer in the political scene—which I was at that time—the opposition party is going to do
everything they can to keep you less visible, less effective. . . . I could see the
handwriting on the wall."[1]

Moreover, many times Norma found herself chafing at the procedural
constraints lawmakers faced: a six-month session every two years, with no
power to call themselves into session (that was the governor's prerogative),
and the bustle and confusion of reorganizing the legislature after every election. As she told a 1976 meeting of the Republican Women's Club,

Each time it's a whole new system and all we do is pile programs on top of programs. Because we handle the tons of "new" bits of legislation in such a frantic fashion, and because we have that "power" only six months, these matters are passed on to some agency to implement the laws, and there's no one on hand to ride herd on these administrative agencies. The system forces this practice, but it is not representative government.[2]

That system, she felt, undermined the very reasons she had entered politics in the first place. She yearned for a setting in which she could really get things done.

TOUGH RACE

The 1976 campaign for secretary of state was grueling for both candidates. After beating John P. Kelting in the Republican primary, Norma faced her Democratic opponent, legislator Blaine Whipple, in what reporter Steve Forrester called "the hottest and closest statewide race" on the upcoming November ballot.[3] Forrester (whose paper later published a popular columnist's endorsement of Whipple[4]) minutely traced each candidate's itinerary in the first post–Labor Day issue. Whipple had taken his race south to "logger country" in Grants Pass, stopping by Sutherlin to meet the town's newspaper publisher and greet voters on the street before spending a full day of interviews, campaign stops at mills during shift changes, and a Kiwanis meeting.

Norma had left her Salem home in her white campaign van in time to meet workers at a 7:30 a.m. shift change at Hyster Corporation in northeast Portland. Her schedule that morning included a one-hour newspaper interview and a tour of the Cascade Corporation's plant. Then she delivered a midday speech to a Kiwanis Club in the Montavilla neighborhood, and afterward headed south to Polk County for more meeting and greeting, ending the day back in Salem with a dinner speech to the Professional Mortgage Women of Marion County.

Forrester devoted many column inches to details of each candidates' resume, issues, and funding specifics. He also noted differences in their personal qualities: Whipple's demeanor was "solid but somewhat gray," in contrast to Norma's more relaxed and "colorful" personality. Forrester contrasted Norma also with Betty Roberts, Oregon's most recent female candidate for statewide office. Roberts's appeal, he judged, "suffered from a hard

Norma with Nelson Rockefeller and Clay Myers; Norma introduced Rockefeller at a Portland rally where Rockefeller quipped that he usually gave cuff links with the Vice Presidential Seal to the men who typically introduce him. He gave Norma a pendant necklace with the official seal and claimed she was the first woman to receive it for such an introduction, October 16, 1976. Official photograph, the White House, Washington 130C76G2362-02A.

edge in her appearance, which was reinforced by a hard edge in her speech," whereas Norma's softer presence coupled with her forthright speech probably made for "a more saleable combination."

In the arena of nonverbal communication, Whipple again came up short, his "somewhat stiff" demeanor contrasting unfavorably with Norma's "looser, hip body language." The reporter had no choice but to admit Norma's charm, without actually calling it that. "It must be observed," he concluded with a certain reluctance, "that while placing a hand on the arm of the listener is an ancient politician's move, it does achieve a new dimension when the politician is a woman and the listener a man."[5] By the time the article hit the streets, Norma was doubtlessly too busy to dwell on that historic aspect of her body language. Her key objective in the nearly eight weeks ahead was to boost her face and name recognition throughout the state.

In the primary campaign against her Republican opponent, John Kelting, Norma's organizers had focused on speaking engagements. They worried that unless voters met Norma face-to-face, they wouldn't regard her as a serious candidate. "Because where they didn't know either of us," Norma said, "they'd choose the man." Consequently, Bob Packwood's strategy of broadening name recognition through lawn signs and campaign slogans had been less emphasized.

Norma now felt that the meet-in-person strategy had cost her in statewide visibility. It had been, she believed, the biggest shortcoming of her primary campaign. Although she won the primary handily, she was not going to make the same mistake again. She hired Karen Whitman, who had handled Lee Johnson's 1972 run for attorney general and Bob Packwood's 1974 reelection campaign. Whitman's first move was to transplant Norma's campaign headquarters from Salem to Portland, renaming the Salem post the Home Office. The new headquarters in the Benjamin Franklin building on Portland's Southwest Front Avenue lent greater visibility and access to leadership.

Whitman raised $120,000 and devoted most of it—$90,000—to television and radio advertising and outdoor boards, including twelve thousand lawn signs. She launched canvassing that reached 60 percent of the homes in the state.[6] Norma's faith in Whitman paid off in a victory that appeared to come off without a hitch. But at her election-night party at the Benson Hotel, Norma was feeling the strain of having kept herself acutely visible for the better part of a year. While she had been confident she would win, Norma didn't find the reality of it as exciting as her epiphany when she first decided to become a public official. As the revelry swirled around her, Norma felt nothing more profoundly than exhaustion. "I don't remember really being really excited or elated," she said. "I was tired, and it was fun to have all my supporters be happy, but I don't have any really vivid recollections of it."[7]

She looked forward to relaxing a little before being sworn in, but her rest was short-lived. Bill had planned a surprise trip to Russia for shortly after the election, and hadn't mentioned it to Norma until ten days before. In other circumstances she would have leaped at the chance. Russia was not welcoming American tourists then, so Bill had arranged for them to join a study trip sponsored by Willamette University. He'd hoped the promise of the trip would keep Norma going through the grueling last days of the campaign. "And I thought, God, November, going to Russia. All I wanted to do was come home."[8]

To Fritz Paulus, his dad's secretly planned trip typified a dynamic in his parents' relationship. Norma and Bill delighted in gifting each other unexpected, extraordinary experiences. On this occasion, while Fritz grants that Norma might not have been completely delighted at first, he recalls that she was soon wholeheartedly won over by the idea of traveling behind the Iron Curtain, an unusual undertaking in those days.

Norma being sworn in as Secretary of State in January 1977 by the Honorable James Burns, Federal District Court Judge. Judge Burns was Norma's boss as District Attorney of Harney County when she was nineteen years old. Bob Ellis/*The Oregonian*. Oregon Historical Society, OrHi105568.

CLEANING UP THE ARCHIVES

Soon after her inauguration, Norma discovered that her office's most recently acquired responsibility—archiving of state records—was beset by serious issues. "When I got to be secretary of state, I was absolutely astonished to learn that we were paying millions of dollars in storage fees to store these records," she said. "As a legislator I was never told this, and nobody ever asked about it."[9] The workings of the archives division make up one-third of the secretary of state's portfolio—the other two are the audits division and the elections and public records division. Oregon's first archives division was created in 1945, and the state archivist's statutory duties were legislated along with full funding in 1974. The archives were originally established as part of the Oregon State Library. In 1973 they had been transferred to the purview of the secretary of state, who supervised the state archivist.[10]

David Duniway, state archivist from 1946 to 1972, had played a major role in how the duties of the office evolved. Duniway was renowned for scavenging for records stashed in random locations around the state, and even in the subterranean tunnels of the Oregon State Hospital. There, among mummified cats and rodents, he had found quantities of historical state documents and records stored in cages.[11] While the retrieval of vital and potentially confidential records such as tax returns, personnel files, and welfare records was important, an

Tom McCall of Oregon

Nov. 4, 1976

Dear Norma (and Bill):

    Next to beating the buzzards on Measure #10, your
victory was our greatest Election Day thrill. I so
greatly distrust Whipple that his election would have been
a disaster--but to win with Norma as the bonus, that is the
best of all worlds. And, gosh, what a landslider you are!
And a landslider who never became a backslider on any
of the things you hold dear .

    I'm the one who needs advice now -- whether to retire
to news and the speaker's trail...or Carter-it...or run for
governor --all decisions that are up in the air now.

    Anyhow, if I do run--and win-- I can die happy in the
knowledge that a great governor would be ready to step up
from only one heart beat away . Warm best wishes from
both of us .

                   Loyally

                   Tom

            Tom (and Audrey) McCall

Personal letter from Governor Tom McCall congratulating Norma on becoming Secretary of State. Norma Paulus Papers, Willamette University Archives and Special Collections_NP074.

effective process for storage and disposal had yet to be developed when Norma stepped in. Such sloppiness offended her sense of orderly, thrifty housekeeping. Proper storage and orderly destruction of the state's paper files was important, not least because "it involves a lot of money."[12] Depending on the nature of the information they contained and on legal requirements, different types of records needed to be saved for different lengths of time, and it was the archivist's job to figure out the best system for storage, retrieval, and destruction.

Norma came to see that this was a first-order logistical challenge, and all the more because the state's functions were growing in scope and complexity.

"We were just being bound up in this mass of paper that we couldn't get rid of, and there was no system for keeping a destruction record," she said.[13] Costly records storage was also a problem for many of Oregon's counties.

Soon after taking office, Norma recalled visiting a fifteen-by-twenty-foot storage room in Portland that contained nothing but parking tickets. She soon found there were "all kinds of privately owned spaces in Salem" for which the state was paying monthly fees. In these rooms were stacked personnel records that had stagnated beyond their required retention periods. In county court-houses, old deeds, transaction records, and marital records were haphazardly stacked, often on the floor, in damp, musty places.[14] Norma realized with dismay that she and her archivist were going to have to start from scratch building systems for the safe retention of records, the proper periods for retention, and the destruction of records that could legally be let go.

After Duniway retired, Norma's predecessor, Clay Myers, had hired J. D. Porter, who was committed to establishing a real, effective records-management system. Porter, Norma, and her deputy Greg McMurdo went to work, with Porter developing a program and McMurdo drafting the necessary legislation and administrative rules. The process was gradual, but over the years, the three of them set up a different system for each department with its individual needs. For example departments such as the State Police, the Department of Agriculture, and the Oregon Arts Commission would have a diverse array of requirements for retention and destruction of records. Norma's tedious and difficult job was to devise the appropriate protocol and schedule for each department and organize extensive training sessions for records managers in each part of state government.[15]

The next step was to buy, "with very little money," some means of destroying the records. For this mission, Norma turned to the Garten Foundation and found a solution that would help both the state and some of the state's disabled citizens. Norma had become acquainted with the Garten Foundation while she was in the legislature, making a name for herself as a passionate recycler. The foundation, which advocates for people with disabilities, operates a recycling business to train disabled people in job and life skills. In 2003 the foundation honored Norma as Oregon's "Mother of Recycling."[16]

Norma and the foundation set up "a wonderful partnership" to tackle the mountain of outdated records. They had to acquire a machine to shred and pulp them, and space in which to house it. This proved challenging, but the right secondhand contraption was finally found and installed in an old flaxseed warehouse on Liberty Street near the intersection with Broadway.

It was a bare-bones rented space, totally inappropriate for document preservation. Although Norma oversaw the installation of fans and dehumidifiers to ameliorate the building's less-than-optimal conditions, she was unable to convince the legislature to buy the huge facility and properly retrofit it for both destroying records and storing still-valid ones. If the legislature had done so, she said, it would have saved the state all the rental fees spent on widely scattered, privately owned storage spaces that were never managed beyond the continual addition of records.

Norma's efforts to clean house in the state archives resulted in solutions that she knew were effective in the short term, but were still just stopgap remedies. Before leaving office, she tried to ensure that the momentum she achieved would continue. She put together a committee headed by Cecil Edwards, state historian, and J. Wesley "Wes" Sullivan, longtime *Statesman-Journal* editor. The committee made a "thorough and non-partisan" analysis of what the archivist needed, again urging the state's purchase and further renovation of the Liberty Street warehouse. It could have been "bought for a song," Norma said, providing ample space for both retention and destruction of documents and allowing the archivist to consolidate the records stored in rented space.[17]

Although the committee's recommendation was set aside in favor of a different solution—the construction of the Cecil L. Edwards Archives Building in 1991—Norma's success as the first secretary of state to develop archive protocols is indisputable. Her efforts demonstrated to legislators and voters alike the need to protect state documents, with the result that Oregon's once widely dispersed records now securely rest under one roof.[18]

THE PROPERTIES

Norma saw the secretary of state's role as that of a defender—defending the state's properties, accounts, and ethics against careless handling or deliberate depredation. She had made this vision clear from the outset of her candidacy, and when she was sworn in she announced that her office would start the new year with a series of "modern-day 'wolf meetings.'"[19] The expression harked back to the gatherings held by Oregon Trail pioneers in the early 1840s to discuss and formulate a governmental solution to the problem of attacks on livestock by wild predators, wolves among them.[20] It made sense that Norma would cite this instance of early Oregonians striving to keep the wolf from their doors by founding a government where there once was none. She saw several modern-day incarnations of the wolf at the door in Oregon.[21]

Paulus family campaign photo, 1976. Family archives.

One wolf she saw threatening Oregon's historical legacy was governmental disregard and misuse of state properties, from furniture to diplomatic gifts—even doorknobs embossed with the state seal. Norma's awareness of abuses surrounding state properties and artifacts was stirred early in her first term. As a passionate "antique nut and junker," she conceived the idea of furnishing her new office with relics of the state's past.[22] Her reverence for the props of history was not something Norma was born to. When she married into the Paulus family, Norma recalled that history was simply not on her radar. At that time, "I was not interested in antiques. I had nothing in my background that would make me aware of the value of antique furniture or artifacts. My family didn't own anything, they didn't have anything, there wasn't anything really to preserve or cherish, so I hadn't grown up with that."

Besides, Norma believed multigenerational Oregonians were so accustomed to watching history living among them—such as the people she saw as a child at Burns's Pioneer Days who had actually come over the Oregon Trail—that they didn't grasp the importance of nonliving artifacts. Once, early in her marriage, she held a big garage sale at Bill's parents' house and unwittingly sold, for a few dollars, a family heirloom, a campstool that had come across the country on a wagon. Norma didn't know what it was, and at the time she didn't care.[24]

By now, though, her view of all things historical had changed, and she was hitting her stride in the study, pursuit, and collection of antiques. When the time came to furnish her office, Norma remembered the supreme court building's attic, filled with antique furniture abandoned by incoming justices who preferred contemporary-style desks and chairs. She decided to search amid these fine old pieces for a desk and chair. She was astonished to find the attics empty. Where had all the furniture gone? Norma's coincidental forays into antique shops had already unearthed some discarded state treasures, like bronze doorknobs embossed with the state seal. In investigating the emptied attics, Norma learned that, in the 1971 remodel of the capitol building's basement into office carrels, the salvage company had been allowed to remove and sell for its own profit items that were not going to be reused. Many items, such as the discarded chandeliers and doorknobs, were gone forever—which was even more galling because the doorknobs later cost $120 apiece to replace.

"It was perfectly legal," Norma said, "but the people who were running the legislature were men. They had no appreciation for this, and they didn't pay any attention to details."[25] The wholesale removal meant that valuable bookcases and desks, even those formerly used by Governor Oswald West, were sold in public auctions, sometimes "literally for a song," to antique dealers or anyone who wanted to buy them. Norma discovered that some legislators were taking their office furniture home, evidently assuming that after years of use they were free to do so. "There are hundreds of examples like that," Norma said. "It was all just disappearing in front of our eyes."

"So outraged and disturbed" was she by the disappearance of these historical treasures that she went to Governor Victor Atiyeh and informed him she was going to introduce a bill to create a Historical Properties Commission. Norma intended to chair the commission herself, and would further require a half-time employee, to be paid not from her budget but from the executive branch's surplus property unit. Norma and her new hire would be authorized to "go out and put red flags on what few things were left of our history, to ensure the property management's system wasn't selling them." Once tagged, the properties could be registered on a Department of General Services database. The "tagging legislation," as it came to be known, ensured that if a piece of state property appeared for sale or in private hands, it could be returned to its rightful place.[26]

Norma's plan for the new commission was legislated into place by 1979 with the help of Senator E. D. "Debbs" Potts and Representative Glenn Otto—two Democrats who, Norma knew, were keenly interested in history.

Norma on the job as Secretary of State, circa 1977. Norma Paulus Papers, Willamette University Archives and Special Collections_NP074.

She selected her commission's advisory committee with equal care, enlisting three or four women "who knew something about politics but a lot about antiques." She also tapped Cecil Edwards, for whom the job of legislative historian was created in 1975, and Captain Terry Aitken, head curator for the Oregon Military Museum. She wanted someone with military connections because, as she said, "I wanted the National Guard to help me. They had manpower and trucks and cranes."[27] With transportation provided by the

Guard, Norma and her recruits combed through the capitol, including all the buildings on the Capitol Mall, as well as the prisons, the universities, and a building that at the time was a Pendleton mental hospital and is now a prison.

Although most of the reclaimed items amounted to a "pretty pitiful" assembly, Norma recalled a few exciting finds. After her first uneventful trip to the Oregon State Hospital, she received a tip from a hospital employee that there was a treasure trove of antiques, amassed by a former superintendent, Dr. Dean Brooks, cached in the tunnels under the buildings. Dr. Brooks was an antique collector and famous in Oregon for his part in hosting the cast and crew for the film adaptation of Ken Kesey's novel, *One Flew Over the Cuckoo's Nest*, in 1975. Dr. Brooks had retired in 1981, and his successor, James C. Bradshaw, was the man standing between Norma and an apparently huge collection of uncatalogued state properties.

When Norma, along with Cecil Edwards and Alfred C. Jones, the half-time employee who was hired to catalogue historical properties, returned to the hospital, the superintendent said he didn't know about any secreted relics, but agreed to show them through the tunnels. A dazzling array of antiques and curios awaited them, even things left from the Lewis and Clark Centennial Exhibition of 1905.[28] The most notable find was a dusty portrait, painted in oils, of a distinguished-looking man. Norma didn't recognize him, but the portrait was so distinctive that she was intuitively moved to take it with her. When the superintendent protested, she reminded him of her constitutional authority over all state property.

Back in the capitol, nobody could identify the subject of the painting, until one day she invited the director of the Oregon Historical Society, Thomas Vaughan, to come to see her. Vaughan walked through her door, spotted the painting, and exclaimed, "My God, this is Oswald West!"[29] The discovery of a lost portrait of Oregon's fourteenth governor (1911–1915) caused a stir in the media. Norma began a quest to find all surviving gubernatorial portraits. She got another tip from a witness to the fire that had destroyed the old capitol building in 1935. Her informant had seen Willamette University students carrying paintings out of the burning Hall of Representatives and stashing them on the Willamette campus, adjacent to the capitol grounds.

Norma consulted Fred Paulus, her husband's uncle and a former deputy state treasurer. Uncle Fred was an Oregon old-timer who in 1935 had rushed into the burning capitol just long enough to stuff a desk with valuable public-funds investment documents and mobilize students to help him carry it out. Uncle Fred readily confirmed the witness's account. He clearly recalled seeing paintings propped up against trees on the Capitol Mall and even being carried across the street by students, but he didn't think all them had been saved. Norma searched the Willamette buildings and found no portraits. But around that time she attended a meeting at MacLaren Youth Correctional Facility in Woodburn, and happened to spot a large oil painting hanging on the wall there. She learned from MacLaren personnel that the painting had been brought over from Willamette, but that was all they knew. Norma ordered a glass case built to transport the portrait to the capitol, and again consulted Tom Vaughan. He identified the subject as T. T. Geer, Oregon's tenth governor (1899–1903).[30]

One day she got a call from a Coos Bay man, Edward G. Sewell, who told her that a long time ago he had been paid $3,000 to paint a portrait of Julius Meier. Meier was Oregon's twentieth governor (1931–1935), and a member of the prominent Portland family that had started the department store Meier & Frank. Sewell had later traveled to the capitol to visit his portrait in the Capitol Wings, a 1976 addition that was intended, among other things, to house the state's art collection. But Sewell couldn't find his painting of Julius Meier anywhere in the building. Norma called Julius Meier's son, Jack Meier, a fly fisherman whom she knew from their mutual commitment to environmental issues. Did Jack know anything about the painting's whereabouts? He did. He had been contacted by capitol staff, he told her, and asked to come and take the painting away. The new capitol, he said, "was designed so they wouldn't have any of that stuff." Meier had retrieved the painting and hung it in the basement of the downtown Meier & Frank store. He agreed to release it to Norma so she could restore it to its rightful place near the governor's office.[31]

In the early 1980s, when Tom McCall was dying of prostate cancer, Norma was in her second term and busy with other duties—"all of the timber stuff and the auditing and the election stuff." But her work on the portraits had become "an avocation I'd created for myself," and she realized the urgency of painting McCall from life before it was too late. After getting Governor Vic Atiyeh's approval, she raised enough money from twenty-seven private donors to pay an artist. Then she turned once more to Tom Vaughan as her guiding light in the search for the right painter. She told Vaughan, "I've got some money, I've made the decision, we're going to get Tom's portrait painted, and I'm not even going to ask anybody, because we don't have time."[32]

Vaughan recommended several painters. Norma was impressed with the monumental nature of Henk Pander's work: "He was the only artist who

Campaign photo taken of Norma in the North Umpqua River, 1976. This photo was a nod to the photo of Tom McCall in the same reach of the river in the early seventies also taken by Dan Callaghan and later used as a model for the statue of McCall in Salem's Waterfront Park. OSA Norma Paulus Photos, 17/19, Miscellaneous & Oversized.

could immortalize Tom McCall." After hiring Pander, Norma talked to McCall's wife Audrey and asked if she could bring the artist to visit McCall and make preliminary sketches. Permission was granted, and Pander came in and drew McCall "as rapidly as he could sketch."

When the portrait was finished, Norma arranged a private viewing for Tom and Audrey McCall. Pander's portrait is a large work, "surrealistic" in Norma's and others' view, that highlights McCall's ravaged face as he stands in a suit and dress shoes on the beach, one foot on sand and one in the ocean. McCall smiles, his right hand extended in welcome, while behind him a red-and-white pole erected in the surf and a flying helicopter signify the visit McCall made with surveyors and scientists on May 13, 1967, to publicize the importance of free public access made law by the Beach Bill. Pander later said his intent was to portray the governor "as the rescuer of the grandeur of Oregon."[33]

The governor, she recalled, was "kind of shocked" by the painting, "and Audrey just plain did not like it." Norma knew how to defuse the moment. "Tom," she told him, "this painting is going to create so much controversy." McCall laughed. "There is nothing that would tickle me more," he replied, "than to be able to create controversy after I'm dead."[34]

By the time McCall's portrait was secured for posterity, the gallery Norma assembled still lacked portraits of the most recent governors: Mark Hatfield, Bob Straub, and Victor Atiyeh. To fund this objective, Norma hit on a solution that combined her innate frugality with her love of recycling. She knew about a potentially profitable chunk of state property that had been gathering dust since the 1976 Capitol Wings building project. When the wings were added, the surplus property department was left with twelve-foot-square blocks of Carrara marble that apparently couldn't be sold or used. In fact, as Norma learned, "there wasn't a saw west of the Mississippi that could cut it."

The marble was a property-management headache: bulky to store, hard to move. The property people "just griped about it all the time," Norma said. "So being the 'old junker,' I thought to myself, I could sell that marble, and I could take the proceeds from the marble and commission artists to paint Hatfield and Atiyeh and Straub." She went to Governor Atiyeh and told him of her idea. He loved it. "So I told him, 'You check it and run it through your administrative people, and see if they want the marble, if they can sell the marble, or if they can use the marble, and if they can't, then you'll sign an executive order transferring it to the Historical Properties Commission, and I'll have a garage sale.' It wouldn't have worked with anybody but Victor. Victor went to all the garage sales just like I did."[35]

Many were skeptical that Norma could actually sell the marble. But she pushed on, advertising the sale of "Surplus Capitol marble" throughout the state. The National Guard was marshaled again to help buyers lift the blocks onto whatever transport they could provide, and Norma's garage sale proved as lucrative as she had predicted. In the midst of the sale, Norma noticed a handsome young man closely examining the marble but not offering to bid on it. When a lull in the bartering allowed, Norma approached him. His name was Ken Hunt, and he was a sculptor. He could create something wonderful with this marble, he told Norma, but had only $50 to spend. Norma offered a deal. Would he be willing to select a piece of marble that would work for the bust of an Oregon governor, and then carve that bust for $50? If so, she would give him three or four pieces of smaller marble. After another look at her wares, Hunt handed over his $50.

When the dust settled, Norma had sold all the marble and raised enough money to complete her gallery of portraits. She turned to Senator Mark Hatfield as the elder statesman who, given the choice of a painting or a bust, chose the marble as the "more eternal" medium. Norma then called her young sculptor, who deliberately carved the great orator as if speaking, his mouth open. Although Norma never heard Hatfield's opinion of it, the bust now stands in the governor's office. Governors Atiyeh and Straub selected their own artists to paint their portraits, with results she doesn't entirely favor. "I don't like Bob's and I don't like Victor's," Norma said, "but it was their choice, and we paid for that out of the proceeds of the marble sale." The sale also funded a bronze bust of the twenty-first governor, Charles Martin.[36]

Included in the sale of the Capitol Wings marble was a quantity of leftover Radio Black marble trim that caught Norma's ever-frugal eye. She talked it over with Frankie Bell, who had served from the beginning on the Historical Properties Commission and assisted with the marble sale. Frankie ran the capitol gift shop and, Norma knew, was always looking for ways to keep it afloat. Surely there was a way to raise money with that black marble. Could they make something of it? As the two women brainstormed, Norma happened to hear that new projects were needed for Oregon State Penitentiary prisoners. Warden Hoyt Cupp was an acquaintance of hers, so Norma gave him a call. The prison was equipped with the right saws, and one inmate was reputedly good at etching. Before long, several hundred marble paperweights, etched with the state seal and signed by the prisoners who cut them, went on display at Frankie's gift shop, selling steadily at $25 apiece.[37]

A sidebar in the 1981–1982 Oregon Blue Book describes how Norma enlisted a cohort of community members to help restore fragments of the old capitol's Corinthian columns, which had languished in the surplus properties department since the building's destruction in the 1935 fire. These fragments of former grandeur, some reclined and some on brick pedestals, were installed on the capitol grounds in a permanent display formally dedicated on February 12, 1981. In a photograph from the ceremony, a smiling Norma stands in front of a large upright fragment, flanked by Allen Goff, the capitol landscape superintendent, and Cecil Edwards, her right-hand man in all matters historical.[38] By the middle of her second term as secretary of state, Norma had successfully divested the surplus property warehouse of its leftover and salvaged goods by putting them to thrifty uses.

Norma receiving congratulations from Governor Victor Atiyeh on her second election to the office of secretary of state in 1980. Robert Bach/*The Oregonian*. Oregon Historical Society, OrHi 105570.

Chapter 8
Keeping Oregon Honest

By appearing before you this evening, it would seem I am violating the first rule, a cardinal rule, of a good speaker, which is: Know more about the subject matter than your audience. I know very little about accounting, and I sincerely doubt that it will ever be one of my spheres of knowledge. Ladd and Bush Bank could easily attest to that—they have been profiting for years from my overdrafts. But I do know a lot about the political system of Oregon and how to wend my way through it, and that is what it is going to take to bring a uniform system of accounting to the state agencies. Before continuing, I'd like to emphasize one fact: Our state government is clean.

—Norma Paulus

In November of 1977, as Norma was wrapping up her first year as secretary of state, *Bend Bulletin* reporter John Marshall, frustrated by many thwarted attempts to reach newsmakers by telephone, hit upon a provocative question to explore in print: Which public officials answered their phone calls without screening by their underlings? He led the resulting article this way:

"Is Norma Paulus there?"
"Sure, just a minute," said the secretary.
There was a short pause, then a female voice said, "Hello."
It was Norma Paulus, Secretary of State.
If you want to talk to Norma Paulus on the phone, you probably can—with no hassle and no questions asked.[1]

Marshall goes on to list his efforts to call other Oregon VIPs directly. Apart from Norma's, the most welcoming response was a refusal to take his call unless he answered a raft of questions. From former governor Tom McCall's office he got only a curt invitation to leave a message and no promise of a callback. The secretary of state, he added, offered the further courtesy of explaining her telephone policy. "When I took this office," she told him, "I told people who worked for me not to ask who was calling or what the call was about. I've always thought that was presumptuous."[2]

Norma's phone protocol spoke volumes about how she held herself accountable in doing the job she was elected to do. Whether it came from her upbringing in a poor and hardworking family, her struggle to carve out a living on her own, or her love for the law, Norma was passionate about holding government accountable, and she knew she was well placed, as secretary of state, to make that happen. Indeed, it was partly her passion for open government that led her to seek statewide office in the first place. After she'd made up her mind to run for secretary of state, she'd gone to Greg McMurdo, a young man who worked for the Republican caucus and whom she was thinking about adding to her staff. She told McMurdo, "I want you to learn everything you can about the election laws and election system, because I'm going to concentrate on the audit section."

"NO THIEVERY IN STATE GOVERNMENT"

Through her command of the law and the state constitution, Norma knew well the magnitude of the secretary of state's job as the chief auditor of public accounts. As a legislator, her understanding of that task's importance had deepened. Although by her third session Norma was convinced that "we had an honest government," she also saw clearly that "there was no accountability, because there just simply wasn't a system that would allow that kind of accountability." Audits were conducted—they were a constitutional function of the secretary of state—but "nobody paid any attention to them."[3]

Back when she was campaigning, she'd told the *Eugene Register-Guard* that "our present system does nothing more than show there's no thievery in state government." Cities, counties, and school districts, she said, did a much better job of letting voters know how their tax dollars were spent. If elected, she would expand the audit system to do much more than document that state officials weren't "tapping the till."[4]

Norma's first mentor in the area of governmental accountability had been Fred Paulus, her husband's uncle. Fred Paulus was a lawyer and former deputy state treasurer who worked for the Oregon treasury for more than thirty-five years. In the late 1960s, just as Norma was getting into politics, Fred Paulus had uncovered what he considered improper use of dedicated monies from the bond fund that supported the state veterans' loan program. The legislature intended to transfer about $13 million from the veterans' fund to

Fred Paulus, Oregon's deputy state treasurer, retiring in 1960 after thirty-five years of service. He was Bill Paulus's uncle and mentor to Norma on numerous topics while she was in office. OSA Norma Paulus Photos, 16/19, Family & Home Life.

the state's general fund for unrestricted use, through statutes Paulus believed were unconstitutional.

Fred Paulus, then in his seventies, was still a practicing attorney and "of counsel" at Bill's law firm. Furious over this apparent constitutional violation, he came to Bill and Norma for help. Together Fred and Bill sued the state for the return of the money to the veterans' fund on behalf of a local Veterans of Foreign Wars group and eventually won an Oregon Supreme Court decision in 1970.[5] The episode alerted Norma, who contributed research to the effort, to how easy it was for accountability to go astray in state government.[6] When she took office as secretary of state in 1977, Norma asked chief auditor George Renner why his office's audits attracted so little attention. She was told that her predecessors were unwilling to stand up, "because they didn't want to antagonize anybody." The auditors were reporting the same deficiencies year after year, with no response given or action taken. "Nobody ever cleans up the state system," the auditors told their new boss.[7]

This was disturbing enough. Then Norma learned that a general-fund item was being promoted and funded by $1 million a year taken from the veterans' fund—another abuse of the fund similar to the violation uncovered by Fred Paulus. George Renner told her that every year the legislature's chief financial officer had been duly informed that the redirection of funds was a violation of the constitution. The proper response of the officer would have been to ask the attorney general for an opinion on whether what he was doing was legal. But he never did ask, Norma's auditors told her. The chief legislative fiscal officers were "just doing it quietly, every year. And the auditors would report it, but they wouldn't do anything to either correct it or verify that their stance was correct."[8]

She took the case to Loren "Bud" Kramer, the governor's executive assistant and the director of general services. She wanted a "showdown" that would provide him with "a good opportunity to keep the skirts clean." Kramer was willing to hear her out but told her he wouldn't push for the attorney general's opinion. Kramer's demurral galled her: "That left another million dollars in the general fund for the legislature and the governor to play around with." She said to Kramer, "To hell with ya!" Then she went directly downstairs into the capitol press room and announced, "These people are stealing money out of the Veterans' Fund to the tune of a million dollars every year, and by God they ought to stop it!'"[9]

Her remark caused an uproar in the press, but Governor Bob Straub supported Norma's bluntly stated position. The matter eventually did come before the attorney general, who judged the legislative fiscal office's practice unconstitutional. The secretary of state's auditors, who "never had anybody stand up for them like that," had finally found their champion.

Norma followed her own bold precedent for the rest of her two terms. "I never once tried to influence an audit," she said. "What I did was, I took what the auditors came up with, and then I marched them down to the press room to share what they'd discovered."[10]

COZY TIMBER SALES

Once she was sworn in for her first term, Norma's to-do list included plans to look into any possible collusive bidding on timber from state forestlands.[11] This was her duty not only as chief auditor but also as a member of the State Land Board, along with the governor and the state treasurer. The State Land Board managed all the assets of the Common School Trust Fund, including the timber operations that came under her jurisdiction as auditor.

Norma soon found that issues with timber sales were commanding much of her attention. In December of 1978 she released an audit of the state Department of Forestry showing the state had lost considerable revenue because of problems with estimating and appraising the timber offered for sale on state lands, especially in the northwest corner of the state. Norma's audit of the Department of Forestry found that its management of state-forest timber sales had cost the state $383,000 in two years. The audit suggested collusive bidding practices and even theft by purchasing firms.

"What it boils down to is that public timber is either being stolen or the department isn't doing a good job," she told reporters after the release. The response from timber companies, through complaints from Associated Oregon Industries, cited the "inflammatory" nature of Norma's audit. Their objections ignited further debate. Norma brushed aside AOI's implication that she and attorney general Jim Redden were belaboring the investigation to further their careers. If the parties involved had simply admitted that a mismanagement problem exists in Oregon's forests, she pointed out, there would be no big controversy over state timber sales.

When her audit was released, her office was inundated with multiple reports about rip-offs in state timber sales.[12] The reports came from diverse sources—from loggers to log scalers, truckers to government employees. Norma calmly stood her ground while the conflict swirled around her, noting pointedly that prior audits had concluded with similar concerns in the mid-1960s and that auditors in her office had not been firm enough with the forestry department in the past.[13]

Soon after taking office, she had learned that the State Land Board never examined the department's management of state forests. "The department sold the timber, did what it wanted with the money, and if there was something left over it went into the Common School Fund." The land board never inquired about the department's accounting, or for that matter even how state forestlands were managed—whether they were sprayed, what harvest methods were used. In Norma's view the land board was neglecting "all the big controversial issues." Her audit also found that the forestry department had used Common School Trust Fund money for projects unconnected with schools. One such project was the construction of an interpretive center in the Tillamook State Forest—an expense that she said should have been controlled by the legislature through general-fund money.[14]

From her first day in office, Norma suspected that some collusion was taking place when private industry bid on timber sales on state forests. This was confirmed by a Marion County timber and mill owner who reported to federal authorities that mill owners in his area were taking turns on bidding for timber sales in order to keep the prices down. She began to advocate forcefully for a sealed-bid system of sale—a policy that timber owners and the Board of Forestry opposed with equal fervor. As the sealed-bid idea gained more publicity, more and more reports of industry-wide irregularities in bidding procedures flowed into her office.

With the governor's help, she called for the forestry department to present the land board with bills for the costs of managing the forests. If the department refused to do this, Norma said, the land board could hire someone else to manage the timber. This was a heretical idea. The State Land Board had never perceived itself as the manager of state forestlands, even though it had legal responsibility for them. The management job was left to the Oregon Department of Forestry, which operated under the direction of the Board of Forestry. The problem with that, she said, was that the board tended to be dominated by timber-industry players. "Because who else would want to manage timber besides the timber owners and the mill owners?" There was no one, she said, to speak for the financial interests of Common School Trust Fund.[15]

> If I were a mill owner, traditionally, the forestry department would let me win the bid, make a small down payment, and say, "I'll cut it down eight or nine years from now." It was terrible; it was just criminal. It was all for the benefit of the timber industry. No one ever said, "What's best for the Common School Fund?" And that's what I was doing, what the Constitution clearly says you have to do: maximize the income. We, the Land Board, were not doing that.[16]

Norma told the Board of Forestry: "We should enter into a formal written contract with the Department of Forestry and hire them as our agents." In the end, the land board and the forestry department agreed to a contract obligating the department to present annual statements.

Norma's push for sealed bids made it through a trial run before the major players in Oregon's timber industry initiated a boycott. She had ruffled many feathers, including those of L. L. "Stub" Stewart, co-owner of Bohemia Lumber Company in Eugene. Stub Stewart was one of Norma's formerly ardent supporters, but now he withdrew his support, which may have cost her votes in her subsequent runs for office.

The Department of Forestry subsequently revamped its guidelines for state timber sales. The new policies were detailed in the department's October 1979 newsletter. From now on the Board of Forestry would "provide maximum state, county and Common School Fund revenue, in perpetuity, from stumpage sales consistent with the Board of Forestry Land Use Policy."[17] Other guidelines were listed, including this one: "To sell stumpage at competitive prices established by a free competitive bidding method and at a price which equals or exceeds the appraised value. [To] assure sales method will be used which encourages competition among multiple buyers for all major timber sales in both the immediate and long-term future."[18]

The November 1979 newsletter published an article titled, "To Improve Operations, Timber Sale Procedures Reviewed." The article details how "public awareness has been aroused by timber issues in the news," including a "federal case involving collusion in the purchase of federal timber, a state auditor's report critical of department policies and practices, and the increasing action by both public and private landowners investigating suspected timber theft."[19] The article outlined new "cost-effective preventative measures" regarding timber sales, theft, and improved management that was developed in response to the critical audits.[20]

From time to time Norma was accused of using the audits to pave her way to higher office—specifically, the governor's office. Could she have been merely "manipulating the process for her own political purposes" without much good having ever come of the charges she made? No, she said:

> After watching state agencies ignore direct legislative intent and past audits as a lawmaker, Paulus says her belief was that going public with her auditors' results was the only way to force the bureaucracy to listen. "We had a really clean government, but there wasn't any accountability in the system," she says. As a member of the State Land Board, Paulus continued to rankle the timber industry, pushing for and finally getting a contract with the forestry department that spelled out the Land Board's authority to manage state forests for the benefit of the Common School Fund.[21]

SLOPPY PRACTICES AT THE VA

Two years into her second term, an audit of the Department of Veterans' Affairs (DVA) found that the department had overpaid a life insurance company by $663,941 and had not attempted to recover the money. The DVA operated a loan cancellation life insurance program and collected monthly premiums from veterans for the coverage. Norma suggested that the DVA withhold the overpaid amount from future payments to the company.

The audit also found that DVA agents were not thorough enough in checking a veteran's eligibility or creditworthiness for a home loan. The auditors discovered other instances of loans improperly going to surviving spouses of veterans. Loans of more than $50,000 had been made to veterans who had previously owned a home in Oregon, which was against the law. The DVA also lent money for the purchase of a vacation home, to buy land for development of a subdivision, and "other questionable purposes."[22]

The Department of Revenue also came under the secretary of state's audit microscope. The audit found major accounting errors, including $500,000 that was entered in the wrong budget year; the error had escaped notice for almost a year. Records for the department's Amusement Device Tax account showed almost $200,000 in funds that should have been transferred to the general fund two years before. In one quarter, receipts were over-distributed to counties by $1.2 million, an error that was corrected in distribution the following quarter.

Norma noted that out of twenty-four agencies her office had audited, only these two agencies, Revenue and Veterans' Affairs, showed serious problems. The other agencies might be doing a better accounting job because they didn't want to be embarrassed by a negative, and very public, audit report. Norma candidly attributed Oregon's newly uncluttered finances on her watch to her open-book policy. The clean bill of health for twenty-two of twenty-four agencies "shows that press accounts of these audits are making a difference," she said.[23]

She continued to take audit results straight to the press. Previous secretaries of state "didn't even bother to announce when an audit was completed," according to George Bell, assistant secretary to Norma's predecessor, Clay Myers. Norma put the press to work for her in her quest to fine-tune government accountability.[24]

VOTE BY MAIL

In 1977, Norma got a call from Linn County clerk Del Riley, who had some disturbing news to report. On June 28, an election had been held in Harris School District 46, in Harrisburg, a small town south of Albany. The question at issue on Ballot No. 30 concerned the district's 1977–1978 budget. What was disturbing was that the school bond levy was passed by two "yes" votes that were unopposed by the fewer than a hundred voters registered in the district.[25]

Norma had long worried about declining voter participation, not just in Oregon but nationwide. She found Riley's news truly sobering. It could not bode well that just two souls, who happened to be a retired husband and wife,

Norma with Linn County Clerk Del Riley, explaining the details of vote by mail to the public at the Linn County Courthouse on October 1, 1981. Stanford Smith, *Albany Democrat-Herald*.

were the only people who had made an effort to vote on an important expenditure of taxpayers' money. "I thought, holy cow, one of these days we're going to have an election and nobody will show up," Norma said.[26]

Nearly a decade before, during her second term in the legislature, she and others had promoted the idea of voting by mail. It didn't come to anything then, but maybe the time was more propitious now. She asked Ray Phelps, the state elections director, to search throughout the country for any elections being conducted by mail. Phelps found an upcoming citywide election in San Diego. It was the city's first experiment with mail-in ballots. Norma put together a reconnaissance team. The House elections committee's chair and vice-chair, Glen Whallon and Kip Lombard, along with Phelps and Riley, observed the San Diego election in May. Their report was more than favorable: the election had "worked like a whistle."[27]

The Oregon House was considering a bill, House Bill 2418, to allow county clerks to conduct elections by mail. After the report of the successful election in San Diego, Norma asked for an amendment that would allow her, as chief elections authority, to have total supervisory power in any vote-by-mail trial, rather than give such discretion to Oregon's thirty-six county clerks. The amendment would give Phelps and his staff strict control over the experimental elections. Norma knew the stakes were high. She didn't want thirty-six county clerks handling it in their different ways; she wanted to oversee the thing herself, "to ensure that the election comes off without a hitch," she said.

Norma explaining legislative redistricting maps and process, October 1981. Claudia J. Howell/*The Oregonian*. Oregon Historical Society, OrHi105571.

"The first time we use a vote-by-mail system, it has got to work very well, so the public will have full confidence in it."[28]

In October the legislature approved a two-year trial of vote by mail. Norma announced that the first vote-by-mail election would take place in Linn County on November 3, 1981. Her choice was made on the basis of the high-level enthusiasm exuded by Albany postal officials, and especially by Del Riley, "one of the best [county clerks] we had in the system." Riley's voter-registration rolls, moreover, were up to date.[29] Norma also felt that Albany was "the most civic-minded community in the state," judging from the generous turnouts she'd observed at some community meetings.[30] The ballot would list five measures: four school bond issues concerning Albany, Scio, and Stayton, and a request from Brownsville voters to revise the city's charter. Norma was hoping the experiment would double voter participation and halve the cost of the election—this had happened in the San Diego vote-by-mail election. A lot was riding on this first attempt: "If it doesn't work here, we won't get another shot at it."[31] Nevertheless, she told a reporter, she felt "very confident Mr. Riley can pull this off."

Ballots were mailed out on October 14, a little more than two weeks before election day. Less than a week later, Norma's confidence in Linn County was rewarded when 29 percent of the voters participated—and some of them returned their ballots early. Not perhaps an overwhelming endorsement of vote by mail, but a great trial run, Norma thought. It signified that voters not only approved of the experiment but understood the new system with "very little trouble."[32]

By December 1984, as she was about to leave office, Norma declared vote by mail "an unqualified success." In a report she submitted to the legislature, she responded to early skepticism that the system could result in "possible undue influence by family members or others" by citing a survey of 1,500 voters conducted by OSU's Survey Research Center. Only six respondents said that "discussions about their votes made them feel under pressure." No one had reported feeling pressured to vote a certain way.[33] As Norma had hoped and predicted, voter participation in vote-by-mail elections was consistently much higher than in traditional balloting at the polls, with participation in some cases topping 90 percent. "After conducting 58 different elections by mail in 12 counties, I feel I can justifiably declare our experiment ended," Norma said. "I believe that vote-by-mail has earned a permanent place in Oregon's elections system."[34]

By 1998, the people showed their agreement by deciding to expand the system to primary and general elections; the vote was 757,204 to 334,021.[35] In 2010, Phil Keisling, who served as Oregon secretary of state from 1991 to 1999 and who, as a legislator, had been initially opposed to the system, cited the people's embrace of it as one of the state's true "beacons of achievement." Vote by mail has "arguably joined the bottle bill and our public beaches as something to brag about when out-of-town friends and relatives visit for the holidays."[36]

THE VOTER'S PAMPHLET

Norma also handled the smaller tasks, such as the biennial *Oregon Blue Book* and the voters' pamphlet, with the same focus on improvement. It was on her watch, she said, that both these publications went out for the first time without errors. As part of her quest to improve voter participation, Norma mailed her first pamphlet to every household in the state, not, as before, only to registered voters. With the help of her assistant, Jordis Schick, a graphic artist, Norma changed the pamphlet "to make the darn thing more attractive," she said.[37]

The mailing consisted of twenty-five different pamphlets, newly—but modestly—adorned with photographs on the cover and throughout the booklet. By law, candidates' photographs were required to be no older than one year, and all photo backgrounds were disallowed. Norma was consequently forced to reject even Governor Straub's first photo offering because there was something pictured on the wall behind his head.[38]

Finally, Norma found a frugal way to make use of blank spaces in the pamphlet: she filled them with excerpts from Oregon's election laws. This was educational for the voter, she said, and gratifying for her. Her next push would be to seek changes in election laws to grant her the authority to simplify the statements describing ballot measures, which were now too rife with "legalese," she thought.[39]

SHARING A JOB

During her campaign for secretary of state, Norma had promised her colleagues in the Women's Political Caucus that she would strive to make job sharing a workable option for women. "There was no job sharing in the public sector, and none in the private sector," she said. Although sharing a job would make the lives of many women in the work force easier, as they juggled work, home, and children, "it was a concept unheard of" at that time.[40]

Once sworn in, Norma found a new urgency to the fulfillment of her promise. As secretary of state, she was allowed to hire only two people, her personal secretary and her deputy. Norma wanted to keep Ann Lau, her legislative secretary, on staff, but the House position had only lasted through the legislative sessions, and Ann wasn't sure she wanted to work full-time year-round. "I've got to have job sharing," Norma told Ann. "It should be done at the clerical level, where the job is the same every day, and the tools used are constant. But I can't create a new job, so I'll have to do it with your position." When Ann agreed she would prefer to work half-time, Norma asked her to find someone with her skills to take the other half of the job.

Ann contacted Phyllis Elgin, who had worked for a senator in a job similar to Ann's. She was agreeable to sharing the position as Norma's secretary. After the two women were on board, however, Representative Gretchen Kafoury, a strong advocate for the job-share thrust in the women's caucus, advised Norma to back away. "Don't try that with your executive secretary," she told Norma. "It will fail." Norma assured her it would work. Her deputy, Greg McMurdo, also lobbied strenuously against it; the logistics were too complicated, he believed. Norma admitted it would be difficult for the two women working on alternate days to transmit all the details of her tightly packed schedule back and forth. But she was convinced it could be done.

When it came time to make the arrangement official, however, the personnel department dug in its heels on the subject of splitting the benefits. Ann

Norma with office staff: (L-R) Phyllis Elgin, Ann Lau, Donna Morgan, and Sue Hoagland, with Norma on far right. Al Jones Collection, Willamette Heritage Center, 2007.001.1614.

tried three times to convey to the department Norma's insistence that she and Phyllis both receive full benefits. After the third futile conversation, Norma visited personnel with a few choice questions. "I went down there and said, 'Look, you want me to go to the *Oregonian* and say this is what we're trying to do? Do you want me to unleash the women's political movement? Do you want me to have a press conference?'"[41] After a siege of a month or six weeks, the department was convinced that benefits could be split to provide full recompense to two people, even if it had never been done before.

With Ann and Phyllis sharing the position, Norma found both women worked harder, and she enjoyed the advantage of "two people's strong points, the input and thought of two people—a fresh viewpoint."[42] Nearly everyone, including McMurdo, agreed that Norma's secretarial staff was more than the sum of its parts:

> Phyllis and Ann were the pioneers and they made it work. Pretty soon, the *Statesman* ran an article about it, and the next thing I knew, the banking association asked if my secretaries couldn't come

Statesman Journal photo by Gerry Lewis

Ann Lau, left, and Phyllis Elgin meet on the Capitol steps to transfer their job.

Norma's aides, Ann Lau and Phyllis Elgin, on the Capitol steps, job-sharing in 1977. Gerry Lewin, courtesy of the *Statesman Journal*. Reprinted from the *Statesman Journal*, p. 45, 3/13/77.

and talk to them about it, because they were thinking it would be a good idea for tellers. Our purpose in doing it was to give women with children more options, so Ann and Phyllis were just delighted to do it. They gave little seminars around the state and it just caught on like wildfire.[43]

The arrangement had worked seamlessly. "I never knew who was going to be there," Norma said. "I just knew one of them would be."[44]

By the end of her first term as secretary of state, Norma Paulus had "streamlined, reorganized and modernized" the office into a model state agency, "managed like a business and responsive to the needs of its citizens."[45] She had conducted more audits, and publicized their findings more, than any previous secretary of state, forcing state agencies to get their houses in order. When she ran for reelection in 1980, she had a solid record to stand on.

Norma listening to Rajneesh lead attorney, Swami Prem Niren. Max Gutierrez. Oregon Historical Society, OrHibb009326.

Chapter 9
The Rajneeshee Affair

> The people of this state are most grateful to the lawyers who volunteered to preserve the integrity of their ballot box (particularly after learning that they were to pay them only $5 apiece). No wonder Shakespeare proclaimed that, in order to undermine the practice of fairness and right, "first, the lawyers" must go, because without them there is no protection for any of us or the ideals we hold so dear.
>
> —Norma Paulus

In the summer of 1981, in one of the more bizarre episodes of Oregon history, scarlet-clad disciples of the Indian guru Bhagwan Shree Rajneesh came to Oregon with a dream of making the desert bloom into a garden paradise. The dream turned into a nightmare of clashes with neighbors, run-ins with the law, even mass poisoning. And it produced a voter-fraud crisis that landed squarely in the lap of Secretary of State Norma Paulus.

Rajneesh was a philosophy professor in India who had reinvented himself as a guru. Throughout the 1970s he attracted many educated and wealthy Western followers willing to pay lavishly to hear his lectures and participate in his group-therapy workshops. In 1974 he founded a commune in the Indian village of Poona that eventually grew to six thousand members. Rajneesh taught his followers to embrace sexual freedom and unfettered surrender to all loving and joyous pursuits. But authorities cracked down on his "unseemly and illegal behavior," including smuggling and tax fraud.[1]

In May of 1981, Rajneesh, his chief lieutenant Ma Anand Sheela, and seventeen followers—called sannyasins—secretly left the village. Rajneesh, a diabetic, was granted a medical visa to visit New York.[2] Sheela left him there and scouted ahead for a new refuge. She found one in the Muddy Ranch, one hundred square miles of rangeland north of Madras, Oregon. (After the Rajneeshees took it over it became the "Big Muddy" to everyone but the locals.) The closest settlement was the town of Antelope, eighteen miles to the west. By July, Sheela had closed on the purchase of the property.

"NICE ENOUGH," . . . MAYBE

The first sannyasins quietly settled in on the ranch. They were friendly to the locals, letting their new neighbors know they came there only to work the land. They couldn't help but stand out, though, with their red and purple clothes and their beaded necklaces, or *malas*, hung with a pendant displaying Bhagwan's likeness. Margaret Hill, then mayor of nearby Antelope, recalls seeing red-clad young men buying beer in the village store and thinking that "they seemed nice enough."[3] Mayor Hill did express a wish that the newcomers respect Antelope's history and culture. "I feel there is perhaps a lack of sensitivity on their part to our feeling about where we live," Hill told the reporter, "and I think their presence here has changed our lives in subtle ways they don't understand." Even so, "all the people I have met have been charming, really, and certainly not threatening," she said.[4]

"Charming" was just the impression Sheela was hoping to make. Upon her arrival in Oregon, she threw a party for her neighbors in Madras, where dancing continued till dawn. She bought fifty head of cattle from a Wasco County commissioner, although the commune was strictly vegetarian.[5] Sheela had promised Rajneesh they could build "the commune of his dreams," complete with homes, warehouses and support buildings, and a commerce center filled with lucrative enterprises. But Sheela had bought the ranch—which was agricultural land zoned for exclusive farm use—with no understanding of state and county land-use rules governing how many buildings could be built or how many people could live on rural land.[6]

Sheela set up a meeting with Wasco County planners, intending to obtain permits for the new homes that were allowed for farmworkers and their families. She and two sannyasins kept the appointment in plain clothes, with their *malas* tucked away. One Wasco County planner, Dan Durow, was a Midwesterner new to both the commission and the region. When Sheela described the "farm commune" she had in mind, he approved the idea and agreed the property could be allowed development for ninety to 150 workers to be brought in for the restoration of the range and its riparian area.[7] When Durow asked if her group was a religious organization, she quickly denied it. "We celebrate life and laughter," Sheela told him. "We are simple farmers."[8]

The commission granted the Rajneeshees permits for fifty-four mobile homes on the ranch, intended for temporary worker housing.[9] Durow initially looked with favor on their proposed changes. But when he later traveled to the ranch to monitor progress, Durow found dormitories being built rather than the promised temporary housing. Mattresses and other evidence reflecting the size of the commune's membership were stowed before his arrival.[10] His discoveries led to closer scrutiny that resulted in the denial of future permit applications.

A team of Rajneeshee lawyers informed Sheela that Durow's authority could be skirted if the commune became a city. They advised that she befriend 1000 Friends of Oregon, an environmental watchdog group founded to help secure the aims of the land-use planning system made law by Senate Bill 100. Sheela and a few others from the commune traveled to Portland and met with two lawyers from 1000 Friends. She described the city they wished to build in order to tend to the "thousands" who would be moving there. Transforming the ranch into a working farm was proving a bigger task than anticipated, she said.

"The environmental lawyers applauded the desire to restore the land, but they saw no need for a city," wrote Les Zaitz in a 2011 *Oregonian* series on the Rajneeshee affair. "As their resistance became apparent, Sheela asked whether their opposition would dissolve if the Rajneeshees joined 1000 Friends with a substantial contribution." When the bribe was brushed off, "Sheela turned snide," Zaitz wrote. "Observing the modest furnishings in the Portland office, Sheela said she was not surprised by 'shabby' work being done by people working in 'shabby' surroundings. The crack was needless, but it was trademark Sheela."[11]

ROLLS-ROYCES AND BULLETPROOF VESTS

Bhagwan arrived in Oregon on August 29, 1981. His observation of a vow of silence taken earlier in the year meant that Sheela functioned as his voice, from him to his followers, including high-ranking sannyasins, and to the world. Rajneesh held frequent audiences, silently sitting on a stage as his devotees beheld him. He took daily drives over the rough roads, selecting his vehicle from a fleet of ninety-three Rolls-Royces they purchased for him. Sheela's life as Rajneesh's second-in-command was far less contemplative. As more zoning roadblocks rose before her, she became adept at using the press to her advantage. Inflammatory sound bites from her interviews sold newspapers and won viewers, not just for the news but for her appearances on the *Phil Donahue Show* and *Nightline*, "where her sharp tongue cut into the enemy of the day," according to Zaitz. "She seemed to spit insults with every breath."[12]

When other prominent commune leaders protested, informing Rajneesh that Sheela's tactics weren't helping to remove impediments to building their city, the guru erupted in a rare show of fury. Sheela was his agent; she spoke for him. Though the commune was supposedly governed by a hierarchy of officers, Rajneesh directed these sannyasins to inform the members that there was to be no challenge to Sheela's authority from them or from anyone else at the ranch.[13]

Wasco County residents had in general reserved judgment on the Rajneeshees, but then a film circulated in Oregon theaters that supposedly showed violent scenes from a therapy session in Poona. The Rajneeshees protested that the scenes were taken out of context, but the locals were disturbed.[14] With each rejected permit application, the Rajneeshees more readily pointed fingers, accusing the citizenry of ignorance and bigotry. "At some point," explained Milt Ritter, a KGW videographer, "people stopped talking, and they just started screaming. Nothing was going to get done in that environment, and nothing got done."[15]

The sannyasins' efforts to thwart Durow's inspections grew more audacious. On one trip he found the single road into the ranch blocked by a bulldozer. No one could explain how it got there. The sannyasins' reactions to housing violation citations he issued grew more threatening. Durow took to wearing a bulletproof vest and taking a police escort along on his visits.[16] In 1982 the Rajneeshees, who had been buying property in the town of Antelope, announced they would place candidates for the Antelope city council on the ballot in November. The city council responded by calling a special election to disincorporate Antelope and dissolve its government.

From the other side of the mountains, Norma, Governor Vic Atiyeh, and Attorney General Dave Frohnmayer were watching the situation with cautious alarm. "We didn't want the rest of the country to think that Oregon was made up of wild people who persecuted these strong environmentalists who loved the earth," she recalled.[17] But the announcement of the disincorporation election put everyone on high alert. Norma considered the big picture. While the Rajneeshees' neighbors had long since lost patience with them, the press and many Oregonians, Norma believed, were still pro-Rajneesh. Yet reports on Sheela's behavior and the sannyasins' documented attempts to dupe the planning commission convinced her that the Rajneeshees were capable of manipulating the election. Norma prevailed on former Governor Bob Straub, retired state supreme court associate justice Jake Tanzer, former state supreme court chief justice Arno Denecke, and Portland attorney and municipal judge Herb Schwab to travel to Antelope and monitor the voting. To ensure their safety, she arranged for all of their food and drink to come from Salem, and put them up in rented mobile homes around Antelope.[18]

The Rajneeshees carried the day, and the town remained intact.[19] Then in November, several Rajneeshees were elected to the council, and one was elected mayor. Two longtime councilors resigned, leaving only one who was not a Rajneeshee. After the election, the town of Antelope was renamed

Rajneesh. By then, Bhagwan's city at the ranch, Rajneeshpuram, had grown to dwarf Antelope/Rajneesh, with predictions that its population would reach four thousand by the turn of the century.[20] Rajneeshpuram boasted a mall with assorted retail shops, a pizza parlor and cafes, and a disco. Tours were offered to curious Oregonians, who were bused in from Antelope and guided around the ranch by comely Rajneesh hostesses known as "Twinkies."[21]

Ranchers living nearby were not inclined to view the new city as a tourist attraction. The Rajneeshees' plans had changed too often, and their treatment of their neighbors had gotten worse. Long-term Antelope residents endured insults and harassment on the streets of their newly named town, Rajneesh. Rajneeshees photographed people, videotaped their meetings, wrote down the license number of every car that entered the town.[22]

Mike Sullivan, the district attorney in neighboring Jefferson County, told writer Frances FitzGerald that his disapproval of Rajneeshee tactics had nothing to do with their beliefs. It was that, even though he'd advised them to quit their lawsuits,

> they kept making aggressive demands and acting like big-city people and getting everyone's back up. Their style is to come in and bang on the table and say, "If you don't do what we want, we'll sue you." Well, the county judges here are in their seventies. They're tough old birds who've been through World War II and their attitude is, "So, perhaps you confuse me with someone who cares."[23]

By the summer of 1984, the Rajneeshees were trying stronger measures. Bill Hulse and two other county commissioners took a tour one August day and returned to Hulse's car to find one tire flat. While a repair costing twelve dollars was amiably arranged with attending Rajneeshees, the commissioners, sweating under the hot sun, were approached by Rajneeshpuram's nurse, Ma Anand Puja, wearing her medical whites, and accepted her offer of a glass of water. Hulse woke that night vomiting, with crippling stomach pain. He spent four days in the hospital, where doctors told him he would have died without treatment. A second commissioner, Ray Matthew, endured the same violent illness at home.

Upon his recovery, Hulse said publicly he had been poisoned at the ranch. Soon after the incident, patrons of restaurants along Interstate 84 in The Dalles fell ill in alarming numbers after eating from salad bars. When upward of seven hundred people sought medical treatment for salmonella poisoning up and down the Gorge, reporting where and what they had eaten, public opinion accused the Rajneeshees—an accusation that proved to be true.[24]

HOMELESS VOTERS

While rumors surged about the salmonella outbreak, Sheela announced a new humanitarian program called "Share-a-Home." Buses were chartered to transport homeless people, mostly men, from cities throughout the United States to the ranch. Participants in the program were provided with room, board, and beer. Upon their arrival, loudspeakers in ranch halls broadcast an announcement that encouraged all guests to exercise their right to register to vote as Wasco County residents.[25]

Worldwide followers of Bhagwan also crowded onto the ranch, where the gap between outer-fringe street people and wealthy disciples soon opened wide. While the surge of new citizens was reported to the public as a joyful enterprise for both guests and hosts, it was later learned that the sannyasins were fearful of what they saw as a potentially unruly crowd. Some of their guests were mentally unstable and physically ill, and not all of them took kindly to the regimented life they found there. As a safeguard against possible unrest among the street people, the sannyasins spiked the beer kegs with Haldol, an antipsychotic, colorless, odorless, and tasteless, which, according to subsequent investigation by the Oregon Board of Medical Examiners, the Rajneeshees had purchased in large quantities.[26]

By late September, Rajneeshee-watchers statewide were alarmed by the sudden population explosion of new voters at the ranch. Many believed the Rajneeshees planned to launch a massive write-in vote campaign to take over two of the three seats on the county planning commission. Some openly anti-Rajneeshee Oregonians devised their own plan of attack "to get the red out." An Albany-based group led by JoAnne Boies vowed to travel en masse to the Wasco County Courthouse and vote as residents, taking advantage of Oregon's same-day registration law. Boies claimed that about a thousand residents east of the mountains were prepared to risk arrest for voting fraud, while others were expected from Medford.[27]

County clerk Sue Proffitt found herself smack in the middle of a double threat to the integrity of the voting system. The Rajneeshees' plan to pack the election rolls, however nefarious its motives, was in theory protected by the law. And angry anti-Rajneeshee voters throughout the state were ready to break the law in order to protect the principle of free and fair elections. Proffitt's office was flooded with new voter-registration cards. The registrants

Rajneeshee demonstrators near Rajneeshpuram, the former Muddy Ranch, in Wasco County, 1984. OSA Norma Paulus photos, 15/19, Wasco C. Hearings (Rajneesh) 1984, Rajneesh Protestors.

may have been following protocol, but she knew fraud when she saw it. Voter-registration cards were sent in the names of deceased voters, some personally known to Proffitt. Others came from Oregon residents who held vacation homes in the vicinity but legally resided elsewhere in the state. Proffitt knew it was time to take her suspicions to the secretary of state.[28]

POSTCARD REGISTRATION

Back in 1973, as a member of the House elections committee, Norma had been approached by Nellie Fox, head of Oregon's AFL-CIO chapter. Fox told her about "postcard registration," currently in use in some eastern communities, that enabled citizens to register through the mail. The idea appealed to Norma, who had long worried about the sharp drop in participation at the polls. While part of the problem was surely disenchantment with government—the country was still fighting an unpopular war, and the Watergate scandal was in the headlines—Norma also suspected that what she called the "Joe Lunchbucket" citizens of Oregon were simply unable to make it to county offices to register during business hours.[29]

As the committee prepared to send the bill forward, Norma spotted a red flag. What if voters gamed the system by registering pets or dead family members? She declined to sign off on the bill until it provided that the county clerk could reject any registration if he or she felt something was amiss—even if it was merely a gut instinct—as long as an administrative hearing was held on the matter within twenty-four hours.[30] Eleven years later, this provision went a long way toward saving the integrity of the election system.

When Proffitt contacted Norma's office with evidence that both Rajneeshees and anti-Rajneeshee Oregonians were in danger of committing
voter fraud, Norma wasn't surprised to hear it. In Salem and everywhere in Oregon, people were talking of little else but the situation out east.[31] Norma told
one reporter, "Quite frankly, I think the presidential election has been totally
eclipsed by the Rajneeshee situation." Letters from angry citizens urged action
against the Rajneeshees. In a September editorial, Norma urged Oregonians
to follow a wait-and-see approach. In response, Lebanon resident Neva Klee
wrote the editor that citizens had waited long enough. "The government is the
people, and we are upset," she wrote. "We elect state officials to do their jobs,
and I really wonder sometimes why we bother."[32] Some people felt Governor
Atiyeh had dropped the ball when he had urged tolerance and patience toward
the Rajneeshees, while refusing to meet with the vocal anti-Rajneeshee people
in Linn County, whom he described as "vigilantes."[33]

Some took matters into their own hands. Norma, McMurdo, and Frohnmayer were targets of sophomoric pranks that were nonetheless threatening.
Packages of animal manure and blood were delivered to Norma's office. The
state police warned her that Liz and Fritz, both attending college in Walla
Walla, Washington, were at risk, and recommended alerting local authorities
as a precaution.

McMurdo found "a satanic-like wreath" on the doorstep of his Salem
home. Frohnmayer was signed up for membership in a club "he prefers not
to name," and was mailed a subscription to a magazine called *Combat Arms.*
Animal entrails were dumped on his driveway in Eugene. A letter on the attorney general's letterhead was sent to the People's Republic of China charging
that a Portland businessman trading with China was being investigated by
Frohnmayer's office. Other letters were sent to the press alleging wrongdo-
ing by Norma, Frohnmayer, and others. Everyone targeted was "identified in
some way with some strong stand on the Rajneesh issue," Frohnmayer said.
This did not mean the guru or his disciples were the perpetrators, he added;
"it could also be someone trying to stir the pot."[34]

Norma was most concerned about the Albany contingent. "I realized
they were growing in numbers and were serious . . . , despite my warning
that they would be committing a crime. . . . The more I pleaded for tolerance
and suggested they remain calm, the redder their necks became. By mid-
September it was clear that we had an election crisis unlike any we had ever
faced in Oregon."[35] Norma considered measures she could take to keep a lid
on the situation. She didn't want to "go overboard and ruin our reputation by

persecuting a religion," she said.[36] As secretary of state, she had the power to halt the registrations. But she knew that would be unacceptably heavy-handed. The best thing, she realized, would be to empower county clerk Sue Proffitt to impose the registration ban, as provided in the 1973 legislation, and then hold hearings within twenty-four hours to validate the registrants' eligibility.

This course posed logistical challenges. The new registrations could number in the thousands. How would they come up with a venue that could accommodate hearings for all those registrants? How would they maintain calm between opposing factions? And how could Norma find enough lawyers to serve as hearings officers so that each challenged registrant could be heard within the twenty-four-hour period required by law?

The answer to that riddle walked up to her on a downtown Portland street. On an early-morning stroll before a Portland engagement—a breakfast-meeting speech on the Rajneeshee situation—Norma paused to look at a jewelry store window and spotted Cliff Carlsen waiting on the other side of the crosswalk. Carlsen was a prominent Portland attorney who'd been a Freedom Rider in the mid-1960s. Norma had always admired his courage as a defender of civil rights in the segregated South. After they exchanged pleasantries and Carlsen strode off, Norma was struck by sudden inspiration. If Carlsen could go to Mississippi to help out with a crisis, Norma thought, why couldn't he go to Wasco County?[37]

Norma spent the better part of that day trying to reach Carlsen. She called his office and was told he had just left. She called his home with no answer. Finally it occurred to her to contact *Bend Bulletin* publisher Bob Chandler, her friend and champion, and, coincidentally, a close friend of Cliff Carlsen. Chandler gave her good news: Carlsen was on his way to have dinner with Chandler in Bend, and he'd have him call.

When Carlsen called, Norma related her dilemma. Could he assemble the dozens of lawyers they needed to follow through, pro bono, on potentially thousands of registrants' administrative hearings? Carlsen replied, "We can do that."[38] At her request, Carlsen joined Norma in Salem the next morning, October 10, for a press conference. Norma sent out a press release to announce the conference: "Everyone is cordially invited, with the exception of Sheela, because nowhere in the contract that I have with the People of the State of Oregon does it say I have to submit myself to the vitriolic and vile epithets hurled by that woman at everybody in this state."[39]

Sheela responded that Norma had long been jealous of Sheela's looks and her beautiful wardrobe.[40] She vowed to attend the conference expressly to teach Norma a lesson, "to let her know she is weaker and I am stronger."[41]

She promised to bring two thousand Rajneeshees with her. This prompted a dress rehearsal by Norma's staff and the state police officers who were always in residence at that time. Strict instructions were issued to all to remain polite and noncombative with every attendee. State police also kept Interstate 84 under surveillance. They reported no increase of traffic that would indicate a crowd of the size threatened by Sheela was traveling to Salem.

A substantial audience—without a single Rajneeshee—gathered for the press conference, along with reporters from across the country. Norma kept her message plain. County clerk Sue Proffitt suspected widespread attempts to perpetrate fraudulent voting practices. Therefore, Norma was empowering the county clerk by administrative rule to require the attendance of all registrants at hearings to validate their residency in her county. In two weeks, hearings officers would be dispatched to The Dalles, where all registrations tendered after October 10 would be vetted and either accepted or rejected, with an immediate hearing granted to those in the latter category. This was the action Oregonians had been waiting for, Norma said. "People were relieved that someone had stood up and said, 'This is it.'" Portland attorney Herb Schwab told her, "Norma, you could be elected queen today."[42]

The Rajneeshees' lawyers filed a lawsuit in federal court claiming that the moratorium on registrations was imposed out of religious bias and bigotry and was an unconstitutional burden on their right to vote. The Rajneeshees also announced the end of their Share-a-Home project.[43]

"VOTE TO SAVE THE RANCH"

Because of its urgency, the Rajneeshee lawsuit was set to be heard over a three-day weekend in Portland, with Judge Ed Leavy of the United States District Court presiding. After she announced the administrative rule, Norma had received two phone calls. The first came from a woman who worked for the Oregon School for the Deaf. She told Norma that one of the school employees had taken to wearing only garments in shades of red, along with the beaded *mala* bearing Bhagwan's portrait. The caller related how this employee told her that she needed a day off in order to go to vote in Wasco and "save the ranch."

The second caller was a man who worked as a scout for the Seattle Seahawks football team. The man told Norma he spent a lot of time in airports, and had lately noticed droves of people, all dressed in reds and purples and wearing some kind of bead necklace, passing through the Salt Lake City airport. Some of them spoke German, the man believed. Of those whose language he could understand, the conversations ran along a consistent theme: they were

Norma with Attorney General David Frohnmayer at a press conference regarding the Rajneesh situation circa 1984. Norma Paulus Papers, Willamette University Archives and Special Collections_NP061.

on their way "to vote to save the ranch."[44] Both callers agreed to testify before Judge Leavy, providing what Norma believed were solid grounds to rebut the Rajneeshee allegation that Norma was simply and groundlessly harassing their right to register legitimate voters.

After the hearing ended on Monday, October 22, Judge Leavy[45] found for the state and upheld Norma's right to conduct the voter-registration residency hearings. While the Rajneeshee lawyers prepared their appeal, Norma focused on completing her arrangements for the transport, care, and protection of the hearings officers marshaled by Carlsen from law firms throughout the state. Carlsen had managed to find hearings officers with surprising ease. As he told the *Hillsboro Argus*, Norma had asked him to line up a hundred lawyers to donate their time for the hearings. Following her press conference, he swiftly accrued more willing volunteers than he needed.[46]

Norma contacted the National Guard and booked the armory in The Dalles for a hearing room. On the night before the first hearings, Norma and Bill met state elections director Ray Phelps and Wasco County clerk Sue Proffitt at the armory to prepare the space, carefully removing all traces of weaponry before setting up twenty fourteen-foot tables. Privacy was provided with large pieces of cut-up cardboard boxes positioned between each hearing officer.

Norma made it clear that everyone who came to the armory should feel welcomed and be received in an orderly fashion. She directed Proffitt to arrange a crew of twenty county staff and volunteers and ten student helpers from the local high school. The students would direct and escort applicants to the

Norma, Antelope city
attorney Keith Mobley,
and officer Bob Brown
closing an Antelope
polling site to the press.
Oregon Historical
Society, OrHibb009328.

proper lines. Rajneeshees would be instructed to hand their documents to the students, who would transport them to the clerk. By this means, Norma hoped to keep all business above suspicion, ensuring that potentially anti-Rajneeshee townspeople didn't get even one hand on "that precious document": a citizen's identification and proof of his or her right to vote.[47]

As part of her effort to keep everyone calm, Norma met with one of the leaders of a citizens' group in The Dalles. Having endured months of threats and harassment in addition to the perils of the salmonella epidemic, this group had developed a telephone network to keep track of the Rajneeshees' activities. Norma explained to the leader that, in order for this hearing process to work, every registrant—Rajneeshee or no—would have to go through the same process, and some people might have to reregister. The leader assented and spread the word throughout her network.[48] When Norma was notified that some Rajneeshees were too ill and indigent to make the trip into The Dalles, she knew the process had to go to them. She asked her volunteer lawyer group who the toughest lawyer in Oregon was. They said Bob Ringo of Corvallis was her man. Ringo went out to the ranch and conducted hearings from the hood of his pickup truck with a band of Rajneeshees dancing and chanting all around him. It took Ringo ten hours to process eight registrants.[49]

Norma secured donated buses and drivers from Pacific Trailways to transport the hearings officers from Portland. As the buses drove east through the Gorge on October 23, the lawyers received instructions on the procedure and the demeanor they needed to maintain. They were to take no food or drink from anyone while on-site; box lunches and bottled water would be provided. In order to receive insurance coverage while on duty, each volunteer would be paid a stipend of five dollars. When they disembarked at the armory, the lawyers were scheduled to meet with four hundred applicants that day, seventeen of whom were from the ranch. Attorney David Rhoten swore in the hearings officers, and the doors opened at 9:30 a.m.[50]

"Things were a bit chaotic as the first people arrived, but we did everything to make them feel welcome and comfortable," Norma said. Taking the role as overseer of the slow process, Norma moved up and down the queued registrants, greeting everyone and bringing mothers who were carrying small children to the heads of the lines. Although processing applications took much longer than expected, people were largely patient. As Norma reported in the *Oregon State Bar Bulletin*, "the people were most courteous and understanding of why they were there." Clearly, "most citizens were grateful that their election process was being protected, and many expressed their appreciation for the attorneys who were donating their time."

When the Rajneeshees arrived in the afternoon, their lawyers insisted the press was to be included in the hearings, although the reporters on-site that morning had agreed not to contribute to crowded conditions in the hearings area. Norma and her staff agreed that to maintain "a tone of cooperation and friendship," they would allow the media to come in just as soon as the last of the locals had finished. When the media moved in, confusion reigned, as Norma had feared, with each officer besieged by two or three cameramen and news photographers recording the event. Norma ruefully also found that her cooperation was used against her in news coverage that made it to television. Though she felt that she was "as hospitable as Perle Mesta" toward the Rajneeshees,[51] a sound bite on the eleven o'clock news that night depicted her gruffly warning entrants, "If you behave yourselves, you can come in; if you don't, you are out." While the implication through the editing was that she had said this to the Rajneeshees, Norma had actually made the statement to the television cameramen.[52]

By the end of that first day, only two Rajneeshee registrations were refused. Norma recalled that when the officer pronounced the first of the two

Norma overseeing Wasco County voter registration, 1984. OSA Norma Paulus photos, 15/19, Wasco Co. Hearings (Rajneesh) 1984.

registrants unqualified to vote, a Rajneeshee lawyer "exploded." Carlsen appeared at the booth and received an on-camera tongue-lashing. As a testament to the younger man who had bravely championed the black vote in Mississippi, Carlsen stood his ground calmly. Both rejections were later reversed in a county court hearing.[53]

Between October 23 and the next hearings, scheduled for November 1 and 2, the Rajneeshees fought on, challenging the court ruling upholding the voter-registration hearings. The appeal required the submission of an affidavit from Norma. In her testimony in the affidavit, she urged the court to uphold the administrative rule in Wasco County, not just to prevent potential widespread voter fraud there, but to quell civil strife that would be a "substantial possibility" if voter fraud were uncovered. She also urged keeping the hearings in The Dalles rather than moving them to Rajneeshpuram, as requested in the Rajneeshee appeal. If the hearings were moved, she and her staff fully expected the plaintiffs would engage in "confrontational tactics," as they had on October 23. "The rejecting hearing officers and particularly the chief officer, Mr. Carlsen, were personally confronted, in the presence of the media, by the attorneys for the Rajneesh applicants, with yelling, name calling, and violent argument." If the hearings were held at Rajneeshpuram, such behavior would likely happen again, "only on a much larger scale and under much more oppressive circumstances."[54]

OREGON TRIVIA

The Rajneeshee appeals were denied. As the second and third rounds of hearings were set to go forward, the Rajneeshees staged one more rebellious gesture. The media was invited to an October 30 gathering at the ranch to cover an enthusiastic, commune-wide agreement to boycott the upcoming hearings. Norma rallied her volunteers and bused them to The Dalles for the scheduled hearings, only to find that this time Sheela's people were telling the truth. While some seven hundred applications were processed, all came from local registrants and none from the ranch. Ma Prem Sunshine told the *Oregonian* that Bhagwan's followers and the two thousand street people would boycott the hearings entirely. "We thought it would be fun to watch them just stare at each other, 50 lawyers," Sunshine said.[55]

While the officers sat mostly idle and left the armory soon after their box lunches were distributed, Norma made certain to engage the volunteers in profitable down time. She took all who wished to go, including the students, on an excursion to the Maryhill Museum, and launched games of Oregon Trivia to pass the time. On Friday, November 2, the hearings again went on as scheduled, this time with a complete day of no-shows because the 1,900 applicants expected to appear were all from Rajneeshpuram.[56]

On November 4, the Rajneeshees announced they would boycott the upcoming elections. Sheela told media the whole street-people project and election controversy were "just a joke," and that no one understood her sense of humor. On November 5, Rajneesh, who a few days earlier had broken the vow of silence he had maintained throughout his stay in Oregon, announced that "it might have been better if he had not come to the United States." The street people, who had been promised a round-trip ticket to leave the ranch when they were recruited, were taken by busloads into Portland and other cities and summarily dumped.[57]

Norma's strategy had succeeded. Sue Proffitt had received 4,400 new registration cards, a fair few of which proved unattached to actual voters, and only 1,100 applicants appeared for their hearings. Of the rest, Norma could claim, "we called their bluff," and they backed down.[58] Her response to the crisis, including marshaling an army of volunteer attorneys, had protected the state's election system. Although the Rajneeshees' web of criminality would take the courts months to untangle fully,[59] the secretary of state played a pivotal role in keeping Oregon's elections honest.

Norma was able to connect with Oregonians from all walks of life; here she is campaigning for governor in 1986. Norma Paulus Papers, Willamette University Archives and Special Collections_NP12125.

Chapter 10
Heartbreak and Consolation Prize

> I intend to win this campaign by attracting a legion of voters and by relying on the support of thousands of volunteers in every part of our state.
>
> —Norma Paulus campaign newsletter, 1985

Norma ended her second term as secretary of state on a crest of media and public approval. She had been "perhaps the best secretary of state in Oregon history," said the *Eugene Register-Guard*. "Through a combination of a progressive political philosophy and a personal style based on candor, credibility and courage, Paulus was able to accomplish impressive election law reforms, increase the sensitivity of the State Land Board to environmental concerns and vastly improve both the visibility and the effectiveness of the state's auditing functions."[1] Her vigorous audits of state agencies had kept her in the public eye and gained her a reputation as "an undaunted battler with bureaucracy."[2] Her handling of the sticky Rajneeshee situation in Central Oregon had boosted her profile and her popularity. She emerged from the fray with a reputation as an effective public servant, a principled and decisive leader, and the likeliest person to become Oregon's first woman governor.

She had been thinking about it since 1974, when she supported then secretary of state Clay Myers in his unsuccessful bid for the governor's office (he was defeated in the Republican primary by Vic Atiyeh[3]), while she was running for a third legislative term. Three years later, newly elected as secretary of state, she put it this way to the *Bend Bulletin*: "The teller in the bank wants to be president some day. And I'd like very much to be governor."[4]

Norma knew that Straub's two Republican predecessors, Tom McCall and Mark Hatfield, had used the secretary of state's office as a stepping-stone to the governorship. Like them, she had gained popularity as a progressive and independent Republican in a state dominated by Democratic voters. Her personality and politics clearly spoke to voters across party lines. She was getting encouragement from friends and colleagues; several of her friends from the legislature had pledged their support if and when she decided to run.[5]

She was also receiving national attention as one of a crop of gutsy women aspiring to high political office. Many of these women leaders were from western states. The journalist David S. Broder marveled at this in a column that appeared in the *Oregonian* in February of 1985: "For some unexplained reason, the Pacific Coast has been more willing than most other parts of the nation to entrust real political and governmental power to women." Besides Norma Paulus, Broder mentioned former Washington governor Dixy Lee Ray; Dianne Feinstein, mayor of San Francisco (now California's senior US senator); Barbara Boxer, a US representative from California (now a US senator until her term ends in 2016);[6] and Vera Katz, speaker of the Oregon House.[7]

Norma continued to break barriers closer to home, too. In 1981, a Portland chapter of the Lions Club invited her in to give a speech, and afterward they asked her to become a member. They presented her with a gold statuette of a lion on a marble base inscribed "Norma Paulus, Secretary of State." It was a daring move, because the national organization still barred women from becoming members. "These younger guys were challenging the constitution, building a case for the national convention," Norma said. "They were actually using me, which I kind of resented, as a matter of fact." Nevertheless, she accepted with pleasure. "Well, there was some press about it, and I'll be darned if one day some high mucky-muck in Lions didn't come in with the Oregon state president, and they asked me not to accept membership," she said. "Can you believe that?"

The men asked her to return the statuette. "I said, 'There's no way I can do that. You want me to tell people who've given me this honor that I can't accept it? Let me tell you, the only way you're going to survive is if you start admitting women as members.' And, of course, they and Rotary and everyone else found that out."[8]

Norma had a solid reputation on her own merits. It didn't hurt that she was also buoyed by the rising tide of respect for women political leaders nationwide.

CONTENDERS

In early 1985, Governor Vic Atiyeh was serving the last year of his second term and, by law, could not run again. Atiyeh had struggled greatly during his second term with a fractious legislature and an economy in free fall. The embattled governor, said the *Oregonian*'s Foster Church, "has quietly submitted to nearly non-stop abuse from legislators and businessmen and unsubtle ribbing from members of his own party."[9] An example was a derisive bumper sticker that read, "Don't blame Victor. He hasn't done anything."[10] Atiyeh was widely viewed as too mild-mannered and indecisive to be an effective leader.

Republicans were rightly worried about losing the state House. But the party was fortunate enough to have two strong contenders. Norma's likely rival in the May primary was Dave Frohnmayer, Oregon's attorney general. Frohn-mayer, like Paulus, had been propelled into the public eye by the Rajneeshee affair, which had burnished both their reputations. Frohnmayer prosecuted several members of the Rajneesh organization for their crimes. Seven of the cases went all the way to the US Supreme Court, and Frohnmayer prevailed in six of them.[11]

Like Norma, Frohnmayer had solid progressive-conservative credentials. A Paulus-Frohnmayer primary race, said the *Oregonian*, would likely "create considerable drama because both are popular and widely known and share the same moderate-to-liberal political philosophy." The editorialist noted that "Frohnmayer is usually considered somewhat to the right of Paulus."[12] As one illustration of this shade of difference, Frohnmayer questioned the sweeping nature of the land-use planning system that Norma had fought hard to put into place and called for a mid-course correction.[13]

In the spring of 1985, neither Paulus nor Frohnmayer had publicly committed to the governor's race, but the press noted that both were pulling together campaign organizations.[14] Norma wanted to take her time in an-nouncing her candidacy. She was reluctant to come out too early—she knew she needed to pace herself most effectively to avoid fizzling before reaching the goal. More importantly, she knew a governor's race would fling her family into a twenty-four-hour-a-day glare of publicity, and she wanted to postpone that impact.

Her intention was therefore firm, but private, which put her into a some-times awkward position. "It was a very difficult time," she recalled, "because I knew I was going to run. I was the obvious person to run for governor—I had strong polls, strong support, and very high credibility ratings."

> By that time I'd spoken to every Rotary Club, every Kiwanis Club, every Lion's Club. Every institution in the state of Oregon, not once, but several times. I couldn't go anywhere without being recognized. Not anywhere. And I had very high approval ratings because I had done my job very well, and I was clean as a whistle. I was very candid, and people liked that. I was a good speaker. I could easily make people laugh.[15]

"But I knew I couldn't say I was going to run," she added, "because it was too early. It's a strange thing to try to explain to somebody." When a reporter asked her whether she intended to run for governor, she replied coolly, "I just don't think it's the appropriate time to discuss my planning in detail."[16]

POINTING TO THE PRIMARY

Norma announced her candidacy on October 28 at a 7:00 a.m. rally at the Salem airport, in a hangar decorated with flowers, with Bill, Fritz, and Liz beside her. Both of her children would be working on her campaign. There was a band, and coffee and pastries.[17] An invitation flyer showed a smiling Norma with the caption "Norma's taking off from Salem."[18] "You bet I'm running," she told some five hundred friends and supporters.[19] After she made the announcement, she climbed into an airplane and took the news to other communities around Oregon.[20]

On that day, coincidentally, the papers were full of another big story: Bhagwan Shree Rajneesh fled Oregon in his private jet and was arrested when the plane stopped to refuel in Charlotte, North Carolina.[21] "So I got no publicity," Norma said ruefully. "I was at the bottom of the page." Bhagwan's scooping of Norma's big announcement may have felt like a final spit-in-the-eye from the man whose empire she had helped bring down.[22]

The Democrats had a strong contender in Neil Goldschmidt, a young, vigorous, and charismatic politician. Born and raised in Eugene, Goldschmidt was a former Freedom Rider and legal-aid lawyer who had been elected Portland mayor in 1973—the youngest big-city mayor in the country at the time. In 1979 he joined the Carter cabinet as secretary of transportation and served until 1981. He returned from Washington to take a top-level executive job with Nike, the Oregon-based sportswear company.[23]

Not everyone was impressed with Goldschmidt's eclectic resumé. "Unlike Neil Goldschmidt," said the *Statesman-Journal* in an editorial, "[Paulus] has not gained a reputation as shopping around, in state and out, for career opportunities." On the contrary, "Oregon people see her as one of theirs, someone willing to risk her political career, if necessary, to tackle a delicate problem."[24] A poll conducted in early December of 1985 by the national Republican Party revealed that Norma had a significant edge over Goldschmidt. If the two were running for governor, 50 percent of respondents would vote for her and only 35 percent for Goldschmidt. Norma also polled better on voters' awareness of her and their favorable opinion of her.[25]

Goldschmidt's Democratic rival was Senate president Ed Fadeley, a man who expressed his populist, pro-working-class, anti-tax views in a flamboyant speaking style. Fadeley did not have the national stature or the support among urban voters that Goldschmidt had, but mainstream Democrats worried about him as a potential spoiler who would split the Democrats' vote and thereby strengthen the Republicans' grip on the state House,[26] which the GOP had held for forty-two of the past forty-eight years.[27] Fadeley had a rough side to his tongue that offended some potential supporters. After he spoke at a Corvallis Chamber forum, the Corvallis newspaper criticized his antagonistic attitude toward business. "His opponents would do well to listen to his anti-tax, frugality-in-government theme," said the writer, "but Fadeley's performance here didn't do anything to take the luster off Neil Goldschmidt or Norma Paulus."[28]

He also had a reputation as a womanizer, which Norma had learned firsthand

Paulus for Governor campaign brochure. Norma Paulus Papers, Willamette University Archives and Special Collections.

as a freshman legislator, when she served in the House with both Fadeley and his wife, Nancie Fadeley. She tells the story of when Nancie, a fellow freshman, carried her first bill on the House floor. With television cameras rolling, Ed Fadeley walked over to his wife's desk with a bouquet of flowers and presented them along with a demure kiss on her cheek. Then when Nancie got up to speak, Fadeley stepped over to Norma's desk, which was right next to Nancie's. He leaned over and murmured, "How'd you like to meet me at the Village Green? We could have a wonderful time." The Village Green was a resort near Cottage Grove. "I was dumbfounded. Flabbergasted," said Norma. "I just kind of gasped and stared at him. I didn't say anything, and he walked off." She soon learned that "every woman who's been anywhere near him has her Ed Fadeley story. He was always making suggestive remarks to me, as I'm sure he did to everyone else. But this was an out-and-out proposition."[29]

As Fadeley's appeal to working-class voters attested, Oregon's sagging economy was the key issue facing all the gubernatorial hopefuls. The painful shift from a heavy reliance on timber to a more diversified resource and manufacturing economy was well under way. While she recognized opportunities posed by the emerging high-tech sector, Norma was convinced that it was even more important to support timber and agriculture and develop new opportunities in those traditional sectors.[30] A few weeks after her kickoff, Norma and her team developed a detailed position paper called "Cultivating a More Prosperous Future." It was critical, she said, "that government work cooperatively with private agricultural interests to provide assistance and incentives for the preservation and expansion of agriculture's role in Oregon." She proposed creating a marketing program to promote the quality of Oregon's crops, expanding the food processing industry, offering a tax credit to producers to offset high freight rates, and boosting support for agricultural research and marketing.[31]

APPOINTMENT IN MANILA

Early in 1986, President Ronald Reagan asked Norma to join a team traveling to the Philippines to oversee the February 7 presidential election. The team was headed by Indiana senator Richard Lugar, who chaired the Senate Foreign Relations Committee. After more than twenty years in power, the Philippines' autocratic president, Ferdinand Marcos, was being challenged by Corazon Aquino, the widow of a prominent opposition leader who'd been assassinated three years previously.

The United States was in a delicate position. The Philippines, once a US colony, had been independent since 1946, but it remained an essential American outpost in the South Pacific. The United States had maintained a strategic alliance with Marcos since his first election as president in 1965. Marcos's strong-arm and often extralegal tactics, such as imposing martial law in 1972, were credited with keeping a simmering Communist insurgency from reaching the boiling point. Marcos also was willing to maintain two critically important US military bases in the Philippines: a naval base at Subic Bay, Zambales, and Clark Air Base on Luzon, in exchange for generous financial assistance.

No one disputed that Marcos's rule was dictatorial, corrupt, and sclerotic. Aquino's late husband, Benigno Aquino, had been a relentless critic of the Philippine government until he was assassinated in 1983. His murder was found to be the work of high military officials in the Marcos regime. When his widow stepped forward to run against Marcos for the presidency in 1986, her candidacy excited a level of popular support that alarmed Marcos and his supporters.

Paulus family campaign photo, 1986. Jerome Hart. Family archives.

Fears of voter fraud and election tampering were widespread.[32] "There is grow-ing concern in Washington," warned one newspaper, "that a budding commu-nist insurgency will lead to civil war if Marcos is re-elected Friday."[33]

Norma's two terms as secretary of state, overseeing Oregon's (mostly) squeaky-clean elections, may not have been the best preparation for auditing a highly contested election in a country with shaky democratic traditions. "As experienced as she is in election matters," said one newspaper editorial, "there is nothing other than a keen instinct for what's right and wrong to prepare Norma Paulus—or other members of a nineteen-member US team of observers—for objective appraisal of Friday's presidential elections in the Philippines."[34]

Norma expected some corruption; a clean vote, she said, was simply unreal-istic. What she saw was organized cheating on a massive scale. The team witnessed flagrant attempts by Marcos supporters to tamper with votes—and voters—at polling places and tabulation centers. Speaking later to a lunch meeting of Lane County Republican women, she told how she and two other delegates assigned to Llocas Norte province, a Marcos stronghold, slipped their government-appointed "babysitter" the night before the election and went off in search of local opposition leaders. They met with a Catholic bishop who told them how to detect voting fraud, which they saw in abundance the following day.[35]

The cheating on the Marcos side, she believed, was systematic and cold-bloodedly practical, while any fraud on Aquino's side was "the result of

A quilting circle Norma attended during her campaign for governor, 1986. Norma Paulus Papers, Willamette University Archives and Special Collections_NP007.

well-meaning but passionate supporters."[36] Marcos won the election, doubtless because of the voter fraud. Two weeks later, his supporters inaugurated him as president. Aquino was inaugurated by her own supporters on the same day, February 25, leading to a tense standoff. Later that day, President Reagan urged Marcos to leave the country. He departed and went into exile in Hawai'i.[37] Corazon Aquino became the Philippines' president and served until 1992.[38]

The experience renewed Norma's faith in the human passion for self-determination. The depth of support for Aquino, she said, represented an inspiring commitment to democracy on the part of ordinary citizens. "I never in my life thought I would . . . witness people risk their lives to protect the ballot box." In her speeches, she urged church and civic groups in the United States to "reach out and let Filipinos know they support a free and democratic society."[39]

INTO ACTION

When Paulus came home from the Philippines, the May primary was less than three months away. She started recruiting campaign workers and lining up support from the Republican leadership, including Bob Packwood, Mark Hatfield, and Vic Atiyeh and their friends.[40] She won an endorsement from her old friend Bob Chandler, publisher of the *Bend Bulletin*. She made the rounds of former legislative colleagues and got the endorsement of the Women's Political Caucus through their lobbyist, Gretchen Kafoury. Kafoury, a Democrat, became Norma's lifelong admirer and supporter.[41]

Norma liked and respected her presumptive opponent and knew he was potentially a strong rival. But she sensed that the state's Republican leaders preferred her candidacy to Dave Frohnmayer's. She was a strong female candidate—an asset because it gave her a distinctive identity with the progressive core of Republican voters. And her liberal-leaning views gave her considerable crossover appeal with Democrats. More than that, Norma intuited a consensus among party leaders that it was her turn. "Inside the Republican party," she said, "there's always been a kind of feeling that you wait your turn, and you take your turn. So I felt very confident that I would be the Republican nominee."

Then, unexpectedly, Frohnmayer bowed out of the primary race. His young daughter Katie had been diagnosed with Fanconi anemia, a rare, deadly genetic disease. Katie's older sister Kirsten had been diagnosed in 1983 at age ten. Frohnmayer and his wife, Lynn, curtailed their professional lives to care for the girls, both of whom later died.[42]

Frohnmayer's decision left Norma with a virtually clear field. Her closest challenger was Betty Freauf, a Christian housewife who represented the religiously driven conservative politics that was beginning to rise in Oregon. Freauf tried to paint Norma as a well-intentioned politician who "has gone off to the liberal left."[43] Freauf may have been a splinter candidate, but her presence was a troubling portent for the mainstream Republican Party, an early-warning signal of a growing rift between moderates and conservatives, in Oregon and across the nation.

That signal was beginning to register on Norma's acute political radar. In her first run for secretary of state in 1976, she'd won a very narrow primary victory over a little-known opponent, John Kelting. Her razor-thin margin of victory, speculated *Statesman-Journal* commentator Ron Blankenbaker, meant that the Republican electorate was tilting rightward more than Paulus realized: "I've always credited the broad conservative stripe of Republican voters for Paulus' failure to squeak past a politically unknown building contractor . . . by more than the slimmest of margins,"[44] he wrote. But Paulus disputed that interpretation, he wrote, attributing her slim victory to her own inexperience in campaigning.

ANOINTED

Norma and Goldschmidt stumped Oregon in the weeks before the primary, acting very much like the anointed candidates they later came to be. Norma campaigned on making government leaner and more effective, promoting traditional Northwest industries like timber and agriculture, and making the state friendlier for tourists. She called for Oregon to join with neighboring states in promoting a Northwest identity, both to boost the tourism economy and to raise the region's profile with people east of the Rockies. "They also have this vague image of us as wet and green," she told the *Eugene Register-Guard*.[45]

Goldschmidt's platform was not too different on the big issues. For example, Norma's passion had always been education; she spoke frequently on school finance reform—schools were funded mostly through local property taxes then—and promoted a sales tax to furnish some of the needed revenue. Goldschmidt had no issue with this—school finance reform was needed, he believed, and a sales tax was a good idea.[46]

As the two candidates were sometimes at pains to distinguish themselves from each other, they scrapped over smaller issues. Goldschmidt backed a gasoline tax; Norma derided the idea. Norma continued to support land-use planning and environmental regulation; Goldschmidt's views on these questions were less than forthright.[47] Their differences, concluded the *Oregonian*'s Foster Church, were mostly on strategy rather than substance. "Norma Paulus and Neil Goldschmidt paused long enough in their quest for the governorship Sunday night to dine together—or at least take a meal in the same room," and, speaking after dinner to a restaurant-and-beverage gathering, "they disagreed mildly over tourism and economic development issues." The topics were worker compensation (both agreed it was a mess; neither offered a solution), tourism (Oregon needs more of it), and liquor liability for bars and restaurants (the drinker should bear some responsibility).[48]

Ed Fadeley was also on the stump. Although he trailed the other two in the polls, he was a serious opponent, cultivating a small but significant strand of the electorate that was responding coolly to the front runners. In February he followed Norma and Goldschmidt in speaking to the Coos Bay Rotary Club. Fadeley used the occasion to expand on his populist, small-government philosophy. He deplored the monied interests he said were controlling the political process. He recommended abolishing the land-use planning system, reducing property taxes, limiting growth in school spending, and returning economic and political control to local communities.[49] His attack on "big business, big money, and big press," said the *Oregonian*, was bound to strike a chord in this formerly prosperous timber town, "which bitterly resents Portland's economic dominance of the state."[50]

A controversy erupted in early March when Goldschmidt challenged Fadeley and Paulus to a three-way debate. Norma initially agreed, and the debate was scheduled for April 11 at the Salem City Club. Then Norma changed her mind and stepped out, saying that the Democrats first needed to sort out who their candidate was.[51] Not surprisingly, Goldschmidt made hay out of her demurral. "She can run," he said, "but she can't hide."[52] Norma also took some criticism in the press. The *Oregonian*'s Foster Church said the decision tarnished her image of "gutsiness."[53] Ron Blankenbaker, the *Statesman-Journal*'s political commentator, called her excuse lame, and said the real reason was that she was running ahead of Goldschmidt in the polls, and it would not be to her advantage to debate him now.[54]

Well, of course not, said the *Albany Democrat-Herald*. Paulus made a calculated decision—it is seldom a good idea for the front-runner to engage in a debate. And the editorialist agreed that only same-party hopefuls should debate each other before the primary.[55] The debate went forward with just Goldschmidt and Fadeley, and both took pokes at Norma in absentia. The *Oregonian* ran a cartoon labeled "The Cheshire Candidate." It showed Goldschmidt and Fadeley standing at podiums, frowning. At a third podium is a disembodied smile with the balloon caption: "I'll be here in spirit, guys. . . "[56]

It wasn't that Norma was afraid to face Goldschmidt on the stump. He was a spontaneous and charismatic speaker, but so was she. They both could think on their feet, they both knew their material, and they both knew how to work an audience. After the primary they did meet in several debates throughout the state.

AFTER THE PRIMARY

With Frohnmayer out of the race, and with no other serious opposition, Norma won the Republican primary with 77 percent of the vote. She'd learned a lesson from 1976 and worked hard to get her name and face in front of voters statewide. She did not bother to cultivate the sliver of the electorate that appealed to Betty Freauf (who took 13 percent of the vote) and other conservative candidates. For her, she figured they were a lost cause. "Their rationale was, maybe both candidates are terrible," she said, "but it's better to vote for a man than for a woman."[57]

As Norma threw herself single-mindedly into the campaign, her schedule went from rigorous to near-impossible.

> One day I was in five vans, an airplane, two helicopters, a paddleboat on the Willamette River, a sternwheeler, and I don't know how many individual automobiles. I had to be in Coos Bay by car, and going down the beach, and stopping at the different radio stations,

Norma campaigning at the 1986 Pendleton Round Up. The Paris Woolen Mills in Stayton, Oregon, owned by Don Lachman, wove the Norma Paulus blanket. Family archives.

giving speeches, and to be picked up by a helicopter and flown to the Black Bar Ranch in the Rogue Valley over nothing but jagged mountain tops and treetops.[58]

For the first time in her career, she had to raise serious money.[59] She worked the mainstream party network in Oregon,[60] gaining the support of people like the prominent Portlanders John Schwabe and William Love of Schwabe Williamson & Wyatt, one of the Northwest's biggest business-law firms.[61] Love had chaired her 1980 reelection campaign for secretary of state and now headed a group called Friends of Norma Paulus.[62]

Another well-known champion was John Elorriaga, chairman and CEO of U.S. Bank.[63] Elorriaga was an old acquaintance; like Norma, he hailed from eastern Oregon's Basque country. Norma loves to tell the story of the prominent Portland attorneys and some high-level executives taking her up to the fortieth floor of the U.S. Bank Tower so she could be "introduced to" Elorriaga. She walked into his office with her escorts and—much to their surprise—Elorriaga gave her a mock-severe look and demanded, "What's a nice Burns girl like you doing in a place like this?" She smiled and replied, "What's an old Basco like you doing in a place like this?"[64]

She also cultivated donors outside Oregon, raising money from national women's groups. She tapped into a network of well-known figures and celebrities, including the actress Lily Tomlin, who performed at a fund-raiser for her in New York, and aviation pioneer and test pilot Chuck Yeager, the inspiration for Tom Wolfe's book *The Right Stuff*. Yeager appeared at a Paulus for Governor fund-raiser in Portland. Also supporting Norma were William and Mary Gates, who were prominent in the Seattle business community (and, incidentally, the parents of a bright boy named Bill who would later make a big name for himself).[65]

Norma still tried to make time for family. Bill Paulus, a partner with the Salem firm Garrett Hemann Roberts, was busy with his law practice, but he managed to slip away from time to time and meet his wife on the road. After the primary, Fritz, his mother's driver and advance person, got to see Norma more often than her husband did. Daughter Liz had helped open Norma's Portland campaign office in the fall of 1985. She served on the statewide team until after the primary. After a stressful eight months she moved on to work for Powell's Books, and supported the campaign in other ways.[66]

"GOVERNOR OF PORTLAND"

As the campaign moved into summer, debates became a contentious topic. The candidates clashed over how many there should be, and when, and—in particular—where. The disagreement drove Goldschmidt to make a memorable campaign gaffe.

Though an Oregon native, Goldschmidt was widely viewed as a liberal, big-city, eastern-affiliated politician. He had a sturdy following in Portland and the Willamette Valley, but was less well liked east of the Cascades. Norma may not have been born in Oregon, but she grew up in Burns, and her small-town credentials played well with the farmers, ranchers, and small-business owners on the east side.[68] She proposed a debate schedule that included Bend, where these advantages would show up well. Goldschmidt surely knew this as well as Norma did. He was game for the debate but resisted the venue. In an August 6 interview with KOIN-TV in Portland, he said, "Let's do these debates where they'll do some good. Quit pretending a debate in the middle of nowhere and when nobody can watch it is a real debate."[69]

The remark created a righteous furor in Bend and points east. "We do not think of ourselves as living 'in the middle of nowhere,'" wrote H. Bruce Miller in the *Bend Bulletin*, with tongue only slightly in cheek. "On the contrary, we think of Bend as a pretty sophisticated and cosmopolitan place," boasting a

Wendy's, a McDonald's, a Kentucky Fried Chicken, and a Dairy Queen, and "for the more gastronomically adventurous," Mexican, Chinese, and even Polish food. "And," he added, "we are about to get our own full-service car wash."

And another thing: since Bend is approximately in the middle of Oregon, Goldschmidt must think Oregon is Nowhere. "Now, why would a man want to be governor of Nowhere? The only possible reason is that Neil hopes someday to parlay it into another, better job Somewhere."[70] The next day Norma held a press conference and demanded an apology.[71] Later she accused Goldschmidt of wanting to be "the Governor of Portland."[72] Two weeks later Goldschmidt made a special trip to Bend and apologized. "The last two weeks have been painful for me," he said. "If you want to know how painful, it is not easy to dislodge a size-11 foot from one's mouth."[73] The crowd included Paulus supporters waving signs that said, "Nowhere Loves Norma."[74]

In the end the candidates met for six formal debates, "all of which," noted the *Register-Guard*, "were marked with flashes of anger, bitterness and endless attempts to force each other to make the big mistake that could swing the election."[75]

THE LAST BATTLES

As election day drew nearer, Goldschmidt was becoming a more formidable opponent. Going into the primary, Paulus had led in the polls, 47 to 31 percent.[76] Little by little Goldschmidt was gaining on her, and by October he led by a narrow margin: 46 to 43 percent, with 11 percent undecided.[77] He was using the tagline "The Oregon Comeback" to promote his ideas for reviving the economy.[78] The slogan worked to his advantage as he attacked the Atiyeh administration and, by extension, Norma Paulus, for failing to cure Oregon's economic ills.[79] He accused Atiyeh's state-agency leaders of incompetence, indecision, and "cover-ups," and castigated the "dry rot" in the governor's administration. He went so far as to name names, singling out two high-level administrators for particular excoriation.

Goldschmidt's personal attacks sent the usually even-tempered Atiyeh into a state of incoherent rage. "He called Neil Goldschmidt a demagogue, a bureaucrat-basher, ill-informed and reckless," said the *Oregonian*'s Foster Church. "Atiyeh himself trembled and stammered as he read the speech. Afterward as he lit a cigarette, his forehead was filmed with perspiration."[80] Goldschmidt's remarks, mused Church, "often make it sound as if he is running against Atiyeh." But his target was clearly Norma Paulus. Goldschmidt, said Church, "has attempted since early this year to tie Paulus and Atiyeh as

In one of the many debates in the race, Norma Paulus and Neil Goldschmidt appear here at the Washington County Public Affairs Forum in Forest Grove, Oregon. Michael Lloyd/*The Oregonian*.

partners in what he describes as a failed administration."[81] During one of the more contentious debates, Goldschmidt told Paulus, "I am going to talk every day about what you and your friends in the same old Salem crowd have allowed to happen in this state."[82]

Norma knew Goldschmidt was aiming at a vulnerable spot. She needed to distance herself from Atiyeh's economic policies (which, as secretary of state, she didn't have much to do with) without alienating Atiyeh's loyalists and other mainstream Republicans. Without directly defending Atiyeh, she turned the spotlight on the legislature, one of the most quarrelsome in recent memory,[83] saying that it had dropped the ball on fixing several major problems, including a "stifling" permit system, workers compensation policies that discriminate against small businesses, and liability insurance grown to "nightmare proportions." Legislators, she said, had been waiting "for a knight to ride in on a white horse and rescue us all. But the future of the state won't be run that way."[84]

ELECTION COUNTDOWN

Goldschmidt had promised "a clean fight," and mostly it was. Norma remembers a Goldschmidt ad that was supposed to be hard-hitting, but in her view it misfired. During the campaign she'd made a lighthearted comment that she "knew where the bones were buried" in state government—meaning only that her secretary of state's audits had revealed some irregularities. "So they had the damnedest television ad that showed a man digging holes and shoveling,

Norma with her family and supporters at a rally at the Salem airport in the final lead up to election day, 1986.
Randy L. Rasmussen/*The Oregonian.*

the dirt coming out of the holes, trying to make fun of me, but nobody knew what it meant. When people saw 'Paid for by Goldschmidt,' they must have scratched their heads."[85]

Another of Norma's offhanded remarks had more serious consequences. From time to time the campaign staff would get a phone call from a woman who identified herself as the live-in partner of one of Goldschmidt's key strategists. The caller would alert them to what Goldschmidt was planning to do—"she would tell them what kind of dirty tricks they were planning," said Norma. The woman claimed to be a Paulus supporter even though her boyfriend was working for Goldschmidt, but Norma's staff suspected a deliberate disinformation feed from the Goldschmidt camp.

Leaving a press conference shortly before the election, Norma let slip a comment that it "might be dirty tricks time" in the Goldschmidt campaign. A reporter asked her how she knew this. She replied, "Well, we have a mole."[86] Norma is adept at snappy comebacks, but this was one she deeply regretted. "I should have said, 'We have a leak.'" Or better yet, said nothing. The "mole" remark made the newspapers the next day, and the story made it sound as if her campaign had infiltrated Goldschmidt's. The Goldschmidt campaign quickly ran an ad criticizing Norma for stooping to spy on her opponent. "Which just drove me right up the wall," said Norma. "I wanted to respond, but my staff said, 'Don't respond. It'll go away.' And I always regretted that I didn't. We should have stopped and had a press conference right away."[87]

In late October, worried about the slipping poll numbers, Norma's political consultant, Doug Watts, prepared a television ad that accused Goldschmidt of "flip-flopping" on some of his positions. Watts was a partner in Russo Watts & Rollins, the prominent California political consulting firm that had advised Ronald Reagan's 1984 presidential campaign.[88] Puzzlingly, Norma had turned down an offer from the statewide Republican Party to invite the president himself to come to Oregon and campaign for her. She may have felt Reagan's brand of conservatism, with its distaste for government regulation and environmental protection, was too extreme for the voters she wanted to court.[89]

Norma was uncomfortable with the "flip-flop" ad, although it was mild by today's standards, she recalled. But she agreed to release it, hoping it might perk up her poll numbers. In the meantime her campaign staff was picking up disturbing rumors that Goldschmidt was having extramarital affairs. She decided it was best to ignore these.[90]

Along with the "flip-flop" ad, the Watts team had created a second, highly negative piece, titled "Ambition," which portrayed Goldschmidt as an insincere, untrustworthy opportunist. Fritz Paulus remembers the sinister undertones in the ad's presentation that brought it to the verge of character assassination. He tells the story:

> That memory is blazed in my mind. Mom comes home one night in October after a long day of campaigning. All her political advisors are assembled at our house, and they tell her, "We need to talk." Her pollster was there, Bob Moore; also Doug Watts; also Diane Landers, her campaign manager. They were saying, "We need to do something different. We need to go negative here to counter the drop in the polls." They told her, "You'll lose the election if you don't do something different." Mom was tired, and she had to make a decision right then. I remember her asking me, "Fritz, what do you think?" I said, "Mom, it might help, but it's not your style and it could backfire." My dad was there too, and he agreed. So she went against Watts' advice and refused to run the ad. If she'd run that ad, it might have tipped the scales. But ultimately that's not who Mom is, and everybody loves her for that. She didn't get to be governor, but she kept her integrity.[91]

Norma on the campaign trail aboard a fishing boat at the Oregon Coast Memorial Day Fleet of Flowers, 1986. Norma Paulus Papers, Willamette University Archives and Special Collections_NP057.

It's not clear whether her "mole" comment, or the decision not to run the "Ambition" ad, or declining to invite President Reagan, or any one thing, was enough to tip the balance in a heartbreakingly close election. In the end, perhaps, it was a little bit of everything.

While she had an army of enthusiastic volunteers—hundreds working from Salem, Portland, and throughout the state[92]—Norma had struggled from the start to pull together an effective leadership team.[93] Her first choice for campaign manager had been Karen Whitman, whose brilliant strategizing had propelled Norma to the secretary of state's office in 1976. By 1986 Whitman was running her own consulting firm and was not available for full-time managing, although she did help with strategy.[94] Norma originally hired Jim Hulden as campaign manager, but replaced him with Diane Landers in February of 1986, nine months before the general election.[95]

Perhaps more important, her key leaders were not full-time political op-
eratives. "They were people that were stable parts of the community, and they
were willing to work really hard during the election season," Norma said, "but
then they were going to go back and run the hospital, or run the real estate
office. They had lives. I was a part of their life, but I wasn't their life."[96] Goldschmidt had raised more money, enough to outspend her by about a million
dollars.[97] The Paulus-Goldschmidt race would tally up as the most expensive
gubernatorial campaign in Oregon history up to then.[98]

Norma did not get the endorsements she was expecting. She was dismayed that, after meeting with both candidates, the *Oregonian's* editorial board
endorsed Goldschmidt. She acknowledged she was not at her best during
that interview: "I don't think I did very well, and I didn't feel good about it."
The *Statesman-Journal* had also given the nod to Goldschmidt—a significant
sting, coming from her hometown newspaper.[99] Norma did get an endorsement from Senator Mark Hatfield in an ad filmed on the capitol grounds by
Watts's group. "We assumed that Hatfield's stature in Oregon was such that his
endorsement would have a positive effect," said Fritz Paulus, who was present
for the filming. "But I remember that the polling did not go up significantly
after the ad was aired. Which I guess supports the notion that going negative
would have been a better strategy."[100] The unkindest blow was that the Oregon
Women's Political Caucus endorsed Goldschmidt over Paulus—evidently in
the hope that a male Democrat would do more to advance women's issues
than a female Republican with impeccable feminist credentials. "I still can't
forgive them for that," said Liz Paulus.[101]

Which brings up the stubborn fact of her gender. Early in the campaign,
when asked whether gender would become a factor in the race, Norma quipped,
"Whose? His or mine?"[102] Now she faced the sober truth that there was still
a segment of voters who would not vote for a woman—perhaps from simple
prejudice, or perhaps because of a reflexive conviction that a man is a safer bet
in hard economic times. "So many people would say, 'Either one of you would
be a great governor.' It wasn't enough."[103] She'd started with a decisive lead
and ended running a defensive campaign against a forceful and charismatic
challenger of the status quo, a man who promised to cure Oregon's economic
malaise, a man whose deep flaws of character were not yet visible to his public.
She acknowledged that Goldschmidt had a stronger economic message, and
she believed that "in the end, that's what turned things around for him."

Norma was thinking about none of these things during the election-day
countdown. Instead, she was single-mindedly sprinting for the finish line. "I'm

not getting the broad picture at all. I'm not watching any television," she said. "I'm getting in the van, being driven someplace, I'm reading the newspapers, I'm preparing my speech for the next stop, and by the time I've finished the last speech of the day, I go to sleep and get up the next morning and do it all over again."[104] True to tradition, Norma, Bill, Liz, and Fritz spent election night at the Benson Hotel. "I don't remember much," she said. "I remember it was too close to call," and she and Bill went to bed. The next morning she learned she had lost. "The press came in and they asked me what I was going to do. And I said I thought I'd go home and rake leaves." She was exhausted. She had lost weight and strength, and all she wanted to do was sleep.

After a few days at home, she was able to contemplate her defeat in a more philosophical frame of mind. She'd lost a close race—the difference was 42,470 votes out of 1.08 million cast.[105] "Of course I was sorry about it, particularly for all the people who worked so hard for me," she said. "But I can't say I was devastated. As a matter of fact—and this is another thing people will find hard to believe—being governor is not that much fun. It's too intense; it's too confrontational. In a time of plenty, when you've got money to spend, that's one thing. But in a time of need, it is very difficult. The need is real, and there are always real people behind the need. It's a very, very stressful job."

If not governor, then what? Norma considered her future. For the first time in sixteen years, she was out of a job. Where to go now? The answer came from an unlikely quarter.

POWER AND FISH

Soon after the election, Goldschmidt called Norma and asked her to meet with him. They had lunch at the Illahe Hills Country Club, a few miles from Norma's home, causing a mild stir. "People were just beside themselves when they saw the two of us together," Norma said.[106] Over lunch, Goldschmidt told Norma he'd like to put her to work in some capacity that would interest and challenge her. Did she have any suggestions? She told him the only job she would consider taking was an appointment to the Northwest Power Planning Council.

Norma knew about the council and its workings from her old friend Herb Schwab, former Chief Judge of the Oregon Court of Appeals,[107] who had represented Oregon on the council since it was created by the Northwest Power Act in 1980. The council's mission (its name today is the Northwest Power and Conservation Council) is to secure a consistent and reliable supply of energy, and also to protect and enhance fish and wildlife in the Columbia River Basin.[108]

A membership photo of the then-called Northwest Power Planning Council, 1987–88. Back row (L-R): Jim Goller (Idaho), Bob Saxvik (Idaho), Norma Paulus (Oregon), George Turman (Montana), Ted Bottiger (Washington), Ted Hallock (Oregon); front row: Morris Brusett (Montana), Tom Trulove (Washington). Photo courtesy of Northwest Power and Conservation Council.

The Columbia Basin is a huge river system, once containing the nation's richest runs of salmon and steelhead. Today it has the world's largest network of hydroelectric dams—eleven on the Columbia's main stem and hundreds more on tributaries throughout the basin.[109] The tension between generating power and protecting fish has prevailed in the basin since the opening of Bonneville Dam, the Northwest's first multipurpose federal dam, in 1938.[110] For that reason, serving on the Power Planning Council can be a difficult balancing act. Members are appointed by governors with varying views on the economy and the environment, and their constituents represent a host of sometimes-conflicting interests: consumers of the power generated by the dams, farmers who water their crops from the rivers, port towns that need enough water in the river to move their barges of grain and vegetables, Indian tribes exercising their treaty fishing rights, environmentalists committed to protecting fish and wildlife, recreationists who like to fish and water-ski in the reservoirs behind the dams.

Norma started her term in January of 1987, one of eight representatives from the four Northwest states, Idaho, Montana, Oregon, and Washington. The other Oregon representative was Bob Duncan, who formerly represented Oregon's Third District in the US House of Representatives. When Duncan's term expired in 1988,[111] Goldschmidt appointed Ted Hallock, whom Norma knew well from her legislative days, to succeed him.

Norma made something of an entrance at her first meeting with the US Army Corps of Engineers' commanding officer, Colonel Jim Fry. Peter Paquet, then a young fish biologist who worked for the council, was in the room when Norma came in, escorted by Bob Saxvik, a council representative from Idaho. Colonel Fry looked at Saxvik and, somewhat more lingeringly, at Norma. "Hey, Sax," he said. "Who's that? Your new girlfriend?" "The second he said it, the world just went silent," Paquet recalled, remembering his own embarrassment. Then Norma spoke up. "No, sir," she said, "I'm Norma Paulus. I'm the new council member from the state of Oregon." Then, turning to another staffer, she said, not quite sotto voce, "We're going to get these guys."[112]

The council, she recalled later, "dealt with all the issues I knew a lot about and was vitally interested in: power, conservation, global warming, recycling, and fish issues."[113] An urgent priority of the council's wildlife-restoration effort was to bring back wild salmon and steelhead, whose numbers had declined greatly since the dams were built. Norma was pleased to be working on such vital matters in an integrated way, and in a multistate arena.

Because meetings are held in all four member states, Norma spent many bumpy hours in small aircraft. Both Duncan and Hallock disliked flying: Duncan because his hip replacements made it extremely uncomfortable for him, and Hallock because he'd had enough of airplanes after flying combat missions during World War II. "So that left me with flying all over these four Northwestern states," Norma said, in all kinds of weather. "It got to be a hassle."

One morning I left Pigeon Hollow, our home in Salem, and my husband was about to go off to his office. I said that at ten o'clock I'm flying to Portland and then to Spokane to chair a meeting over there for the Power Council and I should be back to Portland by two so we'll be able to go to this event that we were going to that night. . . . Well, I got back five days later. When I got on the plane in Portland, one of the small airplanes, we flew to Spokane and there was such cloud cover that we couldn't land, so we went to all the smaller towns in Idaho and in Oregon trying to find a place to land and we couldn't. We ended up, before we ran out of gas, in Kalispell, Montana. I was there, I think, for four days before we could get out.

On another day my secretary told me I had to be on the plane by such and such a time, and I had forgotten to ask her where I was going. So I get on the plane, and as I'm flying in there, in this small airplane, I'm reading all this stuff, and when we land I get out and I'm stretching around and I say, "Gee, those look like the Tetons." And the federal wildlife expert who was with me looked at me with this strange look and said, "Where did you think you were?" I thought I was going to Idaho, and I was in Wyoming! It sort of gives you a short picture of what my life was like during that time.

At the time Norma joined the council, it was wrestling with a controversial policy question: how to get young salmon and steelhead—smolts—from the upper river down to the ocean. Before the dams were there, the smolts migrated downstream from the tributaries where they were hatched. Now they risked being chewed up in the dams' churning turbines. To protect the young fish, the council was requiring the US Army Corps of Engineers, which operates eight federal dams on the Columbia's main stem,[114] to spill reservoir water over the dams during migrations, rather than holding it back and letting it run through the turbines. This requirement was not popular with power advocates because it posed a significant cost in power-generation opportunities.[115]

To solve the problem permanently, the council's hydrologists recommended installing underwater diversion screens to funnel the smolts away from the turbines. The project would cost the Corps $160 million. Congress had allocated almost $20 million over two national budget cycles toward the project, and the screens would allow more water to go through the turbines, which would generate more power, which could be sold to recover the cost of the project in just a few years, by the council's estimates.[116] But the Corps argued that it shouldn't have to pay for fish-mitigation projects, saying that the cost should be borne instead by regional ratepayers. Besides, it would be cheaper, the Corps maintained, to collect the smolts in barges and ship them downstream—a strategy known in shorthand as "bypass." The Corps dismissed the fears of biologists who believed that barging the fish might stress them and contribute to disease. The Corps maintained that there was no evidence that screens were any better for the smolts than barges.

Norma was dumbfounded at the Corps' position. The screens were the obvious solution, she said. Most people in the region wanted to save the fish and felt that underwater screens were a reasonable use of taxpayer money. And loading all these tender young fish into barges and shipping them down through the locks was a waste of energy; it simply didn't make sense.[117] She had a supply of bumper stickers printed that read "Bypass the Corps." Her

Council members Bob Saxvik (Idaho) and Norma Paulus (Oregon), observing culvert removal for improved fish passage in Middle Fork of Lick Creek, John Day Basin. Norma Paulus Papers, Willamette University Archives and Special Collections_NP112.

feisty attitude tickled native-fish activist Bill Bakke, then with the conservation group Oregon Trout.[118] "I called her and said, 'I could really use a bunch of those bumper stickers. Could you give me some?'"[119]

Bakke agreed with Norma that the council's restoration plans relied too heavily on salmon hatcheries as a mitigation strategy.[120] "Because hatchery fish were expensive and poor in survival, she called them 'wimp fish,'" said Bakke. "She was willing to say that in public. That's something I appreciate about Norma: she takes sides." By this time, too, she had begun to speak out about removing the Columbia Basin's dams to save the wild fish.[121] "After I'd been there about eight months," she said, "I realized something that nobody had told me at the beginning, and that is that the John Day [dam] is constructed so that the silt just builds up behind it so that fish wander around and get lost."

(All dams eventually collect silt behind them.) "So, if you're really serious about saving the salmon, the dams have got to go."[122]

At the end of Norma's first year the council's composition shifted, and the new members were more pro-business, as she remembers. While the Power Act called for equal treatment of fish and power, Norma was (perhaps naively) disappointed to realize that "the power still received more attention in every way."[123] She stepped down in 1989, after three years of service. "By then the whole complexion of the thing had changed," she said; the council had become "dominated by people and their governors who did not want the dams to go, didn't give a crap about salmon. They were concerned about timber, pea farms,[124] agriculture. And they had the political support to kind of cut the council adrift. So it was made toothless."[125]

Bill Bakke had found in Norma a kindred soul, and he was sorry to see her go. He describes his association with Norma as "a blessing." Power council members are political appointees, serving at the pleasure of their states' governors, and "often they really don't understand why they're there," Bakke said. "She did. It's pretty easy to grasp the importance of a secure power supply. It's a little more difficult to grasp the biological intricacies of wild salmon recovery. But she got it." Despite its limitations, Bakke said, the council has done good work in the past thirty-five years. "There's been a lot of benefit to the region in terms of predictable and secure power supply," he said. "There've been significant improvements in salmon survival around dams. And a lot of research has been funded, even though state agencies don't implement it. So there's been a tremendous amount of benefit from the council." And yet the decline of wild salmon continues—a crisis with a tangle of causes and no easy solutions.

After she stepped down from the power council, Norma didn't have any particular plans other than taking a much-needed rest. "I had been living a very fast-paced life for a long time," she said. Fritz and Liz were grown and out on their own, and Norma was ready to spend some time with her husband. "Bill and I had a lot of opportunity to be together. We went to the coast a lot, to our beach house over there, we played a lot of golf on weekends."

Another political race was on the horizon, but Norma wasn't looking that far—yet.[126]

Oregon Supreme Court Justice Betty Roberts swearing in Norma as Oregon's Superintendent of Public Instruction in Salem's Pringle Community Hall, Friday, October 5, 1990. Timothy J. Gonzalez/Courtesy of the *Statesman Journal*. Willamette Heritage Center, X2012.022.010.0129.

Chapter 11
Oregon's Chief Educator

> No matter what job I had, I always said that there was nothing
> more important than the public school system. When I became
> superintendent, I had clout. I ran for the office because I thought
> I'd be able to get a sales tax passed that would support schools.
> Of course that didn't happen. But I was able to get more money
> for the K–12 system than they'd ever had before.
>
> —Norma Paulus

In late 1989, Norma Paulus was about to complete her three-year term on the Northwest Power Planning Council, with no plan to seek another. After the grueling governor's race, she had expressed a desire to maintain a low profile, and the Power Planning Council work had seemed to fit this intention—her travels around the Northwest on council business kept her out of Oregon for a total of fifty-six days during her first ten months alone.[1] But three years of bumping around the Northwest in small aircraft had convinced her that one term was enough.

Since her loss to Goldschmidt, noted one reporter, Norma had "gone from being one of the most visible politicians in Oregon to a woman who avoids the public eye."[2] She had been happy to discuss her work on the council, the reporter said, and she would gladly hold forth on whether she was "healthy and happy, wealthy and wise." But she wouldn't discuss the campaign, the victor, or her reaction to the defeat. Norma did allow that she had healed enough to start reading newspapers again, after a long hiatus during which she "couldn't bear it." She also intimated that she had kept "close contact with her past aides," burning no bridges just in case she chose to run for office again someday. A US Senate contest might be appealing, she told the reporter.[3]

In the meantime, she still had her early passion for education. "When I got off the council," she said,

> I thought, well, here I know probably more than almost any-
> one about the state and its government. I had a really good

understanding of Oregon, its people, its geography, its industries, its rivers. I knew the state like the back of my hand because I'd been traveling around it constantly for years. I have such a wealth of knowledge about Oregon, what should I do? Throughout my political career and involvement as a mother, I'd been trying to find some way . . . some guiding light to get a better system for our schools, because it was one property tax upheaval and revolt after another. Then I thought the thing I had always wanted to do was to get a sales tax to fund schools. If I ran for superintendent and had that under my belt, I'd have a platform to do just that.[4]

Norma had publicly advocated for a sales tax since 1973, when Governor Tom McCall had asked her to co-chair his tax proposal along with Neil Goldschmidt, then mayor of Portland. A sales tax was the necessary third leg on the stool, she believed, without which the school system might wobble and fall.[5] The office of superintendent of public instruction, she thought, would be a bully pulpit from which to push for a sales tax and other reforms essential to preparing Oregon's kids for the future.

Norma's good friend Vera Katz, just ending an unprecedented third term as speaker of the House, had been working on education reform since the early 1970s. She had teamed up with Joyce Reinke, a former primary school teacher at the Oregon Department of Education, on a plan to provide better skills training and job preparation for the changing twenty-first-century workforce. "Vera's emphasis was on the school-to-work part of education, through the high schools and community colleges," Norma said.

The three of them, Katz, Reinke, and herself, would make a good team, Norma thought. She suspected that Katz might want to run for superintendent of public instruction herself, "so when I decided I was going to do it, I called her and told her. It was obvious to me and to her that I would win because my poll numbers were so high and I had a state-wide presence." Norma also told Reinke that after she was elected and Joyce was on her staff, "she could continue whatever she and Vera were doing, and in addition to that, we would make a big thrust for early-childhood education."[6]

On October 3, 1989, Norma announced her intention to run. Immediately she started building a case for her unique qualifications, arguing that what could seem a liability—her lack of teaching experience—was really an asset. Her predecessors may have had more educational training, she said, but dropout rates were soaring, drug problems were increasing, teacher quality was declining, and school financing was a persistent problem. She vowed to hire experienced educators to help with those issues, while she used her formidable political skills to take "sole responsibility" for school funding. "I intend to be at the doorstep of the Legislature every day of the next session, saying, 'I'm here for the kids and we want our money.'"[7]

NORMA'S ARMY

In early April, well ahead of the election, Norma appeared before the chamber of commerce in Redmond and announced her intention to lead a march on the capitol a few weeks after the legislature convened in January. Coverage of her announcement in the *Bend Bulletin* portrayed her quest as a quasi-military mission, "stockpiling political weapons and campaigning to be a general" on the issue of equitable school funding.

The "best-known woman in Oregon politics" told her audience exactly where she would lead them:

> "We will go there [to the Capitol] to tell them that we want education funded first, and that we want that 50 percent," said Paulus, explaining that it will cost the state an additional $400 million a year to pick up half the costs of grades kindergarten through 12. "It won't be easy," she added, "but it can be done." Paulus also believes Oregonians will at last support a sales tax—if the proposal is structured so that taxpayers are certain the money will be used solely for schools and will be a one-for-one offset for property taxes. "It has to be clear that it is a substitute, not a third tax," she said.[8]

Norma was familiar with Oregon voters' strong aversion to a sales tax. Her proposal would sweeten the deal by mandating a referendum vote after three years, "at which time Oregonians could dump the tax if they found it did not deliver what elected officials had promised." She appealed to Redmond voters as the victims of the inequity of Oregon's school funding system, supported by property taxes. "Your children are not treated as fairly as those in Lake Oswego, or Beaverton, or Eugene," she told her audience. "This state does not do right by many children including those in places like Central Oregon."[9] The *Bulletin* reporter noted that Norma was a heavy favorite to defeat her opponent, incumbent John Erickson. Erickson had been on the job only a short time; he'd been appointed by Governor Goldschmidt to succeed Verne Duncan after Duncan's November 1989 resignation. The story also noted

Concerned citizens and volunteers—"Norma's Army"—marching to the Oregon Capitol in support of education initiatives. Gerry Lewin/Courtesy of the *Statesman Journal*. Willamette Heritage Center, X2012.022.010.0048.

Norma's endorsement by the Oregon Education Association, the state's teachers' union.

A month shy of the election, Norma was the shoo-in candidate. It was, she believed, a hopeful, heady time for Oregon schools, and she wasn't going to wait till she was elected to take action. She rallied hundreds of parents, teachers, and other interested parties and created the promised "Norma's army." The first rally, on August 25, brought together "nearly 1,200 citizens from all 36 Oregon counties . . . from every walk of life" to attend seminars and round-table discussions "led by some of the best political and educational minds in the state."[10] "We all worked together," she recalled. "It was the first time, I think, that the unions and the school boards and the superintendent of public instruction were in sync. I was the leader. A lot was written about it, there was a lot of television, a lot of meetings, a lot of marches, a lot of gatherings and people came from all over the state to support it."[11]

Some pundits took issue with Norma's high-profile approach. "Somebody should tell Norma Paulus," the *Register-Guard* editorialized, "that in the battle to reform Oregon's school finance mess, she's a lieutenant, not the general." The proper leaders of the education-reform conversation, argued the writer, were gubernatorial candidates Dave Frohnmayer and Barbara Roberts. Norma was putting the cart before the horse in using her campaign "as a platform from which to assert leadership" on school finance, "rounding up an 'army'" to march on the capitol in January, and holding rallies of her recruits in Salem.[12]

"For a school finance package to have any chance with the voters," the editorial continued, "it must have the firm backing of the governor, and solid majorities in both houses." Instead of trying to command an army, Norma "should use that independence to become a vital part of the team that creates and sells a workable reform" of school finance.[13] The writer also acknowledged that Frohnmayer and Roberts had been conspicuously silent on the subject of education—perhaps out of deference to Norma for her loss in the governor's race four years before, and perhaps also out of a general unwillingness to offend her.

Jimi Mathers, a Republican and a Paulus supporter, came to Norma's defense. She said Norma was the obvious leader in the movement to reform school finance, because neither the legislators nor the governors had done anything about it, whereas Norma had "done more in this last year (even before taking over the job) than any of the other superintendents did in their full terms." Moreover, Norma had "never claimed to be a general."[14] In an editorial response in the *Register-Guard*, Norma said she felt she had to focus on signing up citizens willing to "go for the throat" when the legislature convened. "Thus the 'army' was born," she explained, adding, "I dislike the term, but at the time we were unable to come up with another one."[15]

The August 25 rally had already prompted the Corvallis school board to support Norma's proposal for a sales tax, she said. The legislature had tried many times to pass a sales tax, and she applauded them for that. "But we will never succeed unless the effort is initiated by the voters, not politicians or the education lobby."[16] In the depths of the 1982 recession, she added, school support totaled 33 percent of school operating costs, while in the last session, "when the state was awash in tax dollars," support had dropped to 29.8 percent. Only a sales tax would solve the problem. She said a sales-tax measure should be locked into the constitution, so that only a vote of the people could change it. She also reiterated that her proposal had an option for repeal after a three-year trial run.[17]

Norma won effortlessly and was scheduled to take the helm on January 1, 1991. Then the incumbent, John Erickson, announced that he intended to step down on October 1. Norma and most people expected Goldschmidt to appoint her immediately, which would put her in office three months early. But Goldschmidt didn't. In fact, he'd told her pointedly in August not to assume anything.[18] Even as late as September, he was still keeping mum on the subject, despite frequent queries by the media.

The *Statesman-Journal* attributed Goldschmidt's "slow" and "reluctant" handling of Erickson's absence to his preoccupation with a new state budget—although the writer alluded to unsavory "residue" left from the 1986 governor's race.[19] The writer also noted the obvious advantage to Norma's

Norma releasing Oregon's first statewide report card for schools, Pringle Hall, Salem, 1992. Timothy J. Gonzalez, courtesy of the *Statesman Journal*. Willamette Heritage Center, X2012.022.014.0206.

stepping in early: it would give her valuable time to prepare her education and financing proposals for the upcoming 1991 legislative session. She went ahead with plans to move into borrowed space in the Department of Education office on the Monday after Erickson's departure. Michael Holland, the department's director of community colleges, had agreed to let her set up shop in his conference room, two floors below the superintendent's office that she would eventually occupy.[20]

Goldschmidt waited until September 28, Erickson's last day in office, to appoint Norma as interim superintendent. He told reporters that it was "a subject he tried not to think about" because the job was not vacant until October 1.[21] She kept Greg McMurdo as deputy superintendent. McMurdo had been her closest aide since her first term as secretary of state, and she greatly valued his legislative knowledge and experience. Robert Burns, who had been Duncan's associate superintendent, stayed on as a deputy focusing on education reforms and, after 1995, on State Board of Education relations.

Norma decided she needed a third deputy to help her handle the biggest budget she had encountered in any of her jobs. "I needed somebody I could trust that would come in and handle all the financials for me, because more than any other I had been involved in, more money came through the

Department of Education—millions of federal and state dollars." She found her man in Rick Burke, a former fiscal officer for the legislature. "Not only did he know where every dollar and penny was, but every morning he'd walk around and keep track of what everyone who worked for us was doing."[22]

BOMBSHELL

Norma was eager to get to work. She reiterated her intent to "ask the next legislature to make education this state's number-one priority, and to come up with a predictable, fair method of paying for schools."[23] Then came a bombshell in the form of an initiative petition called Ballot Measure 5, a property-tax rollback law that radically changed Oregon's way of financing its schools. Measure 5 was approved in the November 1990 general election by about fifty-three thousand votes out of more than a million cast.

Inspired by the same tax-revolt sentiment that had produced California's Proposition 13 in 1978, Measure 5 was a constitutional amendment that capped property taxes dedicated to school funding at $15 per $1,000 of assessed property valuation per year, starting in 1991-1992, and lowered that amount to $5 per $1,000 by the end of the succeeding five years. The new law had the effect of forcing the state general fund to pick up the majority of school funding, shifting the burden from local property owners to statewide income-tax payers. Some Measure 5 proponents hoped that shifting funding responsibility to the state would equalize funding across school districts, in addition to lowering local property taxes. Some also hoped that it would help voters see the wisdom of a sales tax as a needed "third leg" of support for education. Opponents warned of massive cuts in support for education.[24]

A fraction of school funding was already coming out of the state general fund. Norma put it like this: "What the legislature did before Measure 5 passed was, they would fund everything else and then they'd turn the money bucket upside down, and whatever fell out went to schools."[25] Now, public schools would have to rely on the state for most of its funding—competing with hundreds of other priorities in the state budget. Norma assembled influential figures from her network of public servants and got them talking to each other. She enlisted John Danielson, lobbyist for the Oregon Education Association, and John Marshall, Ozzie Rose, and Chris Dudley, representing school boards and district administrators. She enlisted Jim Scherzinger, former legislative revenue officer. "We tacitly decided we'd overlook any past rifts in order to get the funding system put together," she said. "And we started plotting how we were going to get more money out of the legislature. Because suddenly we were putting these how-many-million school kids into the general fund, and that had never happened before."[26]

Norma credits her work with Scherzinger and Rose, director of the Confederation of Oregon School Administrators, for the successful development of a school funding formula that, in 1991, produced more money for Oregon schools than anyone expected.[27] Unfortunately, in the 1993 session, one of the most contentious and lengthy in state history, the preeminent issue of school funding became entangled with the ramifications of the third and fourth years of the five-year plan to phase in Measure 5. Led by House speaker Larry Campbell, both the House and Senate initially agreed on the need to cut $640 million from the schools budget for 1993 to 1995. While the House approved a one-year cut as part of the bill, the Senate rejected it. Campbell retaliated by splitting up the House–Senate budget committee, wiping out its nearly two months of work. Then he formed his own House budget committee and forced the Senate to do the same.[28] Senate president Bill Bradbury first sought a new school funding plan from the Senate Democrats. When after nearly a month they were unable to find agreement, Bradbury crossed party lines and accepted Senate Republicans' proposal to add up to $48 million to school budgets. Campbell agreed on the Senate's funding bill, which was more generous than the plan on which he forced his members to vote.[29]

In the end, total funding for schools was reduced by 5 percent for the years 1992–1993 to 1993–1994. For the first time in Oregon history, elementary and secondary schools operated with fewer actual dollars than in the previous school year. Chris Dudley, a member of Norma's staff and the executive president of the Oregon School Boards Association, noted that the session's resolution simply underscored, as Norma and many other pundits had said all along, "the need for lawmakers to consider a sales tax earmarked for schools."[30] By the time the 1993 legislature began, sales-tax measures had been rejected by voters on eight occasions.[31]

REFORMING EDUCATION

Norma also turned her attention to the education-reform plan being crafted by Vera Katz and Joyce Reinke. They were building on an approach to improving Oregon schools that began in the 1970s, when public education began changing from a system that emphasized the means and methods of instruction to one that emphasized educational outcomes. In 1984 the Oregon State Board of Education had adopted an Oregon Action Plan for Excellence, a call to arms for what came to be known as outcome-based education. Educators were expected to set goals defining what students should know and be able to do, the means by which student performance could be measured against those goals, and corrective actions that could be taken when necessary to help students achieve the goals.[32]

Reinke's and Katz's ideas drew on nationwide concerns about a general decline in public education,[33] especially in its function of preparing young people for productive work.[34] A 1990 report from the National Center of Education and the Economy titled "America's Choice: High Skills or Low Wages!" is worth quoting here at some length, because it provided a rationale and something of a model for reforms that Norma and her team eventually championed.

> Work force growth will slow dramatically in the 1990s. To ensure a more prosperous future, productivity and competitive position must be improved. New high performance forms of work organization operate very differently from the system of mass manufacturing. These work organizations require large investments in training. The approach to work and education must fundamentally change. Recommendations include the following: (1) a new educational performance standard should be set for all students, to be met by age 16, with the standard established nationally and benchmarked to the highest in the world; (2) states should take the responsibility for assuring that virtually all students achieve the Certificate of Initial Mastery (CIM), with new local Employment and Training Boards creating and funding alternative learning environments for those who cannot attain the CIM in regular schools; (3) a comprehensive system of Technical and Professional Certificates and associate's degrees should be created for the majority of students and adult workers who do not pursue a baccalaureate degree; (4) all employers should be given incentives and assistance to invest in the further education and training of their workers and to pursue high productivity forms of work organization; and (5) a system of Employment and Training Boards should be established by federal and state governments, together with local leadership, to organize and oversee the new school-to-work transition programs and training systems.[35]

Norma with Superintendents of Public Instruction from 1960–1998: (l–r) Verne Duncan, Leon Minear, Norma Paulus, Dale Parnell, Jesse Fasold, (John Erickson not present). Norma Paulus Papers, Willamette University Archives and Special Collections_NP052.

The Katz–Reinke reform plan was eventually shaped into a legislative bill, House Bill 3565, that was intended as a comprehensive rebuild of Oregon's framework for K–12 education. It spelled out high standards for performance at each grade level, and it contained an assessment system to determine whether the students' performance was meeting the standards. "What was happening—and it was unthinkable to my mind and I didn't even know it was happening—was a lot of these kids were never being tested," Norma said. "I felt Oregonians were entitled to know exactly how their schools were doing in reading and writing, math, and science, and there had never been a comprehensive way to produce this."[36]

The new law also established a statewide apprenticeship program for students who wanted to pursue job training instead of a college-preparatory program after tenth grade. A 1990 study by the US Bureau of Labor Statistics had projected a healthy growth rate in technical, professional, and health-industry jobs that did not necessarily require a college degree but required more skills than current high school graduates had. Oregon was lauded by the *New York Times* as the first state in the nation to address this problem by approving and establishing school-to-work apprenticeships. The law established the two milestones for educational achievement detailed in the America's Choice report: the Certificate of Initial Mastery (CIM), to be earned by tenth graders, and the Certificate of Advanced Mastery (CAM), to be earned by high school seniors in addition to their traditional diplomas. The CIM-CAM provision was perhaps the most controversial in the whole package. With Reinke's guidance and Katz's legislative clout, HB 3565, titled Oregon Educational Act for the Twenty-First Century, passed into law in June 1991. Norma was pleased, and a bit surprised, at the ease of the passage, "just like that, with only three negative votes in the House and Senate."

Norma rounded out her staff by hiring her supporter and friend Joyce Benjamin as associate superintendent for federal programs. Like Norma, Benjamin had gone to law school as an older student; she'd made a career change after nearly twenty years as a sheep rancher near Eugene. She had served on the Oregon State Board of Education and in the Academy for State and Local Government in Washington, DC. Benjamin supported Norma's run for superintendent, believing she would bring necessary tenacity to the office after a long stretch of superintendents who, while "very nice," had the "backbones of jellyfish." Benjamin believed Norma's gift as a leader was that "she didn't have to agree with the people she hired."[37]

Benjamin's expertise in handling federal education policy and relations with the State Board of Education, along with her network of influential people in Washington, helped to put Oregon's education reform on the national radar. "She knew everyone, and she was my liaison with the federal government," Norma said. "That worked out very well."[38] Among Benjamin's connections were Lamar Alexander and Richard Riley, who served as secretaries of education in George H. W. Bush's and Bill Clinton's cabinets, respectively; and Robert Reich, Clinton's secretary of labor.[39] Benjamin considered it her role to "stand in for Norma and make life better for her" in the federal government arena.[40] She recalled later that Senator Mark Hatfield had also proved a valuable connection in the federal government when Norma wanted more flexibility in spending federal dollars allotted to Oregon schools. "The federal money that we got, which was millions, always had these strings attached," Benjamin said. It was "a very regimented system and didn't allow any flexibility." It would be much better "if we could spend all the federal money we got in the way that we deem best for our students and our system."[41]

Norma approached Hatfield and explained her quest to achieve spending flexibility for Oregon's federal funds. Hatfield agreed to introduce a bill on her behalf. Although ultimately the bill was delayed until the next term, she recalled that it was passed overwhelmingly. "We became the first state in the nation to have flexibility with federal funds," Norma said.[42]

SPEED BUMPS

In February of 1991, soon after she took office, Norma had directed her staff to conduct a survey of students in grades three, five, eight, and eleven. It found that Oregon children were in danger of becoming "couch potatoes" unless the school system demanded more of them.[43] The survey revealed that, as the students progressed through school, they tended to lose interest in reading and mathematics. Several college-bound seniors said they had seen many of their peers lose interest in school because they felt it was irrelevant.[44]

Newspapers were watching the progress of the reform measures with interest. "The media was carrying stories about what we were doing and what was happening in the educational system almost weekly, sometimes two or three times a day," Norma said. "For instance, at one time our eighth-graders were judged the leaders in science; there was a big article about that." Meanwhile, results of the first statewide tests of students in grades three, five, eight, and eleven, conducted in the spring of 1990, were ready for release. Larry Austin, Norma's public information officer, recalls the "teachable moment" when she orchestrated the announcement. "Norma was big on public announcements," he says, "especially when it came to testing. Board members and administrators were nervous and wanted the information before it was released. We released it to them a bit early and then held a major press conference."[45]

The school administrators "just went berserk," Norma recalled. "I said I'd already told the *Oregonian* that we're going to do this, but what I will do is have the assessments delivered to each superintendent the day before they were released to the press, so they would have time to look at them. Well, that wasn't very mollifying either. The fact that this was going to be public and you could look at every school and find out what they're doing—it was just unheard of."[46]

The education reforms had begun to hit speed bumps as the first statewide assessment was being conducted. Business leaders hailed Katz's school-to-work option as a big step toward preparing a new workforce for the coming technology revolution. But the whole education-reform package continued to draw fire from educators and other critics. Many educators were concerned that the apprenticeship program would stigmatize students in the job-training track, and would discourage young people from pushing themselves to try the college path.[47] Some alleged that the reform marked a return to "the tracking system of the past," although others said tracking was a current problem that reform would fix. Black United Front leader Ron Herndon, for instance, dismissed claims of tracking by noting, "Teachers are the only ones raising that issue out of their own selfish interests. They are worried about losing jobs if teachers have to learn new skills."[48]

Some educators and school officials said the business and professional component of the curriculum placed unrealistic expectations on public schools. Teachers and others also worried that funding could be withheld by future legislatures, allowing school officials to abandon parts of the plan, such as early-childhood programs, that had proved unpopular among voters because they were expensive.[49] Many parents couldn't see the necessity for or relevance of the Certificates of Initial Mastery and Advanced Mastery.[50] More-vigorous objections came from religious conservatives, including a group led by Ron Sunseri, a former state representative and one of the few legislators who had voted against HB 3565 in 1991. Sunseri had published a book through a Christian publishing house that excoriated the plan's so-called outcome-based education. It was, he wrote, a sham that deemphasized academics, reduced parental involvement, increased control by government and education bureaucrats, and forced students to learn specific attitudes and beliefs.[51] Among the book's claims was that students would be indoctrinated by computers on specific values—the computer would "go to work to change your children's convictions and values to make them conform to a pre-determined standard." Sunseri further alleged that school officials would have the right to go into a student's home for an evaluation if the student wasn't performing adequately.

This was utter nonsense, Norma replied. "There's no way the school district has the authority or wants the authority to do such an outrageous thing."[52] She had not read Sunseri's book, she said, but she was familiar with his arguments, and she rejected them.[53] Some of the allegations were not only false but had nothing to do with the reform act—such as his allegation that it precluded the teaching of phonics, or sounding out words, in learning to read. This just wasn't true, Norma said: "There were some kids who learn that way and some who don't. We give schools flexibility."[54] To Sunseri's condemnation of "outcome-based education," Norma countered that the term meant simply what it said: expecting better outcomes from schools. "We want to expect higher standards in all the academic studies, particularly in math and science. . . . Students should be evaluated on what they can do with what they learn, rather than on how well they memorize facts and figures."[55]

As the criticism gathered momentum, Norma found herself once more leading a campaign. She traveled around the state promoting the reforms to students and parent-teacher organizations. She joked that she'd changed clothes in every gas station in Oregon. By early 1994, in the midst of campaigning for her second term, Norma was still talking about the movement. Before her tenure, the superintendent's doings had seldom been controversial. But now, the Associated Press reported, Norma "doesn't mind if her re-election campaign becomes a referendum on the education reform law." That seemed to be the intent of her opponents, she told the *Seattle Times*: "Their platform is to tear apart the school-reform effort and my platform is to implement it."[56]

Notwithstanding the controversy at home, Norma's stock was rising across the nation. Soon after HB 3565 passed, US Secretary of Education Lamar Alexander visited Oregon to check out what he hoped might be an educational model for other states. "Oregon, more than almost any other state I've heard about—maybe more than any—has been willing to think boldly, to take a pioneering step," he said, "and America will be watching and learning."[57] Soon after her reelection in 1994, the *New York Times* praised Norma's tenacity in putting education reform into action and her success in forging ties between the teachers' union and the business community for "the first time in anyone's memory."[58] The writer credited Norma's two decades of public service for giving her "access to officials that previous school chiefs did not enjoy."[59] With the school-to-work program, Norma was "leading one of the most cutting-edge reforms of any state," according Alex Medler, an analyst with the Denver research group Education Commission of the States.

When Bill Clinton was elected president in 1992, his labor secretary, Robert Reich, and education secretary, Richard Riley, also kept Norma and Oregon on their radar. They enlisted her help to spread the word about the reform to groups of educators all over the country and around the world. She accompanied Riley to an Asian-Pacific conference on education, and she traveled to London to represent the American school system at meetings in Harrogate in Yorkshire and at Oxford University.[60]

A SIDEWAYS TURN

Norma's political path took a sideways turn in the fall of 1995, when Oregon's junior US senator, Bob Packwood, resigned in disgrace after being publicly accused of sexual harassment by former staffers. Three days later, Norma announced that she was a candidate for the open seat. She had never concealed her ambition to run, someday, for nationwide office. She'd expressed an interest in serving in the Senate as early as 1984, and while the long plane rides and weeks away from home didn't appeal to her, she felt confident of her qualifications. The intervening decade, however, had presented no real opportunity.

The US Senate was effectively sewn up, with Oregon's two seats filled by long-serving Republicans of Norma's progressive bent, men who had mentored her throughout her career. Any challenge to them from her would have looked egotistical and, worse, naïve.

Now Packwood's seat had suddenly become available, and she felt her time had come. At sixty-two, with twenty-five years of public service on her record, she was a household name in Oregon, and her accomplishments as secretary of state and superintendent of public instruction had given her a national reputation. Four other candidates declared for the open seat: US representatives Peter DeFazio and Ron Wyden, both Democrats, and Oregon Senate president Gordon Smith and state labor commissioner Jack Roberts, both Republicans. Norma was confident that she was the right one for the job. "I know more about Oregon and all its attributes than any of the other candidates," she declared.[61] When critics cited her reputation for a quick temper and a rock-hard will fueled by largely unbridled impatience, Norma conceded she was "outspoken, bold, even brazen," but "certainly not hot-tempered."[62] And those other qualities were assets, she argued, particularly when combined with her experience. "Oregon's reputation has been sullied by the Packwood debacle," Norma said. "This state will want to make certain it sends someone back there who can represent all Oregonians."[63]

Norma had spent four years in the superintendent's role, which was effectively nonpartisan in outlook and focused mainly on statewide concerns. The practical politics that had served Norma so well at the beginning of her career had been eclipsed by a trend toward ideological conservatism nationwide and at home. In 1994, editorialized the *Seattle Times*, the moderate Republican stance on protecting the environment, spending public dollars responsibly, and addressing conflicts pragmatically was "in decline—or at least on the defensive."[64] Norma had been undone in the governor's race partly because she hadn't reckoned with the rightward current of her party. Over the intervening decade that current had become a torrent, leaving moderate, pragmatic Republicans like her marooned on her party's left bank. In the Republican primary for Packwood's Senate seat, held December 5, 1995, she lost to the more-conservative Gordon Smith. Ron Wyden won the Democratic primary and went on to win the general election.

There is a certain irony in the fact that the special-election primary represented the nation's first vote-by-mail election for a congressional seat, and it saved the State of Oregon about half a million dollars.[65] The election served as a good model of Norma's brand of practical conservatism, something the

Republican Party seemed to be leaving behind. Her promised "one and only bid" for the US Senate lost, Norma returned to work as superintendent with no thought of ever trying again. "This is it," she said.[66]

EMBRACING TECHNOLOGY

In 1997, Norma told the *Portland Business Journal* that most Oregon high school students did not possess the basic math skills to get jobs in the high-tech industry then burgeoning in Portland. Her department had developed new math standards with the aim of mastery by 75 percent of high school graduates within five years. "High-tech produces skilled jobs and high wages," Norma said, "and the education system is not producing people to fill these slots."[67]

When Vice President Al Gore gave the Oregon Department of Education a $1 million grant to invest in Internet connectivity in the schools, high-tech companies like Intel, Mentor Graphics, and Tektronix also pledged support to the cause. Norma and three other superintendents from around the country were invited to join Gore in radio interviews, discussing the importance of getting kids connected to computers and the Internet. "This whole business was something that the school system had never been involved with until the Clinton administration and Vice President Gore really started pushing it," she said. "It seemed like overnight we were making great strides. We got lots of grants with the help of the high-tech firms, because they saw the wisdom in it and the need for it. So they got behind us one hundred percent."[68]

The fast-moving technology kept Norma on her toes. When Intel donated one of the newest and biggest computers available, Norma didn't know what to do with it. "I didn't have anybody in the K–12 system that could even interact with it." She made a deal with the president of Reed College to house the computer there, giving Reed students free access to it and bringing in public school personnel to learn from the Reed students. "There were so many examples of that kind of partnership effort," Norma said. "They saw Oregon as the leader in all this."[69]

In 1996 Education Secretary Richard Riley named Norma to the National Assessment Governing Board. During her final year in office, on February 17, 1998, when Riley delivered his fifth State of American Education address from Seattle (carried live by webcast on the Internet—a sign of the times), Norma was there with him. He introduced her by name and called her "Oregon's chief educator."[70]

Norma in the Oval Office discussing education policy with President Bill Clinton, November 21, 1997. Official photograph, the White House, Washington 21NOV97 BK P058460-016.

REACHING OUT TO TEACHERS

Any reform scheme is by definition a critique of the status quo. The old education system was a necessary casualty of the reform bill, but Norma's criticism of it had won her few fans in the educational establishment. Sometimes the hostility verged on the personal. North Clackamas teacher Trish Johnson alleged that Norma cared only about her political future while endeavoring to cut teacher retirement benefits. "At the very least, I think we should all take a ruler and slap her," Johnson said.[71] The Oregon Education Association, which had endorsed Norma on her first campaign, refused to back her for a second term. OEA's president, Bruce Adams, said, "We feel that we're the ones in the classroom and that we should be listened to when we say this doesn't work."

The union had gone public with its qualms about the reform almost as soon as it was signed into law—urging legislators in 1993 to repeal the act. "The reformers have decided that we need to turn things upside down, without any data to support that change, and we think that's ridiculous," said Karen Famous, then OEA president. Norma riposted with, "I don't think the legislature will repeal a reform act that's being used as a model across the nation just because the teachers' union got its nose out of joint."[72] This was the kind of flip response Norma was known for, and it embodied much of the problem teachers had with her. They grumbled that she'd stepped in to take over for educators when she was not an educator herself. They felt she was too quick to fix a system that wasn't broken, and complained that the reforms were costing them hours away from the classroom for professional development and re-training, and more hours spent in the classroom preparing students to take the assessment tests.[73] It galled them that she could dismiss their broad-ranging concerns in a single folksy quip.

While she felt sure of her own path, Norma was aware of the education establishment's lack of regard for her personally. She knew teachers felt left out of the decision-making process, and that she needed "to be more supportive of teachers" in general.[74] She acknowledged this sentiment. "I get more frustrated than angry," she told the *New York Times*. "I'm proud to say that I've never held a grudge, but I yell a lot," which, she admitted, was "unseemly in education circles." Described "by friends and foes alike as sometimes impatient and brusque," she defended herself against her critics in classic Norma Paulus fashion. "I'm impatient with people who can't see the big picture, who can't grasp onto a vision, and who don't have the discipline to stay with it."[75]

She tried to mend fences. Her predecessor, Verne Duncan, had initiated the state's participation in the annual Milken Educator Awards in 1988, and Norma carried the tradition forward. Each year she was in office, four to six educators were selected by their peers to receive the award, which came with an unrestricted $25,000 cash prize. The teachers and their families were flown to Los Angeles and feted with all-expenses-paid accommodations and entertainment. One year the pop singer Michael Jackson spent a day at the festivities, rehearsing with high school students on a musical number that was performed for a banquet that night. That event "took teachers out of all the humdrum of their lives," Norma said, "and they were really treated like princesses and princes. I thought it was a really extraordinary thing for teachers. They came back just really pumped, and they learned a lot."

In the interest of lighting an inspirational fire in the field of mathematics, Norma facilitated a special event for K–12 math teachers. For years she had been going to annual lectures organized by the Institute for Science, Engineering and Public Policy in Portland. She noted that the series' 1997–1998 program would feature the Oxford physicist and mathematician Sir Roger Penrose. Penrose's diverse resume included a 1965 proof that singularities (such as black holes) could be formed from the gravitational collapse of immense, dying stars. Norma thought Penrose would be the ideal main attraction at her Math Summit. She got hold of Paul Risser, president of Oregon State University, and made her pitch. Could she hold a Math Summit for teachers on the OSU campus? And could OSU's math professors help her put it on? And by the way, since OSU was now sponsoring the lecture, could Risser invite Penrose to speak?

Risser loved the idea. His answer: Yes, yes, and yes. Now all she had to do was pay for it. She approached George Passadore, Oregon chairman of Wells Fargo bank, and came away with a pledge of $300,000 with no strings attached. Much later, Passadore said that was the first and last time his company allotted its entire yearly philanthropic contribution to one effort. He had been convinced by Norma's political reputation, her personal credibility, and her "good, solid Oregon roots." Frankly, he added, "it wouldn't have mattered what she intended to do with the money."[76]

The Math Summit was held on October 2, 1997. "When the math department at Oregon State heard Sir Roger was coming to speak," Norma said, "they sent emails all over the country, and pretty soon other leading mathematicians wanted to come out too." Nearly four hundred teachers came to hear Penrose, along with Ivars Peterson, a Canadian science writer; Ralph Abraham, a mathematician; and Keith Devlin, a British mathematician and writer from Stanford University. The all-day event included discussion groups and an evening banquet. "It worked out to be an extraordinary gathering and a really stimulating time," Norma said.[77]

LEAVING THE FRAY

Norma retired in January of 1999 after two terms as superintendent of public instruction. She was charmed when Education Secretary Richard Riley wrote her a thank-you note. "One of my proudest moments as Secretary of Education," he told her, "was announcing to your state legislature that, through your efforts, Oregon had led the way in obtaining greater flexibility for the use of federal education funds. . . . By improving education in Oregon, you have made your state a model for other states and contributed greatly to progress in education all across the country."[78]

Norma knew she was ready to retire. She'd fought the good fight for Oregon's kids. The education-reform effort was fully launched, although it continued to be controversial.[79] As for stabilizing the financing of education, Oregonians seemed to have as much distaste for a sales tax as ever. "We're still struggling to finance education," Norma observed ruefully in 2010. And many of us—Republicans and Democrats—still talk about a sales tax. It still makes sense to have that third leg on the stool, but it's still a hard sell with the voters."[80]

Norma in front of Oregon State Capitol. Norma Paulus Papers, Willamette University Archives and Special Collections_NP 004.

Chapter 12
A Legacy of Service

A call to our Grand Old Party: come back to the mainstream.

As Republican former Governors, Senators and public officials, we urge our party to renew its allegiance to the proven, common sense values which unite America.

Instead of partisan ideology—which increasingly has led moderates to leave the party—what's needed is a speedy return to the pragmatic, problem-solving mainstream. Here's how the President and Republican-majority Congress can send that clear signal to the nation:

Stop weakening environmental law—and once again protect our air, water and public lands as Teddy Roosevelt and other great Republican leaders intended;

Restore fiscal responsibility—with "pay-as-you-go" budget discipline to end record deficits that jeopardize economic growth;

Put the health of millions first—and clear the way for embryonic stem cell research;

Appoint mainstream federal judges—and respect the Constitution;

Make America safer—and protect cities and towns, still vulnerable three years after 9/11, by securing chemical and nuclear plants and shipping containers;

Rebuild our alliances—with real partnerships and restore America's standing in the world.

By returning to the mainstream in these ways, our party can regain the trust of a divided nation and earn a vote of confidence in November.

—*New York Times*, August 30, 2004

When Norma Paulus stepped down from her post as superintendent of public instruction in January 1999, she and the rest of Oregon may have thought her public service was at an end. As it turns out, that conclusion was premature.

After thirty years of being in the public eye—and the past eight of them in a hot-seat position where the issues and constituents seemed to be getting more polarized every day—Norma was ready for a breather. "I'm going to try something I've never been," she told the *Statesman-Journal*'s Steve Law on the eve of her retirement, "and that's a private person."[1]

By most accounts she ended her second term as the head of Oregon's public schools with high marks. She'd been "a forceful advocate for improving student performance, teacher training, and school accountability," said the *Statesman-Journal*, although "her candid remarks didn't always win her friends."[2] She was sixty-five, an age at which most people are ready to retire. But Norma had a more compelling need: to gather her strength to care for a sick husband. Bill Paulus had been diagnosed with a brain tumor six months earlier, in July of 1998.[3] Surgery revealed it to be a diffuse, fast-growing cancer called a glioblastoma multiforme, whose tentacles were invading the tissues of his speech center and causing him to grope for words.[4] Doctors gave him two years at the most.

The diagnosis was a shock. Bill had seemed robustly healthy. The symptoms had cropped up suddenly, at an education-foundation conference in Los Angeles.[5] While Norma was at her meetings, Bill liked to play golf at the resort's course. On a particular evening, Norma came back to the hotel room and found Bill back from golfing, relaxing in a chair. He gave her a big smile, which she returned with a kiss. She said, "I'm a little late and the cocktail hour and the program starts soon. So what I'll do is I'll get in the shower first, because I've got to wash my hair, and I'll get dressed, so then you can get in and get a shower, and by that time I'll have myself together."

Bill sat quietly for a moment, and then he replied, "Why don't you take a shower and wash your hair? And I will sit here and then I will take a shower?" And he gave her another beatific smile. Norma gazed at him quizzically. "Bill, that's what I just said."

They went down to cocktails, joining the gathered crowd. It was a beautiful night. Bill fetched two glasses of red wine and handed one to Norma, then turned away to chat with someone. She heard a commotion, and, turning, saw a woman standing near Bill with a wet purple splotch down the front of her dress. Norma looked at the woman, who seemed distressed, and then at Bill. He was chatting with someone else nearby, holding his empty wineglass.

They sat down to dinner. Their table companion was Susan Castillo, a member of the Oregon House of Representatives and Norma's guest at the conference.[6] During the dinner she said to Bill, "My husband is having a very

Bill Paulus was Norma's greatest supporter. His sudden illness and death in March 1999 coincided with her contemplation of retirement from public office. Family archives.

difficult time with my notoriety now that I have been elected to the legislature, and I've always marveled at how you handled your wife's success. Do you have any hints for me?" Bill said nothing, just continued to eat his dinner. Norma was deeply embarrassed, and when they got back to the room she let him know it. "That was very rude of you, you know." "What? What was rude?" Norma repeated Castillo's question. Bill scratched his head. "I didn't hear her say that," he said. "There's no way you didn't hear her," Norma said, but now she was scared.

After they got home Bill continued to miss cues and say things that didn't make sense; for example, "I'm going to go out and mow the driveway." She told him, "Bill, this is getting worse. We need to find out what's wrong with you."[7]

NO QUITTING

When the bad news came, Norma's first thought was to leave her superintendent's post early to care for Bill, but he would not hear of it. In the words of longtime friend Janet Boise, "Bill said, 'Absolutely no, nobody in this family ever quits.'"[8] It was typical of the unflagging support Bill had given his wife over their forty years of marriage. His embrace of her public life was solid and complete and without reservation, rooted in a private cherishing of her, a sustained delight in the very being of Norma Jean Petersen Paulus.

Bill's love for his wife went beyond pride in her accomplishments. His equable temperament anchored Norma's restless one, and his courtliness—stemming perhaps from being the scion of a prominent and respected family and a man with nothing to prove—balanced some of her parvenu striving. At those moments when she was inclined to take herself a bit too seriously, Bill's wry humor helped Norma laugh at herself. "My husband told me throughout my political career that he'd never apologize for what I said," she told the *Portland Business Journal* in 2001, "but frequently he felt compelled to apologize for the way in which I said things. I've yet to learn patience."[9]

"My mom was the dominant voice in the family," said their son Fritz. "That's not to say my dad was weak, but he was just a little more refined, a little more diplomatic." Fritz's wife, Jennifer Viviano, added, "He was gentler, had softer edges."[10] Bill supported his wife, but he did not take a backseat to her. He was a leading citizen in his own right, a distinguished lawyer and partner in a well-established Salem firm. His work as counsel for the Salem-Keizer School District 24-J often put him, too, in the public eye.[11] He had a full life, a successful career, a happy family, and enough friends to fill a stadium.[12] He could afford to get out of the way and let his wife be the force of nature that she is.

Norma was a match for him in every way—not only his intellectual equal, but equally driven, passionate, outgoing, and high-spirited. While neither of them was sentimental or demonstrative—"they weren't huggy-kissy," said Fritz—it was plain to their children that they remained deeply in love throughout their married life. Fritz describes the relationship as "graceful." Jennifer agreed: "It was graceful, but it was also funny. There was a bit of Hepburn and Tracy in their relationship." Bill loved ribald greeting cards and invented occasions to send them to his wife. "Dad was famous for these cards he'd give her," said Fritz. "They'd crack her up. She's kept a whole box of them." When Norma, golfing at the Neskowin course, got a hole in one, Bill went looking for a trophy for her, but found only male statuettes. So he bought a six-inch-high wooden man, dressed it in a skirt and wig, and presented it to Norma. The inscription reads, "Norma Paulus, July 5, hole in one."

The Pauluses were prominent in Salem society. They were an attractive and intensely social couple, moving easily through overlapping circles: political and legal colleagues, business and volunteer acquaintances, neighbors, old friends from younger days. They liked to throw parties. They liked to go skiing or to the beach with friends who had kids the ages of their own. Fritz remembers multifamily weekend getaways to Neskowin, with the kids tearing around on the beach and the adults drinking cocktails on the deck as the sun went down. Norma and Bill belonged to a domino club and two dance clubs, one called the Subscription Club and one called the Terrace Club. "They called it the Tear-Ass club," said Fritz, "because it was more of a party crowd. And they had fun. They really had fun."

Bill liked to whisk his wife away on romantic getaways. After her first election as secretary of state in 1976, he surprised her with a trip to the Soviet Union. Back then, ordinary American tourists were not welcome, but Bill had arranged for the two of them to be part of a special tour sponsored by Willamette University. "They had a wild time," Fritz said. "Mom tells of walking out on a snowy evening, zero degrees, Red Square, no one out there, marveling at St. Basil's Cathedral, dancing with sailors, drinking in Leningrad. It was magical for her, and for him." A decade later, as Norma flew home from the Philippines after observing the Marcos-Aquino elections, she touched down for a routine layover in Honolulu and was surprised to find Bill and close friends waiting for her. They spent a week relaxing in Hawai'i, letting Norma recover from the Philippines sojourn.[13]

Sometimes Norma surprised Bill with her own quirky plans. There was the time when she entered him in the International Whistle-Off Competition in Carson City, Nevada. "Dad was a great whistler," said Fritz. "She called all their friends and got them on a bus. I remember it pulling up at the end of our driveway." The crew, which included Bill's stepmother Lou McCormick Paulus, dubbed themselves the Whistle Punks and headed to Nevada, where the group led by Bill won an award for "novelty accompaniment." Lou wore a T-shirt that read, "Whistler's Mother."

Then there was the time that Norma bought a caboose. It happened on a family vacation trip back to her hometown of Burns. Her brother-in-law Chuck Clark was the brakeman for the railroad that ran from Seneca, in the Ochoco Mountains, to the Hines Lumber Mill. "We took a ride on that train when we went back in 1970, or whenever it was," said Fritz, "and there was this caboose for sale, and Mom said, 'I'm going to buy it.' She wanted to convert it into a beach house at Neskowin." She bought the caboose for $500 and made arrangements to have it shipped to Salem and thence to the coast. Things started to go haywire around Sisters, when the route took the caboose under a low trestle. "So it couldn't go under this bridge over by Black Butte," said Fritz. "And there was something about the snow, and it got off the road." Before the caboose got anywhere near Salem, Norma learned that there was no way the authorities at Neskowin would allow her to turn a caboose into a beach house. Regretfully, she abandoned the project.

"They had this sweetness about them," said Fritz.

Bill's tumor was diagnosed in July of 1998. He died in March of 1999.[14] "We were lucky to have him for nine months," says Jennifer. There were small mercies: Bill was not in pain, and his zest for life seemed hardly diminished. He loved getting together with friends—they'd take turns coming over and taking walks with him, although the walks had to stop after Bill fell a couple of times. Friends urged them to come to Hawaiʻi, and because Bill wanted to go, they went. Then he was invited to come to California by another group of friends. Norma said, "If you want to go, I'll take you." They went. He had a grand mal seizure and was hospitalized in Palm Springs. A friend flew Bill, Norma, and Fritz back to Salem in his personal airplane. When they got home, Norma checked Bill into the Salem Hospital. He died a few days later. She said, "For a long time I kicked myself because I didn't pick up on the symptoms sooner. They tell me it wouldn't have done any good anyway."[15]

A few weeks before he died, Bill Paulus received the Wallace P. Carson Award for service to the community from the Marion County Bar Association. John Hemann, a senior partner in Paulus's firm, described him as one of the luminaries in the Salem legal community. He and others praised Bill's service on numerous civic organizations including the Salem Hospital Fund and Friends of Pioneer Cemetery. They also mentioned Bill's mentoring of many local lawyers.[16] In the last months of his life, Bill received letters from hundreds of grateful clients and associates, thanking him for all manner of services and kindnesses—many of which were a surprise to Norma, said her daughter-in-law Jennifer. "He was—they both were, and she remains—incredibly down-to-earth, committed public servants, committed to egalitarianism and fairness in the world."

The depth of their relationship was revealed more fully after Bill died, when Norma suddenly had more time to spend with her children. "Not that we didn't spend time with them before," said Jennifer. "We had many planned and spontaneous times together. But after he died we really could see how knitted together they had been, and how much they'd enjoyed each other."

AN AMBASSADOR

Norma finished her second term as superintendent of public instruction in January 1999.[17] The next two months were devoted to caring for Bill. Moving through her grief in the weeks after he died, she came to realize that within the space of three months she had lost the two roles that had most fully and enduringly defined her: public servant, and wife of Bill Paulus.

Norma, director of the Oregon Historical Society 2001–2003, dedicating the institution's new pavilion. Evan Schneider. Oregon Historical Society, OrHi104699-12A.

So when Chet Orloff called and asked if she would consider being the head of the Oregon Historical Society, she quickly said yes. Orloff, who had directed the society for the previous ten years, was planning to step down. He'd told the board that they ought to hire Norma to succeed him.[18] "I'd known her for a long time, probably 20 years," Orloff said. "I was just a young staff member when I first met her. I felt that here was someone who should be the first woman governor of the state. I had a high regard for her because of her work as secretary of state and superintendent of public instruction. I knew she was interested in the Historical Society. Plus obviously she had great administrative skills." And because of her own and Bill's deep family roots, "she personally had a strong interest in Oregon history," Orloff said. "She seemed a logical person to take over the job."

Norma realized that directing the Oregon Historical Society—which is not a public agency even though it is partly supported by public funds— would be quite different from being either a state legislator or a top state-agency administrator. She saw it as an opportunity to be an ambassador for a cause she deeply believed in. Although Norma had not given history much thought growing up, she came to appreciate it as a young adult. Throughout her public life she encountered many Oregonians who still didn't appreci-ate their state's history, because, she said, Oregon was still so young. "I can remember growing up and going to the city park in Burns for Pioneer's Day, and I would see the people who actually came over the Oregon Trail, and then their sons and daughters, and they were viewed as real pioneers. So if you are living it, it's not history."

She'd come a long way since that day in 1961[19] when she unwittingly sold a Paulus family heirloom, a camp stool brought across on the Oregon Trail, at a garage sale. As a legislator she had helped pass the law that provides tax breaks for restoring historic buildings.[20] As secretary of state she'd created the Historical Properties Commission, and had unearthed governors' portraits and other historical artifacts from archives and restored them to prominence. In this effort she'd become acquainted with Tom Vaughan, longtime director of the Oregon Historical Society and the man who had transformed the society into a respected scholarly institution during his thirty-five-year tenure.[21] It was Vaughan who had identified the face of Governor Oswald West in the dusty portrait Norma had unearthed from the catacombs of the Oregon State Hospital. Norma came to admire the man and the organization both. The society had marked its centennial year in 1998. Oregon had been fortunate, she thought, that, when barely out of the pioneer stage, it had produced citizens with the education, means, and vision to preserve precious history before it was forgotten.[22]

Orloff told Norma he was stepping down in part because he and some board members didn't see eye-to-eye and because there were conflicts within the board. He told Norma that he was confident her strong, positive personality would be a unifying force. Norma picked up two of Orloff's key initiatives and brought them to completion. One was a major permanent exhibit, the award-winning "Oregon, My Oregon."[23] The second, which required her to raise significant money, was the remodeling of the main entrance of the society's Portland headquarters. She agreed with Orloff that the society needed a dramatic entryway to welcome visitors and boost public confidence in its mission. "She was able to raise the funds and create the new admissions area on Park Avenue," he said. "That was gratifying to me, that she was able to carry forward with those two projects." Before her departure Norma also created a K–12 educational history project that won a national award from the American Library Association, and she worked toward developing similar programs for the Oregon Coast Aquarium in Newport and the High Desert Museum in Bend.

After leaving the Oregon Historical Society in 2003, Norma Paulus remained active as a private citizen. Throughout the 2000s she served on numerous boards, including those of the Oregon State Capitol Foundation, the High Desert Museum, the Oregon Coast Aquarium, The Oregon Garden (to which she helped move the Gordon House, the only building by Frank Lloyd Wright in Oregon), the Portland City Club, Providence St. Vincent's Foundation Council of Trustees, and the World Affairs Council of Oregon.

She was a trustee of the Oregon Graduate Institute of Science and Technology and an overseer at Whitman College, the alma mater of both her children. She is a lifetime trustee of Willamette University. She has been awarded honorary doctorates from Willamette and from Whitman, Lewis and Clark, and Linfield Colleges.[24] In 2003 she received the Governor's Gold Award, celebrating greatness in Oregonians. In 2004 she received a Distinguished Service Award from the University of Oregon. In 2005 she and former Governor Barbara Roberts were named Statesmen of the Year by the Oregon Business Association.[25]

In 2008 Norma led a fund-raising campaign to commission a statue of Tom McCall to honor his environmental and political legacy. She remembered that he'd told her, toward the end of his life, that if anyone ever wanted to make a statue of him, he wanted the sculptor to model it after a cherished photograph of himself in flyfishing gear, wading out of the North Umpqua River with a trout clutched in his fist. That photo, which adorned the cover of McCall's autobiography, *Tom McCall: Maverick*, was taken by his fishing buddy Dan Callaghan, Bill Paulus's law partner and a good friend of the Pauluses. The thousand-pound, ten-foot-tall statue was sculpted and cast in bronze by Troutdale sculptor Rip Caswell. Caswell researched his subject for a more than a year. He asked Norma to introduce him to people McCall had known, and even had her track down McCall's fly rod and waders so he could get the details right. The statue, dedicated in 2008, stands on the bank of the Willamette River at Salem's Riverfront Park.[26]

In 2012 the Oregon Historical Society gave Norma the History Maker's Medal, given to "people who have shaped state history and culture in a positive way."[27]

SHIFTING WINDS

Norma still made headlines after she retired from public life. In 2014 she came out for Democratic senator Jeff Merkley in his reelection bid against his challenger, Portland physician and first-time political hopeful Monica Wehby. Norma was one of five co-leaders of the group Women for Merkley; the other four are prominent women in politics—Democrats all—including former Governor Barbara Roberts and former Superintendent of Public Instruction Susan Castillo.[28]

Norma and sculptor Rip Caswell at the dedication of the Tom McCall statue in Salem Waterfront Park,
September 26, 2008. Photographer unknown. Family archives.

That Norma Paulus would endorse a male Democratic incumbent over
a female Republican challenger says a lot about how politics has shifted in the
last forty years. Norma was a progressive Republican at a time when such a
stance had broad appeal across the Oregon electorate. She was a member of
a well-regarded political tribe that included leaders like Tom McCall, Mark

Hatfield, Bob Packwood, and Dave Frohnmayer. "Those were days," Frohn-mayer said, "when you didn't have to worry about crossing a party line for a good idea. Most of us who served then remember that with great fondness."[29] McCall was the acknowledged chief of that tribe, and Norma has been com-pared to McCall.[30] Like him, she had intelligence, wit, good looks, political chops, and a larger-than-life personality (although in that category McCall probably had her beat). Both of them were well equipped to shine during this particular moment in the state's history.

That Norma was a woman gave her an opportunity to expand the Re-publican Party's embrace and soften its more masculine edges. For example, her tireless advocacy of public schools gave her common ground (at least early on) with teachers and their union, the Oregon Education Association. It also made a persuasive case for public support of education to more con-servative citizens who may not have approved of teachers' unions. "She made a lot of things respectable" in the Republican Party, said Frohnmayer, who worked with her on the Rajneeshee affair when he was attorney general and she was secretary of state, and briefly opposed her in 1986 for the Republican governor's nomination. "Or maybe a better way to say it is, she made a lot of things permissible, in public and private dialogue, that weren't before. She was one of the people who continued to carry the torch for environmental concerns, for open government, for decent treatment of union people." These were issues that had not particularly rallied Republicans before Norma ar-rived on the scene.[31]

Similarly, she was able to embody feminism's potentially divisive agenda from a centrist, nonideological stance. "She led the way in terms of women running for statewide office," said Frohnmayer. As a Republican, "she didn't fit the stereotype of a feminist, but she was very much a supporter of women's rights. She made [feminism] not only acceptable but mainstream, in a way that it couldn't have been if it had just been a liberal, Democratic, urban phenom-enon. . . . Norma made it acceptable for a lot of Republican women to be more assertive." Gretchen Kafoury, the Democratic activist and lobbyist who worked with Norma and other women in the legislature to pass historic women's rights legislation, said, "She epitomized femininity, and also toughness."[32]

Throughout her career, Norma's progressive ideas were very much of a piece with her conservative instincts. Her conservatism shows in her deep-seated sense of the democratic ideal, her faith that ordinary people can be trusted to decide what's best for themselves and their community. She believed in keeping power local and vesting it in the hands of elected representatives instead of state administrators or federal agencies. She often warned of the dangers inherent in an impotent legislature, and said that strengthening the state legislature was the best way to "keep the federal government out of Oregon's hair."[33] Her reflexive distrust of bureaucrats showed when she castigated highway administrators for spending taxpayer money on tourism ads, and when she uncovered the forestry department's cozy timber-sale practices.

Yet she is no small-government libertarian. She strongly believes in the bond of community, and in people's responsibility to care about their neighbors. If private virtue is not getting the job done, she has no qualms about using state power to secure the welfare of society's less powerful citizens. That shows clearly in her tireless work for equal opportunities for Oregon's women and people of color, educational excellence for Oregon's children, and protection for Oregon's environment.

She tells a story on herself that—maybe more than she knows—illustrates her special take on the proper balance of public regulation with private responsibility. Having worked hard as a legislator to make public facilities accessible to disabled people, she drove into a store's parking lot one day and noticed a car pulling into a spot reserved for disabled drivers. A disabled-parking permit hung from its rearview mirror. She watched as two able-bodied young men got out and loped into the store. Norma parked her car, marched in after them, and patrolled the aisles until she caught up with them. Then she gave them a furious dressing-down. The young men, abashed, went out and moved their car.[34]

In sum, Norma's character, personality, and skills were perfectly adapted to a particular historical moment in Oregon, a time, she said, when "you could hardly walk through the Capitol because there were so many citizens there," people who had traveled from all corners of Oregon to get directly involved in the governing of their state.[35] Coming into her own at this moment, Norma's convictions and political savvy made her extraordinarily effective. Even though a member of the minority party for most of her legislative career, she was instrumental in passing groundbreaking laws that protected women, consumers, and the environment. As secretary of state, she had, among many other accomplishments, held state agencies fiscally accountable and warded off voter fraud without compromising the right of every citizen to vote his or her conscience.

As Norma entered the mature middle of her career, there were signs that the progressive half of her conservatism was becoming a liability. The

Norma at the March 30, 2015, signing by Oregon Governor Kate Brown of SB333, designating each March 22 as Tom McCall Day. To the left of Governor Brown (center) is Senator Betsy Johnson (D-Scappoose), whose father, Sam Johnson, served with Norma in the Oregon House of Representatives. Ron Cooper.

Republican Party of her youth had been "exciting," full of people who were "the good thinkers, the moderates . . . in government for all the right reasons." Now the party seemed to be sliding out from under her. How that happened is a long and complicated story that is beyond the scope of this book. But by 1994, the year she started her second term as superintendent of public instruction, the Republican Party had veered to the right in Oregon and nationwide.

That was the year of the so-called Republican Revolution, when the party won enough seats in the midterm election to take control of both houses of the US Congress for the first time in forty years.[36] A year later Norma was trounced in a December special primary to fill the US Senate seat vacated by Bob Packwood, who had resigned in the wake of a sexual-misconduct scandal. Her more-conservative opponent, Gordon Smith, beat her by more than two votes to one.[37] Paulus's progressive views were now "in decline—or at least on the defensive—pushed back by growing numbers of conservatives," said one commentator.[38]

One of these was state representative Marylin Shannon, a Republican who maintained that the educational changes that "Norma's army" had lobbied for in 1991 were unproven fads, light on subject matter and heavy on social engineering.[39] Shannon also thought Norma abrupt and cold and believed Republicans would be better off without her. "Our party has grown by leaps and bounds," Shannon told the *Oregonian* in 1999. "I think it has sort of passed her by." Norma, unbowed, shot back that the party was "doing itself in," and added, "I don't want to have anything to do with them. They don't like me and I don't like them."[40]

She considered leaving the party and registering as an Independent, but her sense of loyalty forbade it. "I kept hoping things would change," she said. Today she jokes that she's an embarrassment to her son, daughter, and daughter-in-law, Democrats all, even though her views are not too far to the right of theirs. She says it lightly, but with a tinge of regret.[41]

TRUTH TO POWER

Norma's supporters and detractors agree on one thing: Norma was a politician of integrity and remains a person of integrity. She made history without betraying her values or pretending to be someone other than who she was. She was one of those people, said environmental activist Bill Bakke, who "make their own path and speak from the heart and have impeccable core values that are based on the health and happiness of the community. And she recognized that the community reaches well beyond humans and represents the fabric of all life."[42] Said Dave Frohnmayer, "She was a progressive voice, and none of it was artificial—it came from her gut." She was plainspoken and direct, "sometimes to the point where your jaw would drop," he said. "It was part of her persona. She spoke truth to power."[43]

Even in old age—she will turn eighty-four in March of 2017—Norma has an abiding conviction that hard work, self-discipline, reason, and a positive attitude will prevail over pessimism, irrationality, and selfishness. She once said, "If you're smart enough, work hard enough, and have a rational debate, you'll win."[44] It may be the closest thing to a creed that Norma, a religious agnostic, has ever confessed. She retains her fierce sense of justice. She embraced the feminist cause for a very practical reason: because it was obvious that women were getting a raw deal under the law. She admires Oregon's early-twentieth-century suffragist and women's-rights activist Abigail Scott Duniway. Shortly after the 1973 session, so supportive of women's rights, she remarked, "If I could see Abby today, I'd have to tell her we've come a long way, but only very recently—because most of the time I've been an adult, Oregon has had some very discriminatory laws."[45] She continues to speak her pro-choice views in an environment in which legal abortion, once apparently secure, is under increasing attack.

Norma is an idealist in this same practical sense, curious and willing to try new ways of doing things. On some matters her thinking has been a bit on the fringe; for example, she once advocated moving Portland's entire port apparatus to Astoria and turning that city into Oregon's main seaport. "And of course, the Port of Portland just put the kibosh on that," she said. (No surprise there.) "But you tell me, does it make any sense for us to have a major seaport 55 miles inland?"[46] But in many of her views Norma has been ahead of her time. During the oil crisis of 1973–1974, she became a vocal advocate of solar energy and energy conservation. While still in the legislature, she visited the home of a self-taught engineer in Coos Bay who said he was getting 85 percent of his power from the sun. If you could capture solar energy along the cloudy south coast, Norma said, you could capture it anywhere. She introduced bills to promote solar power and also geothermal power, but they didn't get far.[47] While on the Northwest Power Planning Council, she advocated doing whatever it took to bring back Pacific salmon—including removing dams. "I'm on the side of the fish," she said bluntly.[48]

She has long favored open primaries—in which Democrats are allowed to vote for Republican primary candidates and vice versa—and pushed for them throughout her career and after she retired from public life.[49] Oregon's primaries remain closed, but the debate endures. An open-primary initiative on the November 2014 ballot would have replaced Democratic and Republican primaries with a single primary open to all registered voters, including the 31 percent who aren't affiliated with either major party. Backers said it would force candidates to appeal to a broader spectrum of voters and reduce partisan divisions.[50] The measure went down by a wide margin, 68 to 32 percent.[51]

A sales tax seems even less likely to come to pass. Throughout her career Norma plugged for a sales tax to fund education—"I had a moral obligation to do so," she told a reporter in 1995—even as Oregonians have made it repeatedly clear that they do not want one.[52]

FOCUSED, DETERMINED, OUTSPOKEN

It was not only Norma's political views that secured her reputation as an effective public servant. She also has strong personal qualities that, for better or for worse, made her a distinctive personality within Oregon politics.

Norma is visionary—able to imagine a desired destination and only then concern herself about the details of getting there. Perhaps because of this big-picture view, she is impatient. She often cannot understand why a seemingly obvious solution takes so long and provokes so much foot-dragging. In some matters this trait has served her well—for example, the time she ramrodded through a policy to enable her two secretaries to share a job while she was secretary of state. Her impetuous action set a model for job sharing, proving to public agencies and private employers that it could be done efficiently, and could be advantageous all around.

For her friends, colleagues, and coworkers, her charming and (usually) cheerful manner softened her harder edges, even though her employees sometimes felt the rough side of her tongue. "Everyone who worked for her knew she had a short fuse," said Jennifer Viviano, "and they mostly adored her anyway. The public saw the impatience, but they didn't always see what made her lovable."

At times her impatience cost her, as when the educational reforms crafted by the 1991 legislature—which she strongly favored—bogged down in opposition from teachers and religious conservatives. Never shy about speaking her mind, she sometimes overstated her case, and her language could be intemperate. When opponents of the reform package sued the state in 1996, for instance, Norma accused them of being backed by national right-wing groups intent on finding "a communist under every bed." When skeptical teachers said the reforms were imprecise in content and unproven in methodology, she retorted that teachers weren't doing enough to improve student performance. When Oregon's voters approved a property-tax limitation measure in 1990, she "scolded school board members for 'whining' about tax losses. But then she turned around and criticized then-Governor Barbara Roberts and legislators for proposing cuts in state educational support."[53]

Norma was "a shotgun going off," said a lobbyist for the Oregon Education Association. "You never know when she's going to explode."[54] Norma's response to such criticism: If the teacher's union doesn't "wake up pretty soon and understand that public education has to change—and rapidly—it is not going to be here." She is determined—or, if you will, stubborn. She is willing to go to considerable lengths to get her way, and she's not one to yield for

A reunion of Oregon pathbreakers Norma Paulus, Gretchen Kafoury, Vera Katz, and Betty Roberts at an Oregon Historical Society event celebrating women in Oregon politics, April 2004. Norma Paulus Papers, Willamette University Archives and Special Collections_272.

the sake of keeping the peace. This trait surfaced early in life, in her school accomplishments and her self-driven recovery from polio, and continued to shape her choices throughout her career. And no doubt it's made her the powerhouse she is. Without a generous share of old-fashioned grit, it's unlikely she would have dared to enter law school without a college degree, or become the first woman elected to statewide office.

Here's a story: When the Pauluses built their new house on south Salem's Pigeon Hollow Road in 1967, Norma had her heart set on a high-ceilinged, half-timbered Tudor-style home, massive and open and welcoming. The architect, Phil Settecase, was a family friend. He started with a standard post-and-beam design, which called for stout crossbeams to support the roof. Norma took one look and sent him back to the drawing board. Her vision was of an airy cathedral-style ceiling, with nothing interrupting the eye.

Settecase brought new plans without crossbeams, but with a reduced pitch to the roof. Norma dismissed them out of hand. She didn't want a "cowboy ranch style" roof, she told him; she wanted a big vault with no crossbeams. Settecase patiently explained the engineering constraints; roofs fell down if they didn't have enough support. Norma said, "Come with me." She took him to see a house she admired, with a tall pitch to the roof. Settecase pointed out that the house had crossbeams. "Well, I don't want crossbeams." Her son Fritz was four years old at the time. He doesn't remember this argument, but he does remember his father's stories about bringing Settecase and the next iteration of the house plans home, "and opening the door and throwing them in to Mom," and then closing the door and waiting for the delayed explosion: "Jeezus Christ! This is NOT what I want!" In the end, Norma got what she wanted; Settecase designed the house without visible crossbeams by turning to an engineer to design a hidden steel superstructure.[55]

Norma is intensely focused. "She has an incredible ability for mental control," said Jennifer. She remembers asking her mother-in-law how she kept her cool in the pressure cooker of political life. "She told me, 'I literally do not think of anything except what is right in front of me. I compartmentalize it, get my daily schedule, give it a review, and then I go to the task. And when I'm done, I let it go and go on to the next task.'" "It's a very mind-over-matter attitude," said Jennifer. "She just powers through." Sometimes Norma's single-mindedness gives her an almost supernatural faith in her intuition. On the campaign trail for secretary of state, she got into a vigorous discussion with a Central Oregon resident about dams. This man was a pilot, and he challenged Norma to fly with him in his small plane, "and I'll show you some dams." Norma's aides, fearing for her safety, urged her not to go. Typically, she dismissed their fears and went. The flight was uneventful, and Norma enjoyed the geography lesson. Afterward she said, "I know I'm going to win this election, so how could I die in a plane crash?"[56]

Like most people in politics, she has a healthy self-regard. From an early age, she knew she was gifted: "I don't remember a time when I didn't think I was going to amount to something," she told a reporter near the end of her career.[57] Her tremendous confidence, along with her "staying power," said Chet Orloff, would have made her a good governor. "If [her opponent] had been just about anyone else, she would have prevailed. And between you and me and the wall, she would have been a better governor."[58] At the same time, she is highly principled, which helped her channel her considerable ego into an equally strong service ethic. It is telling, says Orloff, that Norma sought the post of superintendent of public instruction after two terms in the more-public, more-powerful role of secretary of state. "A lot of politicians would have said the superintendent's job was beneath them after that," he said. "But Norma loves public service, and she was happy to be in a position to make public instruction really a strong thing in this state."

She lived her principles at home, too, said Fritz. As an example, Norma and Bill disapproved of using their influence on behalf of family members, especially their children. "I feel like my mom didn't want to show any favoritism. Even though my parents were very well-connected, they didn't go to their friends and say, 'My Fritz, he needs work, can you give him a job in your office?' My parents didn't believe in that. You had to go work in the cannery," which both Liz and Fritz did during their summers off from school. "I hated it," Fritz said, but it was a valuable experience, "because it was a shakeup of my privileged existence."

Another thing that kept Norma's ego in check was her instinctive grasp of the partnering, the compromise and give-and-take, that is essential to getting anything done in politics. From her work on Wally Carson's legislative campaign in 1966, and then on her own in 1970, she'd experienced the power of organized grassroots support. When she got to the legislature in 1971, she forged effective and lasting relationships with allies and adversaries alike. When she was trying hard to get Cape Kiwanda set aside as a state park in 1973, she offered to withdraw her own proposal toward that purpose and let another representative's bill go forward. "I'm not hung up on sponsorship," she said. "I just want to insure that the cape is preserved."

It helps that she genuinely likes people. While she enjoyed the camaraderie of many political acquaintances, she cherishes her true private friends. She kept these spheres somewhat separate throughout her career, and though many of her good friends were also loyal campaigners and supporters, she did not exploit her personal friendships for political purposes. "My mom had her political life and she had her personal life," said Fritz. "Her personal friends were her true friends, her dear friends." Jennifer added, "She is an authentic and genuine person, and for her, loyalty and friendship and gratitude go very deep."

At the same time, she's a bit dazzled by celebrities. Covering the walls of her office in the Pigeon Hollow house were pictures of her with dozens of famous people: Ronald Reagan, Muhammad Ali, Gerald Ford, even Bill Clinton.[59] She likes to tell stories about the time she met Lily Tomlin, or Barbara Walters, or Erma Bombeck, or Bill Gates, or Carl Sagan. Sometimes she would come home and greet her husband with "Guess who I talked to today?" Typically, Bill would reply, "That's nice. What's for dinner?"

Meeting Moshe Dayan, the dashing one-eyed Israeli foreign minister, was "the most electrifying moment of my life." Dayan was an Israeli military leader, veteran of Israel's 1948 war of independence, and defense minister

during the Six-Day War of 1967. In 1978, with the mediation of President
Jimmy Carter, Dayan negotiated a peace agreement with Egyptian leader
Anwar Sadat, which both leaders signed at Camp David, Maryland.[60] Norma
encountered him in 1980, her third year as secretary of state, when she was flying home from a New York gathering sponsored by the *Ladies' Home Journal.*
The magazine had honored her and several other women, including Walters
and Bombeck, as "Women of the Future." They flew Norma out first-class and
put her up in a luxury hotel. They threw a brilliant party for the honorees,
"a very, very glamorous, stunning night," with scores of celebrities, including
Gregory Peck.

Afterward, waiting in the airline's first-class lounge for the flight home,
Norma and the three women who had accompanied her (Bill was not along
on this trip) noticed "these big, swarthy, burly men in suits, very intent on
their mission." Two of Norma's companions were Salem reporters: Shelley
Lewelling from the *Capital Journal* and Gloria Bledsoe from the *Statesman.*
Lewelling got up to get coffee, and sidled discreetly toward the burly men.
When she spotted the man with the trademark black eye patch, she wheeled
around and mouthed, "Famous Jew! Famous Jew! Famous Jew!" "I thought
she'd lost her mind," Norma said. "She was just about to faint. So I get up and
I go around the corner and I see Moshe Dayan, who was the hottest thing
on the planet Earth. And here he was!" After the Camp David peace accords,
Dayan, already a prominent and controversial figure in Israel, had become a
worldwide celebrity. Lewelling urged Norma to go up and talk to him. "I said,
'No I'm not going to do that!' I'd had so many experiences in my own little
small world where people were always doing that to me, and I was not going
to do that."

Gloria Bledsoe said, "Norma, if I go back to the *Statesman* and tell them
that Moshe Dayan was within twenty feet of you and I didn't have a story about
it, I'll be fired." Norma was adamant. "I'm not going to go in there," she said,
but she couldn't help taking another discreet look. She saw that Dayan was
wearing a bulletproof overcoat. Surrounded by his security men, he looked
small and, she thought, tired. When her party took their seats in the first-class
cabin, Norma found herself next to the aisle in the row behind Dayan, who had
the window seat. She'd been wondering why he was on this particular flight.
Now she remembered that he was on a speaking tour that included a stop at
Willamette University, where she'd received her law degree and where she was
now a trustee.

She pulled out her secretary of state stationery and wrote a note: "General Dayan: as the Secretary of State of Oregon and a trustee of Willamette University, may I be the first person to welcome you to our great state." She signed her name, sealed the note in an envelope with the Oregon State seal embossed on the flap, and gave it to a flight attendant. "I asked her not to give it to the general himself, but to the security guard who was sitting on the aisle," because letter bombs were starting to become a worrisome terrorist tactic. Then she read and dozed a little. After a while she looked up from her book to see a bouquet of carnations floating in the air in front of her. Dayan was holding them out to her over the back of his seat. Dazed, she accepted the flowers, and heard an accented voice say, "To a very gracious lady, may I thank you."

When Dayan gave his speech in the Willamette University football stadium, Norma was in the audience. She remembers a large crowd, a thrilling speech, and an enthusiastic response. "I can't tell you the effect he had on people at that time," she said. "He was absolutely an electrifying presence."[61]

REPORT CARD

The political process seldom brings closure to anything. Every issue that Norma cared about in 1971 is still being debated in 2017: education, the environment, land use, women's rights, energy self-sufficiency, the economy, the efficiency and effectiveness of government, how to pay for public services. And there are issues today, like climate change and a globalizing economy, that were barely on the radar screen when she entered politics.

When she was supervising Oregon's education system, Norma issued periodic "report cards" on its strengths, weaknesses, and opportunities for improvement. If she were writing a report card on Oregon today, her evaluation might touch on some of these items: The overall political environment is more polarized than it was forty years ago, although this is more evident at the national level. Oregon is still a small enough state that practical matters usually overrule ideology when lawmakers need to get things done. While the capitol may not be the cooperative environment that Norma remembers from her legislative days, the atmosphere is cordial and productive more often than not. However, Norma worries that citizen involvement is on the decline. She remembers when "the legislature was highly regarded and Republicans and Democrats worked together, and the legislative process was respected, and the halls were filled with Oregonians."[62] She doesn't get that feeling when she visits the capitol nowadays.

Oregon's pioneering land-use system is forty years old and a battle-scarred veteran of multiple attempts to overturn or weaken it.[63] Nothing in politics is permanent, but land-use planning has become a fixture of Oregon's political landscape as well as its natural one, even as its provisions continue to be challenged or revised. The system was crafted in an era when Oregon's economy was relatively good and its population relatively small. About two million people lived in Oregon in 1971;[64] by 2010 that number had grown to 3.8 million, and the population is expected to hit 4.3 million by 2020.[65] Oregon's population has grown faster than the US average since 1950, and that's expected to continue.[66] Increasing numbers of people put pressure on Oregon's land and water resources and threaten its livability. And when the economy declines, it's tempting for elected leaders to choose prosperity over preservation. It remains to be seen whether land-use planning will endure as a core principle of the "Oregon story."[67]

Oregon's environment is arguably in better shape than it was forty years ago, but the jury is still out on some things. Most urgently, a warming climate portends significant global disruptions that are very hard to predict at a local or even a regional level. The Willamette River was cleansed of its foul pulp-mill effluent in the 1970s, thanks to the strenuous efforts of Tom McCall and others. Now the river is dirty again, this time from harder-to-regulate sources, including polluted runoff from farms and city streets. Declining salmon stocks have been a target of much concern and millions of dollars in mitigation efforts, but wild populations continue to dwindle. While removing dams is no longer unthinkable—some dams, like the Elwha in northwestern Washington, have been taken out[68] and their free-flowing rivers restored—the big federal dams on the Columbia system are still there and will likely remain for the foreseeable future. Hatcheries are still the main means for securing enough fish for commercial, recreational, and tribal treaty fishing.[69]

Oregon has more federal wilderness than when Norma entered politics, largely thanks to Governor Bob Straub, who went up against Oregon's powerful timber industry in 1978 to recommend wilderness designation for three-quarters of a million acres. (In the end, Congress raised Straub's recommendation by nearly 100,000 acres.)[70] Straub also persuaded the Board of Forestry to regulate herbicide spraying, a position that had Norma's approval. "I was with Bob on that one," she said. "We were right but it wasn't easy to take on the timber companies."[71]

Oregonians today still exhibit a conservation ethic. People line up at bottle-return machines outside every grocery store, and curbside recycling

A photo of Norma taken in anticipation of being awarded an Oregon Historical Society History Makers Medal in 2012. Vivian Johnson.

is available in most Oregon cities. At least one town has banned disposable plastic grocery bags, and stores encourage customers to bring their own reusable bags. An organic-farming movement flourishes in Oregon and, while not an economic powerhouse, it makes up a significant fraction of the state's agricultural economy.[72] Many towns have farmers' markets, and a "buy local" movement has taken hold across the state.

The school-reform package of 1991 remained more or less intact for seventeen years. In July of 2008, the Certificates of Initial Mastery (tenth grade) and Advanced Mastery (twelfth grade), probably the most divisive elements of the plan, were phased out. School report cards and student assessment testing remain in place. Audits of state agencies are now routine. The secretary of state's office now has an audits division, headed by an appointed deputy. The secretary of state website invites visitors to read recent audits, search for archived audits, and report government waste and fraud. It publishes audit standards and practices and offers help for local governments in conducting their own.[73]

Women's rights are more established in law and practice than they were forty years ago. In November 2014, Oregon voters, by a nearly two-to-one margin, reinforced their commitment to equal rights for women by adding these words to the state constitution: "Equality of rights under the law shall not be denied or abridged by the State of Oregon or by any political subdivision in this state on account of sex."[74] However, conservative elements are nibbling around the edges, although more in other states and at the national level than in Oregon. Pro-life groups are seeking to overturn *Roe v. Wade* and restrict abortion rights in several states. A US Supreme Court decision in July of 2014 gave for-profit businesses, along with churches and religious charities, the right to exclude birth control services from their employees' health coverage.

At the same time, it is no longer bizarre for a woman to aspire to high office. When Norma ran for governor, she perceived Republican women as a strong bloc of opposition. Today there is no significant anti-woman bias among Republican women in Oregon.[75] Last year, US voters came within a whisker of putting a woman in the Oval Office. If one or two battleground states had voted the way Oregon did, it would have happened, and for that, a good bit of the credit should go to Norma Paulus and women like her, along with the progressive-minded men who encouraged women to enter politics. Today eight of thirty Oregon senators are women. House speaker Tina Kotek shares the chamber with nineteen other women representatives. Oregon's secretary of state was Jeanne Atkins, Atkins until she stepped down in 2017. Oregon's governor is Kate Brown—a former secretary of state—and Oregon's attorney general is Ellen Rosenblum. These women credit Norma for their pursuit of public office and their ability to excel in their jobs.

In all, there is reason to believe that because of Norma Paulus, Oregon is a more progressive, more honest, more environmentally concerned place than it would have been otherwise.

A MODEL OREGONIAN

Just off Highway 97 north of Madras lies a sleepy community that a band of red-clad newcomers once briefly renamed Rajneesh. The town is again known as Antelope. A few miles to the east, the old Big Muddy Ranch, having passed through its identity as Rancho Rajneesh, is now the site of a Christian camp operated by the Young Life organization. The placid, juniper-dotted landscape seems to have quietly absorbed the turmoil that troubled that ground thirty years ago. The newcomers were a political lightning rod. Some Oregonians found it easy to demonize them; others, to excuse their misbehavior in the name of tolerance. The secretary of state steered a decisive middle course. She stood firm on the law and the constitution, set out a clear policy to protect every voter's rights, and enforced it by personally showing up to face her would-be intimidators.

That situation called forth the highest good in Norma: her fairness, her courage, her faith in the democratic process, her instinctive grasp of the heart of the matter. It seems to us that these qualities also describe the best of the Oregon spirit. If you were looking to become an ideal Oregonian, you might follow the example of Norma Paulus. There aren't many greater role models out there.

Secretary of State at the time, Norma overrode her terrible fear of heights to climb the scaffolding to witness the re-gilding of the Oregon Capitol golden pioneer. Funding for the 1984 project was made possible in part by Oregon school children through a penny drive. Photographer unknown. Family archives.

Acknowledgments

We are grateful first of all to Norma Paulus, who was foresighted enough to set down a rich account of her life and times. We are grateful to Clark Hansen of the Oregon Historical Society, whose skill and sensitivity brought out Norma's inner raconteur and distinctive voice. We are grateful to Russell Sadler and the many people he interviewed for their preliminary work on the autobiography. We thank the friends and family members who shared their Norma stories with us, and we are sad that some of them did not live to hold this volume in their hands.

Warmest thanks to reference librarians Mary McRobinson and her staff at the Willamette University Archives and Scott Daniels and the staff at the Oregon Historical Society Research Library, who guided us through boxes and boxes of files, scrapbooks, clippings, and ephemera. Their courtesy and patience with us over multiple visits were much appreciated.

Thanks also to a reviewer of our early draft, who asked to remain anonymous, for many helpful suggestions, and to the two reviewers of the final manuscript, who likewise improved it with their cogent comments. Thanks to Jo Ogden, who helped us and the Paulus family assemble and document the photographs that appear in this book.

Finally, we are grateful to Fritz Paulus, Jennifer Viviano, and Liz Paulus, the ones who know Norma best in the world. They freely revealed to us such inner dimensions of their mother's life as they were privileged to witness, with honesty and generosity of spirit, and they allowed us to portray her in a way that reflects the fullness and complexity of her character. Never did they tell us to sanitize or censor or blur the edges of her life, and the book is much the better for it. Working with them was a joy.

Gail Wells
Pat Amacher
2017

Near the end of her second term as Secretary of State, in November, 1984, Norma takes a moment to celebrate her fifteen years in state government. David Nuss, courtesy of the *Statesman Journal*. Willamette Heritage Center, 2016.023.0041.007. Norma Paulus Papers, Willamette University Archives and Special Collections_NP023.

Notes

CHAPTER 1: THE EARLY YEARS

Epigraph. Russell Sadler draft, pp. 4–5. Norma's response to hearing Senator Wayne Morse speak at her high school.

1 Sadler draft, p. 4; Norma Paulus interview conducted by Clark Hansen (hereafter, "interview by Hansen"), October 2, 1999.

2 Interview by Hansen, October 2, 1999.

3 Interview with Paul Petersen, July 26, 2014.

4 Interview by Hansen, October 2, 1999.

5 Interview with Paul Petersen.

6 Ibid.

7 Interview by Hansen, October 2, 1999.

8 Ibid.

9 Tom Detzel, "She's a Fighter for Her Causes Quite Naturally," *Eugene Register-Guard*, September 21, 1986.

10 Interview with Paul Petersen; interview by Hansen, October 2, 1999.

11 "Possibilities for Petroleum in the Northwestern United States," *Oil Trade Journal* 11, no.2 (February 1920): 106.

12 "Harney County Oil Wealth Fades in Mirage," Jefferson Public Radio, July 13, 2011, www.ijpr.org.

13 Interview with Paul Petersen.

14 Interview by Hansen, October 2, 1999.

15 Interview with Paul Petersen.

16 Sadler draft, p. 3.

17 Interview by Hansen, October 2, 1999.

18 Ibid.

19 Sadler draft, p. 6.

20 Interview by Hansen, October 2, 1999.

21 Interview with Gerri Pyrch, May 1, 2014.

22 Interview by Hansen, October 2, 1999.

23 Ibid.

24 Ibid.

25 Ibid.

26 Sadler draft, p. 7.

27 Interview by Hansen, October 2, 1999.

28 Sadler draft, p. 8.

29 Interview with Gerri Pyrch.

30 Interview by Hansen, October 2, 1999.

31 Ibid.

32 Ibid.

33 Ibid.

34 Sadler draft, p. 9.

35 Sadler draft, p. 5.

36 George H. Bell, "Norma Paulus—Oregon's Cinderella Lawmaker," *Oregon People* 1, no.1 (May 1975). This was the inaugural issue of the magazine; Norma was the cover story.

37 http://oregonencyclopedia.org/articles/yturri_anthony_1914_1999_/#.U-EDWhbXlSU.

38 http://poliotoday.org/?page_id=13. Of the fifty-eight thousand people who contracted polio that year, 3,145 died and 21,269 were left with mild to disabling paralysis. The developer of the vaccine, Dr. Jonas Salk, became a national hero.

39 http://polio.emedtv.com/polio/how-is-polio-spread.html.

40 Interview by Hansen, October 2, 1999.

41 Sadler draft, pp. 11–12.

42 Interview with Gerri Pyrch.

43 Sadler draft, p. 13.

44 Interview by Hansen, October 2, 1999.

45 Sadler draft, p. 14.

46 Interview by Hansen, October 2, 1999.

47 Sadler draft, p. 15.

48 Interview by Hansen, October 2, 1999.

49 Ibid., p. 16.

50 Interview by Hansen, October 2, 1999.

51 Ibid., p. 17.

52 Interview by Hansen, October 2, 1999.

53 Ibid.

54 Ibid., April 19, 1999.

55 Ibid.

56 Bell, "Norma Paulus," May 1975.

57 Interview by Hansen, April 19, 1999.

58 Sadler draft, p. 19.

59 Interview by Hansen, April 19, 1999.

60   Ibid., October 2, 1999.
61   Sadler draft, p. 23.
62   Interview by Hansen, April 19, 1999.
63   Ibid.
64   Sadler draft, p. 21.
65   Interview by Hansen, April 19, 1999.
66   Sadler draft, pp. 25–26.
67   Interview by Hansen, April 19, 1999.
68   Ibid.
69   Sadler draft, p. 29.
70   Interview by Hansen, April 19, 1999.
71   Sadler draft, p. 29.
72   Ibid.
73   Interview by Hansen, April 19, 1999.
74   Bell, "Norma Paulus," May 1975.
75   Interview by Hansen, April 19, 1999.
76   Ray Inouye, "Housewife Nears Law
     Goal," *Capital Journal*, March 27, 1962.
77   Interview by Hansen, June 2, 1999.

CHAPTER 2:
FRESHMAN IN THE HOUSE

Epigraph. Interview by Hansen, June 2, 1999.
 1   Interview by Hansen, November 2,
     2000.
 2   Salem Online History: Mary Eyre,
     http://www.salemhistory.net/people/
     mary_eyre.htm; also interview by
     Hansen, June 2, 1999. Eyre died in 2000
     at the age of 101. "She was my mentor, a
     wonderful woman," Norma said.
 3   Interview by Hansen, April 19, 1999.
 4   Ibid., November 2, 2000.
 5   Ibid., June 2, 1999.
 6   Charles K. Johnson, *Standing at the
     Water's Edge: Bob Straub's Battle for the
     Soul of Oregon* (Corvallis: Oregon State
     University Press, 2012).
 7   "Day Named Hickel Aide; Resigns
     Legislative Seat," *Oregon Statesman*,
     February 12, 1970.
 8   Interview by Hansen, June 2, 1999.
 9   Sadler draft, p. 24.
10   Interview with Wally Carson, December
     10, 2013.
11   Interview by Hansen, October 2, 1999;
     also interview with Wally Carson.
12   Sadler draft, p. 30.
13   Interview with Wally Carson; however,
     one knowledgeable reviewer of this book
     in manuscript was of the opinion that
     political parties in Oregon were more

     structured during this time than Carson's
     observation might suggest.
14   Interview by Hansen, July 6, 2000.
15   A Republican political strategist known
     for his hardball campaign tactics.
16   Interview with Bob Packwood, April 6,
     2014.
17   Interview by Hansen, April 19, 1999.
18   Ibid.
19   Ibid.
20   Ibid., June 2, 1999; also Salem Online
     History: Vern Miller, http://www.
     salemhistory.net/people/vern_miller.
     htm.
21   Interviews by Hansen, July 1, 1999, and
     April 19, 1999.
22   Ibid., July 1, 1999.
23   Ibid., June 2, 1999.
24   Oregon Legislators and Staff Guide:
     1961 Regular Session, http://
     arcweb.sos.state.or.us/pages/records/
     legislative/recordsguides/histleg/
     statehood/1961reg.html.
25   Interview by Hansen, June 2, 1999.
26   Ibid.
27   The hundred-year-old building was
     destroyed by fire in 1971. House major-
     ity leader Roger Martin was staying
     in the hotel at the time. Salem Online
     History: The Marion Hotel Fire, http://
     www.salemhistory.net/brief_history/
     marion_hotel_fire.htm; also The Marion
     Hotel, http://www.salemhistory.net/
     places/marion_hotel.htm.
28   Interview by Hansen, June 2, 1999.
29   "Day Named Hickel Aide; Resigns
     Legislative Seat," *Oregon Statesman*,
     February 12, 1970. At that time
     legislators were elected at large from
     a county. That changed in 1973, when
     single-member districts within a county
     were instituted. In the 1973 session
     Norma represented District 31 in south
     Salem.
30   Charles E. Beggs, "Woman Attorney
     Faces Farmer, Horseshoer in Marion
     GOP Legislative Race," *Oregon
     Statesman*, May 17, 1970.
31   *Capital Journal*, May 1970. Date missing
     from clipping, found in Norma Paulus
     Papers, University Archives and
     Special Collections (hereafter UASC),
     Willamette University, Salem.

32 Interview by Hansen, June 2, 1999. Norma mentions that Rogers had some kind of partnership with Gerry Frank, but the nature of it is not clear.

33 Ibid.

34 In Norma Paulus collection, Oregon Historical Society (hereafter OHS) Research Library, Portland.

35 Ibid.

36 Interview by Hansen, June 2, 1999.

37 "Norma Paulus is escorted at school by young men," photo caption, *Capital Journal*, October 30, 1970.

38 *Oregon Statesman*, undated clipping from 1971. In the Norma Paulus Papers, UASC, Willamette University, Salem.

39 Interview by Hansen, June 2, 1999.

40 Ibid.

41 Ibid.

42 Interview by Hansen, November 2, 2000.

43 Sarah Kliff, "Charts: How Roe v. Wade Changed Abortion Rights," *Washington Post*, January 22, 2013. Prior to Roe v. Wade, Oregon law permitted abortions in some circumstances.

44 "Two Attorneys Battle for Day's House Seat," *Oregon Statesman*, October 26, 1970.

45 *Oregon Statesman*, undated clipping from 1970. In the Norma Paulus Papers, UASC, Willamette University, Salem.

46 Interview by Hansen, June 2, 1999.

47 The first appears to have been Hannah Martin, elected in 1933, the year Norma was born. http://arcweb.sos.state.or.us/pages/records/legislative/records-guides/histleg/statehood/1933reg.html. This gives Martin's name but doesn't confirm that she was the first woman.

48 Interview by Hansen, June 2, 1999.

49 Betty Roberts, *With Grit and By Grace: Breaking Trails in Politics and Law* (Corvallis: Oregon State University Press, 2008), pp. 124–127.

50 Interview by Hansen, June 2, 1999.

51 Ibid.

52 Ibid., July 1, 1999.

53 Ibid., June 2, 1999.

54 Ibid.

55 Undated floor note from a J. P. Anderson. In the Norma Paulus Papers, UASC, Willamette University, Salem.

Fritz Paulus remembers a note from another of Norma's legislative colleagues that said, "Your balls are showing." Unfortunately the authors were unable to track this down.

56 Oregon became the thirty-third state in the Union when President James Buchanan signed the statehood bill into law on February 14, 1859.

57 Interview by Hansen, June 2, 1999.

58 Ibid.

59 Ibid.

60 Ibid.

61 Ibid.

62 Ibid., July 1, 1999.

63 Ibid., June 2, 1999.

64 Oregon criminal law revision records, secretary of state's office, http://arcweb.sos.state.or.us/pages/records/legislative/legislativeminutes/crimlaw/.

65 The Oregon Encyclopedia: Anthony Yturri, http://oregonencyclopedia.org/articles/yturri_anthony_1914_1999_/#.U-EDWhbXlSU.

66 Lee Johnson (Oregon judge), http://en.wikipedia.org/wiki/Lee_Johnson_%28Oregon_judge%29; *Oregon State Bar Bulletin* February-March 2006, Herbert M. Schwab obituary, http://www.osbar.org/publications/bulletin/06febmar/obits.html; Robert W. Chandler, http://en.wikipedia.org/wiki/Robert_W._Chandler). Also Interview by Hansen, June 2, 1999.

67 Interview by Hansen, July 1, 1999.

68 Oregon criminal law revision records, secretary of state's office, http://arcweb.sos.state.or.us/pages/records/legislative/legislativeminutes/crimlaw/.

69 Interview by Hansen, July 1, 1999; "Rep. Rieke Dies in Traffic Crash," *Eugene Register-Guard*, January 27, 1978, http://news.google.com/newspapers?nid=1310&dat=19780127&id=VfhVAAAAIBAJ&sjid=6OEDAAAAIBAJ&pg=5719,6944969.

70 Interview by Hansen, February 17, 2010.

71 Ibid., July 1, 1999.

72 Gambling in Oregon, http://en.wikipedia.org/wiki/

Gambling_in_Oregon. Also interview by Hansen, July 1, 1999.

73 Interview by Hansen, July 1, 1999. Today Oregon allows electronic off-track betting on horse and dog races and "social gaming" in licensed establishments, and there is a state-run, $7 million-a-year lottery. Oregon also has nine tribal casinos. "I'm still sick about it," Norma said. "I opposed lotteries and gambling every chance I got."

74 Interview by Hansen, November 11, 1999.

75 The year after she attended the Eagleton Institute's conference, Norma helped plan and subsequently attended the Institute's first conference for women state legislators, held in 1972 in the Pocono Mountains of Pennsylvania. In 1982 she was invited back as a keynote speaker. In her speech, she told the story of being the sole woman at the Institute's 1971 conference and recounted her adventures in politics in the decade since then. See the transcript of her address in the 1982 conference proceedings, pp. 33-46, http://www.cawp.rutgers.edu/sites/default/files/resources/statelegconf1982.pdf. For more about the Eagleton Institute's Center for American Women in Politics, see http://www.cawp.rutgers.edu/about_cawp/history-and-mission.

76 Interview by Hansen, July 1, 1999. Singer Island (http://www.visitflorida.com/en-us/cities/singer-island.html), which is in Palm Beach County, Florida, is home of the John D. MacArthur Beach State Park (https://www.floridastateparks.org/park/MacArthur-Beach). MacArthur owned the land where the park is and gave it for a park "in the 1970s, after a university study revealed that the property was a biological treasure." The MacArthur Foundation contributed more funds to develop the park and its Nature Center.

77 Interview by Hansen, July 1, 1999.

78 Bill actually served in the US Air Force, his son Fritz recalled.

79 Interview with Wally Carson.

80 Interview by Hansen, July 1, 1999.

81 Ibid., June 2, 1999.

CHAPTER 3:
CHAMPION OF THE ENVIRONMENT

Epigraph. Norma Paulus, reported by Bob Hulen, in "Snow Scene ...," *Oregon Statesman*, April 1, 1973.

1 Interview by Hansen, June 2, 1999.

2 "Political Candidate Gives Ecology Lesson," *Capital Journal*, October 7, 1970.

3 "The Oregon Legislature: 1971," *Capital Journal*, special report, July 16, 1971.

4 Sy Adler, *Oregon Plans: The Making of an Unquiet Land-Use Revolution* (Corvallis: Oregon State University Press, 2012), p. 51.

5 "The Oregon Legislature: 1971."

6 Doug Baker, "Bottle Bill in Danger," column, July 30, 1972. In the Norma Paulus Papers, UASC, Willamette University, Salem.

7 Brent Walth, *Fire at Eden's Gate: Tom McCall and the Oregon Story* (Portland: Oregon Historical Society Press, 1994), pp. 256–257.

8 Interview by Hansen, June 2, 1999.

9 Walth, *Fire at Eden's Gate*, p. 257.

10 Ibid., p. 260.

11 Ibid., p. 262.

12 Ibid.

13 Ibid., p. 317.

14 Ibid., p. 319.

15 Interview by Hansen, November 11, 1999.

16 Walth, *Fire at Eden's Gate*, p. 319.

17 Ibid. It is unclear if Piacentini was speaking before a House committee or floor session, but Norma implies that he was (Interview by Hansen, June 2, 1999), because she says she got up right afterward and attacked S.O.L.V.

18 "Stores Can Force Returnable Containers, IGA Owner Says," *Oregon Statesman*, April 1, 1971.

19 Interview by Hansen, June 2, 1999; also Robert Shepard, "Bottleneck Charged on Litter Campaign," UPI, in *Capital Journal*, March 5, 1971.

20 Interview by Hansen, June 2, 1999.

21 Baker, "Bottle Bill in Danger."

22 Interview by Hansen, November 2, 2000.

23 Walth, *Fire at Eden's Gate*, p. 321; also Roberts, *With Grit and By Grace*, p. 133.

24 Roberts, *With Grit and By Grace*, p. 134.

25 Interview by Hansen, June 2, 1999.

26 Walth, *Fire at Eden's Gate*, p. 322.

27 Interview by Hansen, July 1, 1999.

28 Ibid.

29 "The Oregon Legislature: 1971."

30 Charles E. Beggs, "Environment Vote of Legislature Scored," *Oregon Statesman*, July 19, 1971.

31 "Legislative Grinder Leaves New Solons Strung Out," *Capital Journal*, June 11, 1971. For the younger reader, "solon" is an old-fashioned newspaper term for legislators, after the Athenian statesman of that name.

32 Interview by Hansen, June 2, 1999.

33 Larry Roby, "Paulus Calls for Legislative Power," *Capital Journal*, August 9, 1974. This comment came in a different context—conversation about annual sessions—but sentiment fits here.

34 Bob Smith went on to represent Oregon's District 2 in the US House of Representatives from 1983 to 1995. Robert Freeman Smith, http://en.wikipedia.org/wiki/Robert_Freeman_Smith.

35 Interview by Hansen, June 2, 1999.

36 Ed Grosswiler, "State Had $1 Million Deal for Kiwanda as Talks Folded," AP, in *Oregon Statesman*, February 17, 1973.

37 Press release from office of Norma Paulus, January 19, 1973. Dale Osborn is contact person.

38 Its name was changed to Transportation Commission in 1973. Oregon State Parks was then administered by the Highway Division, which operated under the Transportation Commission's aegis. That changed in 1979 when the legislature made State Parks a separate division under Oregon Department of Transportation.

39 "Preserve Cape Kiwanda," editorial from KATU channel 2 (ABC affiliate), October 12, 1972.

40 Letter from David G. Talbot, Oregon State Parks superintendent, to Representative Bill Markham, May 22, 1973.

41 "Cape Sought for State, but Proposals Conflict," *Oregon Journal*, February 7, 1973.

42 "Solons Ask Highway Board to Reconsider Buying Cape," *Capital Journal*, February 7, 1973. Interestingly, nobody seemed very exercised about the safety of putting a nuclear power plant on a seismically active area of the coast. Arguments against it tended to turn on environmental damage from construction (Norma's reason for opposing) and ugliness of the plant itself. Perhaps this was not so odd given that the Three Mile Island and Chernobyl nuclear accidents were still in the future.

43 "Cape Kiwanda Purchase Sought for Use as Recreational Site," *Oregon Statesman*, February 21, 1973.

44 Interview by Hansen, July 1, 1999.

45 "Strong Support Given for State to Buy Cape," *Capital Journal*, May 18, 1973.

46 "A Waste of Money," editorial, *LaGrande Observer*, February 21, 1973.

47 Ibid.

48 "Cape Sought for State, but Proposals Conflict."

49 Norma Paulus, letter of reply to R. G. Montgomery, editor and publisher of *LaGrande Observer*, March 1, 1973.

50 "Strong Support Given for State to Buy Cape."

51 Ibid.

52 Undated letter from Ray Atkeson, photographer, urging that state acquire Cape Kiwanda. In the Norma Paulus Papers, UASC, Willamette University, Salem.

53 Don Jepsen, "House Beats Purchase of Cape Kiwanda," *Oregon Journal*, May 23, 1973; this and previous paragraph.

54 Larry Roby, "Kiwanda's Owner Renews Bid to State," *Capital Journal*, May 25, 1973.

55 "Cape Kiwanda Placed On Sale," UPI, in *Bend Bulletin*, May 8, 1972.

56 Roby, "Kiwanda's Owner Renews Bid to State."

57 Charles E. Beggs, "State Concludes Cape Kiwanda Deal," *Oregon Statesman*, May 30, 1973.

58 "Environmentalist View: State Didn't Buy Enough of Kiwanda," *Oregon Statesman*, June 3, 1973.

59 "Solution on Cape Kiwanda," editorial, *Oregon Journal*, June 2, 1973.

60 Bob Hulen, "Snow Scene . . . ," column, *Oregon Statesman*, April 1, 1973.

CHAPTER 4: LAND-USE PIONEER

Epigraph. Interview by Hansen, July 1, 1999.

1 Interview by Hansen, June 2, 1999.

2 Ibid.

3 Sy Adler, *Oregon Plans: The Making of an Unquiet Land-Use Revolution* (Corvallis: Oregon State University Press, 2012), p. 14.

4 Governor Tom McCall, OHS, http://www.ohs.org/education/focus/governor-tom-mccall.cfm.

5 Brent Walth, *Fire at Eden's Gate: Tom McCall and the Oregon Story* (Portland: OHS Press, 1994), p. 248: citing the governor's message to the Oregon Senate, February 7, 1969.

6 Walth, *Fire at Eden's Gate*, pp. 313–314: interview with CBS reporter Terry Drinkwater, which aired January 12, 1971.

7 Quoted in Walth, *Fire at Eden's Gate*, p. 246; source of quote is Charles Little, *The New Oregon Trail: An Account of the Development and Passage of State Land-Use Legislation in Oregon* (Washington, DC: Conservation Foundation), p. 13.

8 Walth, *Fire at Eden's Gate*, p. 355, citing various newspaper articles: *Oregonian*, November 21, 1972, p. 12; *Register-Guard*, November 20, 1972, p. 1; *Capital Journal*, November 20, 1972, p. 1.

9 *Oregonian*, January 2, 1999.

10 Charles Johnson, *Standing at the Water's Edge: Bob Straub's Battle for the Soul of Oregon* (Corvallis: Oregon State University Press, 2012), p. 230.

11 Adler, *Oregon Plans*, p.143, sidebar "Urban Growth Boundaries."

12 Ibid., p. 18.

13 Ibid., p. 25.

14 Ibid., p. 26.

15 Interview by Hansen, July 6, 2000.

16 "Day Named Hickel Aide, Resigns Legislative Seat," *Oregon Statesman*, February 12, 1970.

17 Day followed Hickel in leaving the department at the end of 1970, after only a few months of service. Hickel had been sacked after he wrote a letter to President Nixon criticizing the Ohio National Guard's bloody suppression of student protests at Kent State University in Ohio, a debacle that had left four dead the previous April. Day returned to Oregon and worked with legislators on Oregon's land-use planning system.

18 Adler, *Oregon Plans*, pp. 26–27.

19 Ibid., p. 29.

20 Ibid., p. 34.

21 Ibid., p. 37.

22 Ibid., p. 35.

23 Ibid., p. 20.

24 Interview by Hansen, June 2, 1999.

25 Ibid., July 1, 1999.

26 Ibid., June 2, 1999.

27 Ibid., July 1, 1999.

28 Johnson, *Standing at the Water's Edge*, p. 230.

29 Both quotes from Adler, *Oregon Plans*, p. 143.

30 "House Candidate Critical of State Welfare System," *Stayton Mail*, October 22, 1970.

31 Interview by Hansen, June 2, 1999.

32 "House Candidate Critical of State Welfare System."

33 Interview by Hansen, June 2, 1999.

34 Walth, *Fire at Eden's Gate*, p. 355.

35 Walth, *Fire at Eden's Gate*, p. 352.

36 Adler, *Oregon Plans*, pp. 42–43. The Charbonneau project did go forward. In the forty years since that time the Portland metro area has spread south to meet it.

37 KATU-TV, 1972. Cited in Adler, *Oregon Plans*, p. 45; his source is "KATU. 1972. Editorial. November 15. Author's copy."

38 Walth, *Fire at Eden's Gate*, p. 355.

39 Adler, *Oregon Plans*, pp. 44–45.

40 Johnson, *Standing at the Water's Edge*, p. 99.

41 Adler, *Oregon Plans*, pp. 44–45.

42 Ibid., p. 45.

43 Ibid., pp. 46–47.

44 Walth, *Fire at Eden's Gate*, p. 253, citing Little, *The New Oregon Trail*, p. 9.

45 Quoted in Walth, *Fire at Eden's Gate*, p. 353; his source is Little, *New Oregon Trail*, p. 9.

46 Adler, *Oregon Plans*, p. 53; citing Little, *New Oregon Trail*, no page number given.

47 Quoted in Adler, *Oregon Plans*, p. 39, citing Macpherson, 1997, oral history interview 3962, Kami Teramura Masters Project Oral Histories, OHS.

48 Oregon Encyclopedia, http://oregonencyclopedia.org/articles/land_use_planning/#.VLMFV1rXk9c.

49 Adler, *Oregon Plans*, pp. 56–57.

50 Walth, *Fire at Eden's Gate*, p. 356, citing Journals and Calendars of the Senate and House, *House Journal*, January 8, 1973, p. J-313.

51 Johnson, *Standing at the Water's Edge*, p. 205.

52 Ibid.

53 Jerry Uhrhammer, "Solons View 'Scorched Earth,'" *Eugene Register-Guard*, May 30, 1973.

54 Thomas R. Cox, *The Park Builders: A History of State Parks in the Pacific Northwest* (Seattle: University of Washington Press, 2011), p. 158. Liz VanLeeuwen went on to a career in Republican politics, serving eight terms in the House after she was elected in 1980. From Oregon.gov; also Johnson, *Standing at the Water's Edge*, chapter 11, note 27, p. 317.

55 Interview by Hansen, July 1, 1999.

56 Uhrhammer, "Solons View 'Scorched Earth.'" Article doesn't say whether Norma was along.

57 "Bill Prevents Condemning River Farmland for Parks," *Capital Journal*, June 12, 1973.

58 Johnson, *Standing at the Water's Edge*, p. 205.

59 "Bill Prevents Condemning River Farmland for Parks." The bill allowed continuing development of four riverfront parks already in the works: Molalla Park (now Molalla River State Park), Lone Tree Bar Park (now Cottonwood Canyon State Park along the John Day River), Bowers Rocks Park (now Bowers Rocks State Park, a paddle-in park on the Willamette between Corvallis and Albany), and Dexter Park (now Dexter State Recreation Site on the west edge of Dexter Reservoir).

60 Johnson, *Standing at the Water's Edge*, p. 205.

61 Ibid., pp. 205–206. Not clear which vote he's talking about, but seems to be the House vote on SB 100.

62 Walth, *Fire at Eden's Gate*, p. 356.

63 Ibid.

64 Adler, *Oregon Plans*, p. 59.

65 Summarizing Adler, *Oregon Plans*, pp. 51–58.

66 Walth, *Fire at Eden's Gate*, p. 359.

67 Adler, *Oregon Plans*, p. 65.

68 Ibid., citing Hallock, 2000, oral history interview with Ernie Bonner, September 19. Ernie Bonner papers, Portland State University; he also cites Walth, *Fire at Eden's Gate*.

69 Quoted in Walth, *Fire at Eden's Gate*, p. 360; citing author's interview with Fred Van Natta, undated.

70 Oregon Encyclopedia, Senate Bill 100, http://www.oregonencyclopedia.org/articles/senate_bill_100/#.VfDDL4vXm-U.

71 Walth, *Fire at Eden's Gate*, p. 361.

72 Adler, *Oregon Plans*, p. 73.

73 Ibid., p. 75.

74 Contrary to popular memory, women were not a majority on this committee, Fadeley said in a May 12, 2014, interview. "I'm embarrassed to say that I used to say that sometimes. But it wasn't a majority." She looked up the membership in the 1973 legislative record. It listed eleven members, of whom five were women: herself, Vera Katz, Pat Whiting, Mary Burrows, and Norma Paulus.

75 Adler, *Oregon Plans*, p. 75, citing Nancie Fadeley oral history interview 3959, by Kami Teramura. Masters Project Oral Histories, OHS.

76 Walth, *Fire at Eden's Gate*, p. 361, citing interview with Ted Hallock, undated.

77 Walth said it "sailed through the House and landed on Tom McCall's desk," p. 361.

78 Fortieth Anniversary of Senate Bill 100, Oregon Department of Land Conservation and Development, http://www.oregon.gov/LCD/Pages/SB100_40th_Anniversary.aspx.

79 Land Conservation and Development Commission, Oregon Department of Land Conservation and Development, http://www.oregon.gov/LCD/pages/lcdc.aspx.

80 History of Oregon's Land-Use Planning, Oregon Department of Land Conservation and Development, http://www.oregon.gov/LCD/Pages/history.aspx.

81 Goal 15: Willamette River Greenway, Oregon's Statewide Planning Goals and Guidelines, http://www.oregon.gov/LCD/docs/goals/goal15.pdf; also History of Oregon's Land-Use Planning, http://www.oregon.gov/LCD/Pages/history.aspx.

82 History of Oregon's Land-Use Planning, http://www.oregon.gov/LCD/Pages/history.aspx.

83 Johnson, *Standing at the Water's Edge*, p. 204.

84 Ibid.

85 Ibid., p. 207.

86 Ibid., p. 205, citing his own interview with Norma Paulus of May 13, 2007. His placement of the quote is confusing: it's positioned so that it sounds like she's referring to the 1973 debate over SB 100. However, obviously she mentions Straub, so she must be talking about 1975.

87 Johnson, *Standing at the Water's Edge*, p. 207.

88 Ibid., p. 207–208.

89 Ibid., p. 208.

90 Measure 37, which passed in 2004, required the state to compensate landowners or exempt them from compliance if a land-use regulation had the effect of reducing property value. The measure survived a constitutional challenge in 2006, but was modified in 2007 by Measure 49, which narrowed the types of claims a landowner could make.

91 Interview by Hansen, July 1, 1999.

CHAPTER 5:
A JOURNEY TO FEMINISM

Epigraph. Norma Paulus, House speech in favor of ratification of Equal Rights Amendment, February 8, 1973.

1 Interview by Hansen, June 2, 1999.

2 Ibid., June 2 and October 5, 1999.

3 "Women's Rights Are Significant," editorial, *Capital Journal*, July 16, 1971. The writer quotes Eleanor Meyers, director of women's equal opportunity program of Bureau of Labor, on several bills on women's issues. SB 526 (unlinks job qualifications from sex roles), HB 1239 (no-fault divorce), HB 1601 (community child care funding), HB 1228 (child care), SB 591 (birth control information). The 1971 session was "a significant one, mainly because of the thinking that went into the women-oriented issues."

4 Betty Roberts, *With Grit and By Grace: Breaking Trails in Politics and Law* (Corvallis: Oregon State University Press, 2008), p. 124.

5 Interview by Hansen, July 1, 1999.

6 Roberts, *With Grit and By Grace*; also interview by Hansen, July 30, 1999.

7 Roberts, *With Grit and By Grace*.

8 Interview by Hansen, November 2, 2000.

9 Roberts, *With Grit and By Grace*.

10 Ibid.

11 Interview by Hansen, November 11, 1999.

12 The committee also dealt with many important environmental and land-use bills, including Senate Bill 100, the foundation of Oregon's land-use planning system.

13 Interview by Hansen, July 30, 1999.

14 Roberts, *With Grit and By Grace*.

15 Gretchen Kafoury was elected to the Oregon House of Representatives in 1976 and served from 1977 to 1982.

16 Interview by Hansen, October 5, 1999.

17 Interview with Gretchen Kafoury, December 10, 2013.

18 Roberts, *With Grit and By Grace*.

19 Ibid.

20 Interview by Hansen, July 30, 1999.

21 Roberts, *With Grit and By Grace*.

22 Interview by Hansen, July 30, 1999.

23 Norma Paulus, House speech in favor of ratification of Equal Rights Amendment, February 8, 1973.

24 Interview by Hansen, July 30, 1999.

25 Ibid. In fact Elliott represented Multnomah County. Oregon Legislators and Staff Guide, 1973 regular session, http://arcweb.sos.state.or.us/pages/records/legislative/recordsguides/histleg/statehood/1973reg.html.

26 "Legislators Hold Ceremony on Equal Rights Amendment," *Eugene Register-Guard*, February 13, 1973. In the end the amendment fell three states short of the required three-fourths majority required for amending the US Constitution. Which states ratified the ERA and when did they ratify? About Women's History, http://womenshistory.about.com/od/equalrightsamendment/a/When-Did-States-Ratify-ERA.htm.

27 Photo caption in clip from unidentified newspaper, April 20, 1973. In the Norma Paulus Papers, UASC, Willamette University, Salem.

28 Interview by Hansen, October 5, 1999.

29 Ibid., July 30, 1999.

30 Ibid., July 1, 1999.

31 Mary Rieke and her husband, Dr. Forrest Rieke, died in a car accident in Costa Rica in January of 1978, a year after she retired from the legislature. They had traveled there to arrange student exchanges. "Mary Rieke lived her belief." Nancie Fadeley, writing in the *Eugene Register-Guard*, February 6, 1978, http://news.google.com/newspapers?nid=1310&dat=19780206&id=ha5VAAAAIBAJ&sjid=7uEDAAAAIBAJ&pg=2936,1503541.

32 The *Bend Bulletin* noted Priestley's death in September of 1990 with these words: "Wally Priestley's life was politics; the blood of his politics was liberal causes, the more liberal the better so far as he was concerned. He appeared not to care at all that most of his fellows looked upon many of his efforts as tilting at windmills." "Lively If Nothing Else," *Bend Bulletin*, September 16, http://news.google.com/newspapers?nid=1243&dat=19900916&id=clBYAA

AAIBAJ&sjid=wIYDAAAAIBAJ&pg=3890,2632147.

33 Rieke's helper was Representative Paul Walden from Hood River, the father of Greg Walden, currently US representative from Oregon's Second District. Fritz Paulus, personal communication.

34 Sylvia Porter, "Supreme Court's Decision Was Overdue," column, *Oregon Statesman*, April 9, 1975. The story doesn't mention Norma Paulus; it's reasonable to infer that she agreed with the writer.

35 Melinda S. Eden, "Rep. Paulus Says 1975 Legislature 'Conservative' on Women's Rights," AP, March 9, 1975.

36 Watford Reed, "'Women's Lib' Threatens Schools Over Demands," *Oregon Journal*, December 13, 1974.

37 Interview by Hansen, November 11, 1999.

38 Ibid.

39 Ibid., March 23, 2000.

40 Ibid., October 5, 1999.

41 Ibid., February 10, 2010.

42 Roberts, *With Grit and By Grace*.

43 Interview by Hansen, October 5, 1999.

44 Ibid., July 1, 1999.

45 Roberts, *With Grit and By Grace*.

46 "Oregon ERA Stand Reaffirmed," *Bend Bulletin*, February 16, 1977, https://news.google.com/newspapers?nid=1243&dat=19770216&id=YjBYAAAAIBAJ&sjid=7PYDAAAAIBAJ&pg=6809,4980876&hl=en.

47 Interview by Hansen, March 23, 2000.

48 "Women Told to Take Part in Politics," unidentified, undated clipping (but probably 1975) found in the Norma Paulus Papers, UASC, Willamette University, Salem.

49 "Paulus Says Proponents Need 'Mission' for ERA," *Register-Guard*, October 21, 1977, https://news.google.com/newspapers?nid=4pF9x-cDGsoC&dat=19771021&printsec=frontpage&hl=en.

CHAPTER 6:
SUNSHINE IN GOVERNMENT

Epigraph. Paul W. Harvey Jr., "They Say 'No Place for Me,'" AP, in unidentified newspaper,

April 21, 1971. In Norma Paulus Papers, UASC, Willamette University, Salem.

1 Finch had most recently served as California lieutenant governor under Ronald Reagan. A close friend of Nixon's, he had managed Nixon's 1960 presidential campaign, which Nixon lost to John F. Kennedy in a very close race. In 1968, Finch was Nixon's first choice for vice-presidential running mate. When Finch declined, Maryland governor Spiro Agnew was tapped. Nixon chose Finch as his secretary of Health, Education, and Welfare. In 1970 Finch become counselor to the president and was succeeded at HEW by Elliot Richardson, https://en.wikipedia.org/wiki/Robert_Finch_(American_politician).

2 Interview with Dave Frohnmayer, April 21, 2014.

3 Interview by Hansen, October 27, 1999.

4 Ibid., June 2, 1999, and October 5, 1999.

5 Interview with Dave Frohnmayer.

6 "Oregon Public Records Law," Ballotpedia, http://ballotpedia.org/Oregon_Public_Records_Law.

7 Interview with Dave Frohnmayer. The Oregon Attorney General's office (http://www.open-oregon.com/publications/httpwww-doj-state-or-uspublic_recordsmanualindex-shtml/) makes manuals and quick reference guides to the laws available to all citizens.

8 Open Oregon: A Freedom of Information Coalition, http://www.open-oregon.com/publications/guide-to-oregons-public-records-law/.

9 Interview with Dave Frohnmayer; interview by Hansen, March 23, 2000.

10 Common Cause, http://www.commoncause.org/states/oregon/issues/money-in-politics/campaign-finance-reform/campaign-finance-reform.html.

11 Don Jepsen, "Capitol Plan Unit Boosted," Oregon Journal, June 12, 1973. The Highway Department became a division of the new Oregon Department of Transportation in 1969. From "Oregon on the Move: A History of Oregon's Transportation Systems," Oregon Department of Transportation History Committee, p. 62, http://www.oregon.gov/ODOT/CS/bss/docs/oregononmove_final.pdf. The Highway Commission became the Oregon Transportation Commission in 1973; p. 69 of the same document.

12 Capitol Planning Commission organization and functions, http://www.oregon.gov/DAS/CFO/docs/CPC/CPC_History_1949to2003.pdf.

13 Capitol Planning Commission organization and functions, http://www.oregon.gov/DAS/CFO/docs/CPC/CPC_History_1949to2003.pdf.

14 Interview by Hansen, July 1, 1999.

15 Now part of PacificCorp, http://www.pacificorp.com/about/co.html.

16 Larry Roby, "Salem Legislators Seeking Power for Lawmakers," Capital Journal, October of 1974 (date not noted on clipping). In Norma Paulus Papers, UASC, Willamette University, Salem.

17 During the Jackson years, the Highway/Transportation oversaw construction of stretches of Oregon's interstate freeways, many state parks, and the Megler Bridge over the Columbia's mouth at Astoria. The Interstate 205 bridge over the Columbia, joining east Portland with east Vancouver, Washington, was the last big project undertaken during his tenure. Jackson died in 1980, before the bridge was completed. In December of 1982 the first traffic rolled over the new Glenn L. Jackson Bridge. From "'Mr. Oregon': Glenn L. Jackson," Oregon Stater (Winter 2014); also "Oregon on the Move," Oregon Department of Transportation History Committee, p. 143, http://www.oregon.gov/ODOT/CS/bss/docs/oregononmove_final.pdf. Document is undated but its timeline runs through 2008.

18 Interview by Hansen, July 1, 1999.

19 Jepsen, "Capitol Plan Unit Boosted."

20 Ibid. The Highway Commission became the Transportation Commission in 1973. "Oregon on the Move," Oregon Department of Transportation History Committee, p. 69, http://www.oregon.gov/ODOT/CS/bss/docs/oregononmove_final.pdf.

21 Interview by Hansen, July 1, 1999.

22 Ibid.

23 "Oregon on the Move," Oregon Department of Transportation History Committee, p. 43. A 1942 constitutional amendment established the trust fund, which is funded by road user fees and dedicated to the Highway Department, state police, and state parks.

24 "State's Gas Fund Said 'Sacred Cow,'" Oregon Statesman, February 12, 1971.

25 Interview by Hansen, July 1, 1999.

26 Charles E. Beggs, "Committee Approves State Buildings Bill," Oregon Statesman, May 16, 1973.

27 Ibid.

28 Jepsen, "Capitol Plan Unit Boosted."

29 "City Makes Development of Capitol Mall Easier," editorial, Oregon Statesman, June 29, 1973. The writer's use of "fractionating" indicates that McCallisms must have abounded in those days.

30 "Move Would Abolish E-Board, Oust Jackson as Agency Head," Oregon Statesman, December 11, 1974.

31 Larry Roby, "Salem Legislators Seeking Power for Lawmakers," Capital Journal, October 1974.

32 Ibid.

33 Larry Roby, "Paulus Calls for Legislative Power," Capital Journal, August 9, 1974. Story quotes some of Norma Paulus's remarks in a speech to the Salem Optimist Club.

34 Interview by Hansen, June 2, 1999.

35 Ed Grosswiler, "Rep. Paulus: Travel Ads 'Pander to Rich,'" Oregon Statesman, January 30, 1975.

36 "Paulus Sees Red; Assails the Sunset," unidentified newspaper, January 30, 1975, in Norma Paulus papers, UASC, Willamette University, Salem.

37 Ibid.

38 Roby, "Salem Legislators Seeking Power for Lawmakers."

39 Grosswiler, "Rep. Paulus: Travel Ads 'Pander to Rich.'"

40 Harvey, "They Say 'No Place for Me.'"

41 Letter from Norma Paulus to Senator Mark Hatfield, April 19, 1977. In Norma Paulus collection, OHS Research Library, Portland.

42 Vote by mail in Oregon, http://en.wikipedia.org/wiki/Vote-by-mail_in_Oregon.

43 John Painter Jr., "State Audit Finds Faulty Accounting," Oregonian, March 6, 1975.

44 Interview by Hansen, November 11, 1999.

45 Ibid., March 23, 2000.

46 Tom Detzel, "She's a Fighter for Her Causes Quite Naturally," Eugene Register-Guard, September 21, 1986.

47 "Norma Paulus May Run for State Office," Oregon Statesman, October 11, 1975.

48 Maurine Neuberger, US senator from 1960 to 1967, was the first woman from Oregon elected to fill a national office. She was elected to fill the term of her husband, Richard Neuberger, when he died in March of 1960, and was reelected in her own right in November of that year.

CHAPTER 7:
AN HISTORIC ELECTION

Epigraph. Norma Paulus, keynote speech, Conference for Women State Legislators. Conference for Women State Legislators: Report from a Conference June 17–20, 1982. Center for the American Woman and Politics, Eagleton Institute of Politics, Rutgers University, New Brunswick, NJ.

1 Interview by Hansen, October 2, 1999.

2 "Paulus Bids for Strong Legislature," January 23, 1976. Unattributed newspaper clipping reporting Norma Paulus's remarks to the Republican Women's Club in 197. The Norma Paulus Papers, UASC, Willamette University, Salem.

3 Steve Forrester, "Whipple, Paulus Tough It Out," Willamette Week, September 15, 1976.

4 Ralph Friedman, "No Whipple Chauvinism," Willamette Week, October 27, 1976.

5 Forrester, "Whipple, Paulus," September 15, 1976

6 Ibid.

7 Interview by Hansen, March 23, 2000.

8 Ibid.

9 Ibid., April 13, 2000.

10 Staff notes from the office of Oregon Secretary of State, December 2014.

11 "Ex-Oregon Archivist, Historian David Duniway Dies at Age 81," *Eugene Register-Guard*, September 16, 1993. The story comes from his daughter Malissa, and is retold on the Oregon State Archives website, http://arcweb.sos.state.or.us/pages/exhibits/50th/founder/duniwayobit.html.

12 Interview by Hansen, July 6, 2000.

13 Ibid., April 13, 2000.

14 Ibid., July 6, 2000.

15 Ibid., July 6, 2000.

16 Ibid.

17 Ibid.

18 Ibid. Staff notes from the office of Oregon Secretary of State, December 2014, state that Garten disposes of records, but retention is a major core of the program, and the potential storage capacity at the new building is 100,000 cubic feet, almost twice that of the old building on a much smaller footprint.

19 "Paulus Files for State Post," November 22, 1975, clipping from unidentified newspaper. In Norma Paulus Papers, 1953–2006, UASC, Willamette University, Salem.

20 One reviewer of this manuscript characterized the pioneers' wolf meetings as "an excuse to allow politically active residents to establish a preemptive government," and said that "Paulus probably accepted the mythic description of the 1840s meetings."

21 "Paulus Files for State Post."

22 Interview by Hansen, April 13, 2000.

23 deleted.

24 Ibid.

25 Ibid., April 13, 2000.

26 Ibid.; also Henny Willis, "Painting: Private Donations and Determination Result in Unveiling," *Eugene Register-Guard*, February 10, 1983.

27 Interview by Hansen, April 13, 2000; also "Paulus Appointed Chairman of Panel on Old Properties," *Eugene Register-Guard*, October 6, 1979.

28 Interview by Hansen, April 13, 2000. Proper name is the Lewis and Clark Centennial and American Pacific Exposition and Oriental Fair.

29 Ibid.

30 Ibid.

31 Ibid.; The Julius Meier portrait now hangs in the capitol building.

32 Ibid.; also "Painting: Private Donations and Determination Result in Unveiling."

33 Fred Crafts, "A Personal Portrait," *Eugene Register-Guard*, February 10, 1983.

34 Interview by Hansen, April 13, 2000.

35 Ibid.

36 Ibid.

37 Ibid.

38 Norma Paulus, ed. *Oregon Blue Book*, 1981–1982, p. 98.

CHAPTER 8:
KEEPING OREGON HONEST

Epigraph. Norma Paulus, Uniform Accounting System address, undated, Norma Paulus papers in Oregon State Archives.
(Endnotes)

1   John Marshall, "Reporter Finds Contacting Oregon's VIPs by Phone Not Always Easy Task," *Bend Bulletin*, November 11, 1977.

2   Ibid.

3   Interview by Hansen, March 23, 2000.

4   "Paulus Calls for Expanded Audits, Open Primary," *Eugene Register-Guard*, September 10, 1976.

5   "Veterans Fund Ruling Gives Legislature Another Money Problem," *Eugene Register-Guard*, November 19, 1970; also Cross of Malta Building Corporation v. Straub et al. 257 OR 376 (1971).

6   Interview by Hansen, June 2, 1999.

7   Ibid., March 23, 2000.

8   Ibid.

9   Interview by Hansen, March 23, 2000.

10 Ibid.

11 "Norma Paulus Due to Take Oath of Office," *Eugene Register-Guard*, December 21, 1976.

12 Norma gave this information to the Oregon Board of Forestry.

13 "Paulus Criticizes Timber Industry Stance," *Eugene Register-Guard*, April 27, 1979.

14 Interview by Hansen, July 6, 2000.

15 Ibid.

16 Ibid.

17 "Board Approves Guidelines for State Timber Sales," *The Forest Log* 49:3, Oregon Department of Forestry, October 1979.

18 Ibid.

19 "To Improve Operations, Timber Sale Procedures Reviewed," *The Forest Log* 49:4, Oregon Department of Forestry, November 1979.

20 "To Improve Operations, Timber Sale Procedures Reviewed."

21 Tom Detzel, "She's a Fighter for Her Causes Quite Naturally," *Eugene Register-Guard*, September 21, 1986.

22 "Audits Show Deficiencies in Two Agencies," *Eugene Register-Guard*, June 29, 1982.

23 Ibid.

24 Detzel, "She's a Fighter for Her Causes Quite Naturally."

25 Interview by Hansen, February 3, 2010; also interview with Del Riley, August 20, 2015.

26 Interview by Hansen, February 3, 2010.

27 Interview conducted by Russell Sadler (hereafter "interview by Sadler"), March 15, 2011.

28 Henny Willis, "Paulus Puts Stamp of Approval on Vote-By-Mail Idea," *Eugene Register-Guard*, June 6, 1981.

29 Ibid.

30 Interview by Sadler, March 15, 2011.

31 Henny Willis, "Paulus, Linn County Clerk Anxious for Vote-By-Mail Test," *Eugene Register-Guard*, October 2, 1981.

32 "Ballots Back Early in First Vote-By-Mail Election," *Eugene Register-Guard*, October 21, 1981.

33 "Paulus Lauds Vote-By-Mail," *Eugene Register-Guard*, December 22, 1981.

34 Ibid.

35 "Timeline: Oregon Vote by Mail," Oregon Secretary of State, sos.oregon.gov/elections/Pages/votebymail.aspx.

36 George Rede, "Oregon's Beacons of Achievement," *Oregonian*, January 30, 2010.

37 "Voter's Pamphlets Easier to Read, Bit More Artistic," *Eugene Register-Guard*, April 18, 1978.

38 Ibid.

39 Ibid.

40 Interview by Hansen, April 13, 2003.

41 Ibid.

42 Sally Bly, "Share Your Job with Someone You Love," *San Bernardino County Sun*, April 27, 1977.

43 Interview by Hansen, April 13, 2003.

44 Ibid.

45 Norma Paulus, letter to the editor, *Eugene Register-Guard*, October 20, 1980.

CHAPTER 9:
THE RAJNEESHEE AFFAIR

Epigraph. Norma Paulus, "First the Lawyers . . . ," *Oregon State Bar Bulletin*, January 1985.

1 Les Zaitz, "Rajneeshees in Oregon: The Untold Story," *Oregonian*, April 20, 2011, http://www.oregonlive.com/rajneesh/.

2 Win McCormack, *The Rajneesh Chronicles* (Portland: Tin House Books, 1987), p. 11.

3 "Rajneeshpuram," Oregon Public Broadcasting, November 19, 2012.

4 Carolyn Grote, "Few Know Antelope Like the Town's Mayor," *Bend Bulletin*, September 27, 1981.

5 Zaitz, "Rajneeshees in Oregon: The Untold Story." The Rajneeshees needed cattle in order to keep the ranch's BLM grazing permit.

6 Ibid.

7 "Rajneeshpuram."

8 Zaitz, "Rajneeshees in Oregon: The Untold Story."

9 McCormack, *Rajneesh Chronicles*, p. 14.

10 Zaitz, "Rajneeshees in Oregon: The Untold Story."

11 Ibid.

12 Ibid.

13 Ibid.

14 Frances FitzGerald, *Cities on a Hill: A Journey through Contemporary American Cultures*, (New York: Simon and Schuster, 1986), p. 251.

15 Zaitz, "Rajneeshees in Oregon: The Untold Story."

16 "Rajneeshpuram."

17 Transcript of meeting with Clifford Carlsen, Norma Paulus, Judge Edward Leavy, and Greg McMurdo, August 14, 1995 (hereafter "Transcript of meeting").

18 Transcript of meeting, August 14, 1995.

19 "A Town Votes to Remain One," *New York Times*, April 17, 1982.

20 "Guru's Disciples Taking Over in Oregon Town," *New York Times*, December 19, 1982.

21 FitzGerald, *Cities on a Hill*, p. 254.

22 Ibid., p. 259.

23 Ibid., p. 260.

24 Zaitz, "Rajneeshees in Oregon: The Untold Story."

25 "Rajneeshpuram."

26 FitzGerald, *Cities on a Hill*, p. 350.

27 "Anti-Rajneesh Group Plans Voting Blitz," *Spokane Spokesman-Review*, September 28, 1984.

28 Paulus, "First the Lawyers . . .".

29 Interview by Sadler, April 22, 2011.

30 Ibid., March 15, 2011.

31 Newspaper clipping, *Roseburg News-Review*, October 1, 1984. From unprocessed Rajneeshee box, 1983–85. Norma Paulus collection, OHS Research Library, Portland.

32 Unidentified newspaper clipping, September 25, 1984. From unprocessed Rajneeshee box, 1983–85. Norma Paulus collection, OHS Research Library, Portland.

33 Newspaper clipping, *Eugene Register-Guard*, October 5, 1984. From unprocessed Rajneeshee box, 1983–85. Norma Paulus collection, OHS Research Library, Portland.

34 Bill Graves, "State Officials Sent Bizarre 'Gifts,'" *Bend Bulletin*, undated clipping found in Norma Paulus collection, OHS Research Library, Portland.

35 Paulus, "First the Lawyers . . . ."

36 Interview by Sadler, April 22, 2011.

37 Ibid., December 19, 2011.

38 Ibid., April 8, 2011. In interview by Hansen, October 5, 1999, Norma says she tracked Carlsen down with Chandler at Camp Sherman two days after she met him on the street.

39 Transcript of meeting, August 14, 1995.

40 Clipping from unidentified newspaper, October 10, 1984. In unprocessed Rajneeshee box, 1983–85, Norma Paulus collection, OHS Research Library, Portland.

41 "State Tries to Prevent Vote Fraud," *Eugene Register-Guard*, October 11, 1984. As reported in the commune's weekly newspaper, the *Rajneesh Times*, Sheela repeated Norma's prohibition against her attendance at an assembly. Blaming her exclusion on Norma's obvious fear of her "truth-telling," Sheela asked followers if they wanted her to go and represent them to the secretary of state, in an act analogous to "the story of Jesus whipping the corrupt money changers from the temple with a single whip." In response, "the entire assembly of thousands unanimously jumped to their feet, raising their arms in the air." After confirming their wish that Sheela carry to the press conference Bhagwan's teaching that his followers respect everyone, especially the "new residents whose right as Americans to vote was the cause celebrated" by Share-A-Home, the assembly "burst into song and dance to celebrate the death of Oregon and the vibrant life of the City of Rajneeshpuram." "Rajneeshees and Their New Friends Celebrate the Death of Oregon," *Rajneesh Times*, October 12, 1984.

42 Transcript of meeting, August 14, 1995.

43 McCormack, *Rajneesh Chronicles*, p. 12.

44 Interview by Sadler, March 3, 2011.

45 In 2011, Judge Leavy spoke of his conviction that Norma's testimony itself eloquently turned the hearing in her favor "I've said repeatedly that I wished everyone in Oregon could have heard that testimony," Judge Leavy said. "It was an even-handed response to a threat from both sides, at the threats coming from the Albany group as well as the legitimate suspicion of what was going on in Wasco County." It was "one of those cases where it turned out that everything that was suspected of [the Rajneeshees] was the truth." Norma Paulus interview by Sadler, March 3, 2011; also Edward Leavy: An Oral History. Oral History Project, US District Court of Oregon Historical Society, 2013, p. 137.

46 Maynard F. Jensen, "State Should Retain Same-Day Sign-Up Despite Fraud Potential," *Hillsboro Argus*, December 4, 1984.

47 Interview by Sadler, April 8, 2011.

48 Transcript of meeting, August 14, 1995.

49 Paulus, "First the Lawyers . . ."

50 Ibid.

51 Perle Mesta, an American socialite, political hostess, and US ambassador to Luxembourg (1949–1953). She was known as the political "hostess with the mostest," noted for her lavish bipartisan DC soirees up through the Truman years.

52 Transcript of meeting, August 14, 1995.

53 Jensen, "State Should Retain Same-Day Sign-Up Despite Fraud Potential."

54 Affidavit of Defendant Norma Paulus in the US Court of Appeals for the Ninth Circuit, October 29, 1984.

55 Jeanie Senior, "Rajneeshees Boycott Voter Hearings," *Oregonian*, November 1, 1984.

56 Paulus, "First the Lawyers . . ."

57 McCormack, *Rajneesh Chronicles*, p. 14.

58 Transcript of meeting, Aug. 14, 1995.

59 Oregon Attorney General Dave Frohnmayer prosecuted several members of the Rajneesh organization for their crimes. Seven of the cases went all the way to the US Supreme Court, and Frohnmayer prevailed in six of them.

CHAPTER 10: HEARTBREAK AND CONSOLATION PRIZE

Epigraph. "Norma Paulus for Governor," campaign newsletter, vol. 1, no. 1, December 1985. In Norma Paulus files at Willamette University Archives.

1 From "Adieu to Norma, Grattan and Gus," editorial, *Eugene Register-Guard*, January 6, 1985.

2 "Don't Call It Retirement," editorial, *Statesman-Journal*, January 9, 1985.

3 H. Clay Myers Jr., http://en.wikipedia. org/wiki/H._Clay_Myers,_Jr.

4 Charles E. Beggs, "Norma Paulus: She Wants to Be Governor," AP, in *Bend Bulletin*, September 26, 1977.

5 Interview by Hansen, June 2, 1999.

6 http://en.wikipedia.org/wiki/ Barbara_Boxer.

7 David S. Broder, "Oregon Rich in Able Women," column, *Oregonian*, February 20, 1985.

8 Interview by Hansen, July 30, 1999; also "Norma Paulus to Join Portland Lions Club," October 6, 1981, https://news. google.com/newspapers?nid=1310&dat =19811006&id=crRQAAAAIBAJ&sjid =VOIDAAAAIBAJ&pg=6789,1463689 %5C&hl=en.

9 Foster Church, "Atiyeh's Anger May Carry Him into Paulus Campaign," *Oregonian*, March 23, 1986.

10 Interview by Hansen, July 6, 2000.

11 From Wikipedia, http://en.wikipedia. org/wiki/David_B._Frohnmayer, and he confirmed it in our interview.

12 "Likely Governor Rivals Plan, Prepare but Withhold Promises," *Oregonian*, March 14, 1985.

13 "If I Were Governor . . ." Notes for speech given by Frohnmayer on February 14, 1986, to the Portland City Club, in Norma Paulus files at Willamette University Archives. Its cover note contains a warm greeting to Norma Paulus. In an interview of April 21, 2014, Frohnmayer remembered making this statement after the primary.

14 "Likely Governor Rivals Plan."

15 Interview by Hansen, July 6, 2000.

16 Ibid. Quote is from Tom Detzel, "GOP Top Runners Jockey for Position," *Register-Guard,* March 27, 1985.

17 Planning materials for the October 28 announcement rally show committees for flowers, decorations, food, and hiring the hangar, plus a small army of telephoners. In Norma Paulus Papers, UASC, Willamette University, Salem.

18 A tearsheet of a campaign ad, in Norma Paulus Papers, UASC, Willamette University, Salem.

19 "Norma Paulus for Governor." In Norma Paulus Papers, UASC, Willamette University, Salem.

20 Ben Winton, "Paulus Says School Financing Top Priority," *Daily Astorian*, February 21, 1986.

21 From a profile of Bhagwan in Oregon History Project, on OHS website, http://www.ohs.org/the-oregon-history-project/biographies/Bhagwan-Shree-Rajneesh.cfm.

22 Bhagwan was returned to Portland and charged with immigration fraud. He

agreed to a plea bargain that called for his deportation. After being denied entry to several other countries, he returned to India, where he died in 1990.

23 Neil Goldschmidt, http://en.wikipedia.org/wiki/Neil_Goldschmidt.

24 "Don't Call It Retirement."

25 "Poll Picks Paulus in Governor Race," article in *Oregon Republican* newsletter reporting results from a statewide poll in early December. From Norma Paulus collection, OHS Research Library, Portland.

26 Foster Church, "Fadeley Has Power to Wreak Worst Kind of Havoc," *Oregonian*, February 9, 1986.

27 Tom Wicker, "The Two Oregons," *New York Times*, January 20, 1986.

28 "Fadeley's Attitude Wrong for Candidate," *Corvallis Gazette-Times*, February 26, 1986.

29 Interviews by Hansen, June 2, 1999, and July 6, 2000. Later, when he was on the Oregon Supreme Court, Fadeley was charged with sexual harassment by a former secretary. "Oregon High Court Justice Faces Sex Harassment Claim," AP, in the *Eugene Register-Guard*, November 30, 1995, http://news.google.com/newspapers?nid=1310&dat=19951130&id=ckhWAAAAIBAJ&sjid=LusDAAAAIBAJ&pg=1987,7099709.

30 Inferred from undated three-page position paper found among Norma Paulus campaign materials at Willamette University Archives. It begins "As Oregonians Look to the Future" and refers to Norma in the third person.

31 "Oregon Agriculture: Cultivating a More Prosperous Future." Agriculture policy statement delivered December 6, 1985.

32 Background on the Philippines election taken from "A Test for Democracy," *Time*, February 3, 1986. Also from Encyclopaedia Brittanica online, http://www.britannica.com/EBchecked/topic/364302/Ferdinand-E-Marcos.

33 "Manila Bound," *Register-Guard*, February 16, 1986.

34 Ibid.

35 "Witnessing Philippine Election: Paulus Calls Experience Unique," *Eugene Register-Guard*, undated clip in Norma

Paulus collection at OHS Research Library, Portland.

36 "Paulus Pleads Filipinos' Case," *Statesman-Journal*, February 15, 1986.

37 Ferdinand Marcos, Encyclopaedia Brittanica, http://www.britannica.com/EBchecked/topic/364302/Ferdinand-E-Marcos.

38 Corazon Aquino, Encyclopaedia Brittanica, http://www.britannica.com/EBchecked/topic/31280/Corazon-Aquino.

39 "Paulus Pleads Filipinos' Case."

40 Interview by Hansen, July 6, 2000.

41 Interview with Gretchen Kafoury, December 1, 2013.

42 Andy Dworkin, "Gratitude Opens Doors Her Rare Disease Can Close," *Oregonian*, September 26, 2005, http://henrystrongingoldberg.blogspot.com/2005/09/gratitude-opens-doors-her-rare-disease.html. Also David B. Frohnmayer, http://en.wikipedia.org/wiki/David_B._Frohnmayer. Frohnmayer ran again in 1980 and won the Republican nomination. The election was a three-way race with a conservative independent candidate, Al Mobley, also on the ticket. Democrat Barbara Roberts won the election and became the state's first woman governor. Frohnmayer continued as attorney general until 1991, and then went on to become the dean of the University of Oregon school of law and later the university's president. He died on March 10, 2015.

43 Ron Blankenbaker, "Collector Finds a Few More Political Strings," *Statesman-Journal*, January 28, 1986.

44 Ron Blankenbaker, "Paulus Plays It Like the Top Politico She Is," *Statesman-Journal*, January 6, 1985.

45 "Paulus: Promote Northwest," *Eugene Register-Guard*, March 5, 1986.

46 Interview by Hansen, November 2, 2000.

47 Foster Church, "Goldschmidt's Waffling Perplexes Supporters," *Oregonian*, March 2, 1986.

48 Foster Church, "Paulus, Goldschmidt Differ on Strategies," *Oregonian*, April 7, 1986.

49 Foster Church, "Land-Use Board Hit by Fadeley," *Oregonian*, February 12, 1986.

50 Foster Church, "Fadeley Has Power to Wreak Worst Kind of Havoc," *Oregonian*, February 9, 1986.

51 "Paulus Shuns Gubernatorial Debate," *Statesman-Journal*, March 22, 1986.

52 Ibid.

53 Foster Church, "Refusal by Paulus to Debate Hampers Image of Gutsiness," *Oregonian*, March 25, 1986.

54 Ron Blankenbaker, "Paulus Debate Pullout: All Politicians Break Promises," commentary, *Statesman-Journal*, March 23, 1986. Also "Gubernatorial Debate: Paulus Reneges on a Deal," editorial, *Statesman-Journal,* March 26, 1986.

55 "Debates Now Premature," editorial, *Albany Democrat-Herald*, March 25, 1986.

56 *Oregonian*, March 31, 1986. Copy of cartoon is in OHS files.

57 Interview by Hansen, July 6, 2000.

58 Ibid.

59 Ibid.

60 Interview by Hansen, November 11, 1999.

61 Schwabe Williamson & Wyatt, http://www.schwabe.com/about.aspx.

62 "Likely Governor Rivals Plan, Prepare but Withhold Promises."

63 *Reserve Magazine*, U.S. Bank, http://reservemagazine.usbank.com/wealth-transfer/creating-legacy-caring.

64 Fritz Paulus, personal communication.

65 Interview by Hansen, November 11, 1999, and July 6, 2000.

66 Fritz Paulus and Liz Paulus, personal communication.

67 deleted.

68 Wicker, "The Two Oregons."

69 Detzel, "Goldschmidt, Paulus Still Debate over Debates." Also Rick Attig, "Governor Tries Patching Ties in 'Middle of Nowhere,'" *Bend Bulletin*, January 9, 1990 (looking back at the incident from four years later), http://news.google.com/newspapers?nid=1243&dat=19900109&id=LlUPAA AAIBAJ&sjid=eIYDAAAAIBAJ&pg=2577,2540570.

70 H. Bruce Miller, "If Bend Is 'Middle of Nowhere,' Is Oregon Nowhere?" *Bend Bulletin*, August 11, 1986.

71 Detzel, "Goldschmidt, Paulus Still Debate over Debates."

72 Tom Townslee, "Paulus, Goldschmidt Pulling No Punches," UPI, *Bend Bulletin*, October 26, 1986.

73 Ibid.

74 Attig, "Governor Tries Patching Ties."

75 Townslee, "Paulus, Goldschmidt Pulling No Punches."

76 Ron Blankenbaker, "Who's Leading in the Polls," *Statesman-Journal*, April 15, 1986.

77 Wallace Turner, "Nominees for Oregon Governor in Close Race," *New York Times*, October 19, 1986.

78 Oregon Encyclopedia, Neil Goldschmidt, Oregon Historical Society, http://www.oregonencyclopedia.org/articles/goldschmidt_neil/#.Ve3294vXlpk.

79 Church, "Atiyeh's Anger May Carry Him into Paulus Campaign." Also "Goldschmidt Renews Harsh Attack on Top Figures in State Government," *Oregonian Political Notebook*, commentary, April 19, 1986.

80 Church, "Atiyeh's Anger May Carry Him into Paulus Campaign." Atiyeh made his remarks in a speech to Associated General Contractors on March 18.

81 Ibid.

82 Townslee, "Paulus, Goldschmidt Pulling No Punches."

83 Church, "Atiyeh's Anger May Carry Him into Paulus Campaign."

84 Dana Tims, "Paulus Criticizes Lawmakers' Inertia," *Oregonian*. Undated clipping in Norma Paulus collection at OHS Research Library. Norma Paulus is speaking at an Oregon Community College Association convention at Eugene Hilton.

85 Interview by Hansen, July 6, 2000.

86 Ibid. Liz Paulus remembers that her mother made the remark in an interview with Foster Church. Liz Paulus, personal communication.

87 Interview by Hansen, July 6, 2000.

88 James F. Clarity and Warren Weaver Jr., "Briefing: Two for the Tea Leaves," *New*

York Times, October 6, 1985, http://
www.nytimes.com/1985/10/06/us/
briefing-two-for-the-tea-leaves.html.

89 Fritz Paulus, personal communication.
This is Fritz's interpretation.

90 Here is what Norma said: "My staff
knew quite a bit about it, . . . and I had
personally at least five people come up
and tell me about affairs that he was
having with other women, or had had."
Interview by Hansen, July 6, 2000.

91 Fritz Paulus, personal communication.

92 Campaign field team list, from Norma
Paulus files, UASC, Willamette
University, Salem.

93 Interview by Hansen, July 6, 2000; also
"Paulus Replaces Campaign Manager,"
Oregonian, February 26, 1986.

94 Interview by Hansen, November 2,
2000.

95 Fritz Paulus, personal communication.

96 Interview by Hansen, November 2,
2000.

97 Ibid., July 6, 2000.

98 Townslee, "Paulus, Goldschmidt Pulling
No Punches." Townslee writes that
spending in the total six weeks before
election day was a combined $3.2 mil-
lion. In her November 2, 2000, interview
with Clark Hansen of OHS, Norma said,
"I raised 2-point-something million
and he raised about a million more."
The total would come to something
over $5 million, but that number is not
confirmed.

99 "Goldschmidt Stands Out," *Statesman-
Journal*, editorial, October 12, 1986.

100 Fritz Paulus, personal communication.

101 Liz Paulus, personal communication.

102 Cheryl Sullivan, "Women Making
Their Mark in Many 1984 Elections. In
Oregon, Used to Women Officeholders,
Gender May Even Help a Proven
Woman Hopeful," *Christian Science
Monitor*, October 17, 1986.

103 Interview by Hansen, November 2,
2000.

104 Ibid.

105 Steven Carter, "Paulus Bows Out as
1999 Begins," *Oregonian*, January 2,
1999. Vote count from 1987-1988
Oregon Blue Book.

106 Interview by Hansen, November 2,
2000.

107 History of the Oregon judicial department, http://www.oregon.gov/SOLL/
pages/ojd_history/historyojdpart2toc.
aspx.

108 Northwest Power & Conservation
Council mission and strategy, http://
www.nwcouncil.org/about/mission/.

109 Kurt Schillinger, "Over the River
and through the Dam," special to the
Christian Science Monitor, December
29, 1988, http://www.csmonitor.
com/1988/1229/afish.html. Also
Center for Columbia River History,
http://www.ccrh.org/river/history.php.

110 Center for Columbia River History.

111 Robert B. Duncan, http://en.wikipedia.
org/wiki/Robert_B._Duncan.

112 Interview with Peter Paquet, January 21,
2015.

113 Interview by Hansen, November 2,
2000.

114 Schillinger, "Over the River and through
the Dam."

115 Ibid.

116 Ibid.

117 Paraphrased from Schillinger, "Over the
River" and inferred from Norma's oral
history comments.

118 Interview with Bill Bakke, June 18, 2014.

119 According to Bonneville Power
Administration, the Corps of Engineers
continues to barge around some dams,
but are also installing screens, https://
www.bpa.gov/Power/pl/columbia/
stories/magnificent3.htm, e.g.: "To help
salmon along, more screens and better
bypass systems are being installed at the
dams. From April to June, when smolts
need faster flows, extra water is released
from reservoirs upstream. People who
would otherwise want to save that
water—to irrigate farms, float barges and
generate power—have to adjust." This
is part of their undated "For kids of all
ages" site (home page is https://www.
bpa.gov/Power/pl/columbia/page5.
htm).

120 Northwest Power & Conservation
Council, http://www.nwcouncil.org/
about/mission/. The fourth bullet
listed under Fish and Wildlife reads,

"Continue the work to reform artificial production practices so that they are effective in improving production above Bonneville Dam while protecting, and benefitting where possible, naturally spawning populations."

The proper role of hatcheries in salmon recovery is a long-standing debate. Modern-day Pacific salmon species have survived in the wild for about two million years, evolving and adapting to wide swings in environmental and climatic conditions. Hatcheries, developed in the last hundred years, produce fish that are genetically less diverse and probably less resilient than wild fish. Hatchery fish compete with the remnant wild fish for food and other resources, and hatchery populations may pose other risks to wild salmon. Hatcheries are also expensive, although they do provide a reliable supply of salmon for commercial and sport fishing and tribal subsistence fishing. Environmentalists and many scientists caution that hatcheries are not a viable substitute for recovering wild salmon stocks.

121 Interview by Hansen, November 2, 2000.

122 Ibid.

123 Ibid.

124 It may be worth mentioning that Gordon Smith, whose family owned Smith Frozen Foods in Weston, Oregon (http://en.wikipedia.org/wiki/Gordon_H._Smith), was probably the veiled target of Norma's dismissive remarks about "pea farmers" who opposed keeping water in the river to protect migrating smolts. Smith had beaten Norma in the 1995 Republican special primary held to replace Bob Packwood, who had resigned his Senate seat after being accused of sexual misconduct.

125 Interview by Hansen, November 2, 2000.

126 Interview by Hansen, February 10, 2010.

CHAPTER 11:
OREGON'S CHIEF EDUCATOR

Epigraph. Interview by Hansen, February 10, 2010.

1 The Northwest Power Planning Council became the Northwest Power and Conservation Council in 2003.

2 "Paulus Maintains a Low Profile," *Eugene Register-Guard,* January 12, 1988.

3 Ibid.

4 Interview by Hansen, February 10, 2010.

5 Ibid., February 24, 2010.

6 Ibid.

7 Jeff Wright, "Paulus Vows to Ease Woes of Education," *Eugene Register-Guard,* October 10, 1989.

8 Rick Attig, "Paulus Trying to Recruit an Education 'Army,'" *Bend Bulletin,* April 8, 1990.

9 Ibid.

10 Norma Paulus, "Oregon Must Reform School Financing," *Eugene Register-Guard,* September 12, 1990.

11 Interview by Hansen, February 10, 2010.

12 "Paulus Can Help," *Eugene Register-Guard,* September 6, 1990.

13 Ibid.

14 Letters, *Eugene Register-Guard,* September 9, 1990.

15 Paulus, "Oregon Must Reform School Financing."

16 Ibid.

17 Ibid.

18 Bill Graves, "Paulus to Open Office, No Matter Who Governor Picks," *Oregonian,* September 17, 1990.

19 "John Erickson's Departure: Paulus Should Seize the Day," *Statesman Journal,* September 30, 1990.

20 Ibid.

21 "Paulus Gets Head Start as Schools Chief," *Eugene Register-Guard,* September 29, 1990.

22 Interview by Hansen, February 10, 2010.

23 "Paulus Gets Head Start as Schools Chief."

24 From "A Brief History of Oregon Property Taxation," Oregon Department of Revenue, http://www.oregon.

gov/dor/STATS/docs/303-405-1. pdf (9/7/15); also Wikipedia, http://en.wikipedia.org/wiki/Oregon_Ballot_Measure_5_(1990); also "Ballot Measure 5 Turns 20," OPB Think Out Loud, November 8, 2010, http://www.opb.org/radio/programs/thinkoutloud/segment/ballot-measure-5-turns-20/.

25 Interview by Hansen, February 10, 2010.

26 Russell Sadler draft, p. 90; also interview by Hansen, February 10, 2010.

27 Russell Sadler draft, p. 91.

28 Brent Walth, "Gridlock in Legislature Leaves Lawmakers Glum," Eugene Register-Guard, April 26, 1993.

29 Ibid.

30 "Oregon House Bill Makes Deep Cuts in State School Aid," Seattle Times, April 1, 1993.

31 "Schools Need Sales Tax, Roberts Says," Eugene Register Guard, November 14, 1992.

32 Oregon Department of Education, Milestones in Oregon School Improvement, http://www.ode.state.or.us/search/page/?id=2012. Anne Bridgman, "Oregon Board to Vote on Action Plan for Excellence," June 6, 1984, published online at Education Week, http://www.edweek.org/ew/articles/1984/06/06/05490028.h03.html.

33 Joyce Reinke, The Oregon Trail to School Reform (Oregon Department of Education, Publications and Multimedia Center, 1993). This was a pamphlet produced for the 1993-1994 National State Board of Education Annual Conference.

34 Two other notable reports were "A Nation at Risk: The Imperative for Education Reform," by the National Commission on Excellence in Education (1983); and "Workplace Basics: The Skills Employers Want," by the US Department of Labor (1983).

35 National Center on Education and the Economy, abstract from "America's Choice: High Skills or Low Wages! The Report of the Commission on the Skills of the American Workforce" (Rochester,

NY: National Center on Education and the Economy, 1990).

36 Interview by Hansen, February 24, 2010.

37 Interview by Sadler, December 17, 2010.

38 Interview by Hansen, February 10, 2010.

39 Ibid.

40 Interview by Sadler, December 17, 2010.

41 Interview by Hansen, February 24, 2010.

42 Ibid.

43 "Oregon Students on Slide to Mediocrity, Survey Says," Seattle Times, January 20, 1992.

44 Ibid.

45 Interview with Larry Austin, February 1, 2015.

46 Interview by Hansen, February 24, 2010.

47 William Celis III, "Oregon to Stress Job Training in Restructuring High School," New York Times, July 24, 1991.

48 Stuart Wasserman, "Nation Will Be Watching Oregon's 'Pioneering Step': Under New Program, High School Ends at 10th Grade, Followed by Two Years of Specialized Training. It Could Become Model for Future," Los Angeles Times, October 17, 1991.

49 Wasserman, "Nation Will Be Watching Oregon's 'Pioneering Step.'"

50 "Paulus Defends Role in Oregon's New Law on Educational Reform," Seattle Times, March 7, 1994.

51 Tad Shannon, "Ex-Lawmaker's Book Attacks School Reform," Eugene Register-Guard, November 28, 1994.

52 Ibid.

53 Ibid.

54 Ibid.

55 Ibid.

56 "Paulus Defends Role in Oregon's New Law on Educational Reform."

57 Wasserman, "Nation Will Be Watching Oregon's 'Pioneering Step.'"

58 William Celis III, "Profile: A Firm Hand in the Schools," New York Times, January 8, 1995.

59 Ibid.

60 Interview by Hansen, February 24, 2010.

61 Gail Kinsey Hill, "Paulus Demonstrates Calm Determination in Bid for the Senate," *Oregonian*, November 6, 1996.

62 Ibid.

63 "Character Is Key in Ore. Election: Nation Watching Vote to Replace Packwood," editorial, *Seattle Times*, November 12, 1995.

64 "Character Is Key in Ore. Election."

65 "Oregon Mail Primary Sets Up Senate Race," *New York Times*, December 6, 1995. About 1.5 million ballots were cast. The election cost $1.6 to $1.8 million, about half what a regular, polling-place election would have cost.

66 Hill, "Paulus Demonstrates Calm Determination in Bid for the Senate."

67 Courtney Walker, "Paulus Warns of High-Tech Work Force Woes in Schools," *Portland Business Journal*, October 26, 1997.

68 Interview by Hansen, February 24, 2010.

69 Ibid.

70 Full text of speech at http://www.educationworld.com/a_admin/admin/admin052.shtml.

71 "Ore. Teachers' Union Refuses to Endorse State Schools Leader," *Seattle Times*, April 11, 1994.

72 Brad Cain, "Oregon's Ballyhooed Education Act Faces Challenges," AP News Archive, January 23, 1993.

73 Paulus was not the first superintendent who was not an educator. The very first to hold the office, Sylvester C. Simpson (1872–1874), was, like Paulus, a lawyer. All superintendents since Simpson have been trained educators until Norma took over. The superintendents who followed her, Stan Bunn (1999–2003) and Susan Castillo (2003–2012), were also not professional educators. In 2012 the position was eliminated as an elected office.

74 Celis, "Profile: A Firm Hand in the Schools."

75 Ibid.

76 Interview with George Passadore, February 6, 2015.

77 Interview by Hansen, February 24, 2010.

78 R. W. Riley, personal communication, December 16, 1998. Norma served at Secretary Riley's request on the National Assessment Governing Board until September 30, 1999.

79 The Certificates of Initial Mastery (tenth grade) and Advanced Mastery (twelfth grade) were phased out in July of 2008. These were probably the most divisive elements of HB 3565. School report cards and student assessment testing remain in place.

80 Russell Sadler draft, pp. 93–95.

CHAPTER 12: A LEGACY OF SERVICE

Epigraph. Advertisement in the *New York Times*, August 30, 2004, signed by seventeen Republican leaders including Norma Paulus and paid for by an organization called Mainstream 2004. At the bottom of a copy in Norma's files is the notation "Larry Rockefeller Jr. called and asked me to do this," in Norma's handwriting.

1 "Paulus Leaves Lasting Legacy," *Statesman-Journal*, January 2, 1999.

2 Dick Hughes, "Oregon Schools Need to be Kept on Track," editorial, *Statesman-Journal*. Undated clip in Norma Paulus file, UASC, Willamette University, Salem, written about the time Stan Bunn took over as superintendent.

3 Steve Law, "Bill Paulus Faces Cancer Challenge with Grit, Humor," *Statesman-Journal*, October 3, 1998.

4 Ibid.

5 Sponsored by the Milken Foundation. Interview by Hansen, February 3, 2010.

6 Castillo would go on to serve as superintendent of public instruction from 2003 to 2012. Susan Castillo, http://en.wikipedia.org/wiki/Susan_Castillo.

7 Interview by Hansen, February 3, 2010.

8 Law, "Bill Paulus Faces Cancer Challenge."

9 "Norma Paulus," *Portland Business Journal*, March 16, 2001.

10 Interview with Fritz Paulus and Jennifer Viviano, May 1, 2014.

11 Interview by Hansen, November 2, 2000.

12 Law, "Bill Paulus Faces Cancer Challenge."

13 This story, the Whistle-Off Competition, and the caboose account from Fritz Paulus and Jennifer Viviano interview.

14 Interview by Hansen, February 3, 2010.

15 Ibid.

16 "Paulus Praised by Legal Peers," *Statesman-Journal*, February 15, 1999.

17 Norma Paulus, https://en.wikipedia.org/wiki/Norma_Paulus.

18 Interview with Chet Orloff, June 23, 2014.

19 Interview by Hansen, July 6, 2000.

20 Letter from Norma Paulus to David C. Duniway, February 28, 1975, sending a copy of HB 2475, which would give a special tax treatment to people who wish to restore historic homes. Norma Paulus Papers, UASC, Willamette University, Salem.

21 Yuxing Zheng, "Thomas Vaughan, Longtime Director of OHS, Dies at 89," *Oregonian*, December 7, 2013, http://www.oregonlive.com/portland/index.ssf/2013/12/thomas_vaughan_longtime_direct.html.

22 Interview by Hansen, July 6, 2000.

23 "Oregon My Oregon," Oregon Historical Society, http://www.ohs.org/exhibits/current/oregon-my-oregon.cfm.

24 From Salem Online History, compiled by Virginia Green, http://www.salemhistory.net/people/norma_paulus.htm.

25 "OBA's 2005 Honorees: Secretary of State Norma Paulus & Governor Barbara Roberts," Oregon Business Association, October 21, 2011, http://www.youtube.com/watch?v=1ZEs1Qv5VdU.

26 Kathy Aney, "Bronze McCall Stops in Town," *East Oregonian*, September 23, 2008; also Willie Bans, "Honoring a Governor's Legacy," *Statesman-Journal*, June 29, 2007.

27 "Historical Society Names Four History Maker's Medal Winners," *Oregonian*, September 10, 2012, http://www.oregonlive.com/portland/index.ssf/2012/09/historical_society_names_four.html.

28 Peter Wong, "Women for Merkley Include One GOP Name," *Portland Tribune*, June 3, 2014, http://portlandtribune.com/

pt/9-news/222994-84615-women-for-merkley-include-one-gop-name.

29 Interview with Dave Frohnmayer, April 21, 2014.

30 Gail Kinsey Hill, "Norma Paulus: A Profile," *Oregonian*, November 6, 1995.

31 Interview with Dave Frohnmayer.

32 Interview with Gretchen Kafoury, December 1, 2013.

33 Larry Roby, "Paulus Calls for Legislative Power," *Capital Journal*, August 9, 1974.

34 Interview by Hansen, February 24, 2010.

35 Craig Beebe, "Daring Mighty Things: Recapping an Evening with Three Land Use Legends"; "The Latest" (*1000 Friends of Oregon* blog), undated but referring to the first event in 1000 Friends's McCall Society Speaker Series, January 10, 2013, http://www.friends.org/latest/daring-mighty-things-recapping-evening-three-land-use-legends.

36 Andrew Glass, "Congress Runs into 'Republican Revolution,' November 8, 1994"; *Politico*, November 8, 2007, http://www.politico.com/news/stories/1107/6757.html.

37 Dan Postrel, "Paulus Supporters Struggle with Voting Choices," *Statesman-Journal*, January 17, 1996.

38 Hill, "Norma Paulus: A Profile." Gordon Smith lost narrowly to Democrat Ron Wyden in the special general election, held in January of 1996, but beat Republican businessman Tom Bruggere in the regularly scheduled 1996 election to fill the seat vacated by Republican Senator Mark Hatfield, who was retiring after thirty years. Gordon Smith served alongside Wyden until 2009; he was defeated in 2008 by Democrat Jeff Merkley. http://en.wikipedia.org/wiki/United_States_Senate_special_election_in_Oregon,_1996; and http://en.wikipedia.org/wiki/United_States_Senate_election_in_Oregon,_1996.

39 Inferred from Steven Carter, "Paulus Bows Out as 1999 Begins," *Oregonian*, January 2, 1999.

40 Ibid.

41 Interview by Hansen, February 24, 2010.

42 Interview with Bill Bakke, June 18, 2014.

43 Interview with Dave Frohnmayer.

44 James Sinks, "Paulus Never Hid from Fight," *Bend Bulletin*, December 29, 1998.

45 Can't remember where I got this, but I know she said it.

46 Interview by Hansen, November 2, 2000.

47 Ibid., July 1, 1999.

48 Hill, "Norma Paulus: A Profile."

49 George Rede, "Re-Booting Democracy in Oregon," *Oregonian*, June 4, 2008, http://blog.oregonlive.com/oregonianopinion/2008/06/reboot-ing_democracy_in_oregon.html.

50 *Corvallis Gazette-Times*, editorial, July 7, 2014.

51 Election results, November 2014 on OregonLive, http://gov.oregonlive.com/election/.

52 "Paulus Bows Out," *Oregonian*, January 2, 1999.

53 Ibid.

54 Hill, "Norma Paulus: A Profile."

55 Interview by Hansen, April 19, 1999; also interview with Liz Paulus, Fritz Paulus, and Jennifer Viviano.

56 Interview by Sadler, November 30, 2011.

57 "Paulus Bows Out."

58 Interview with Chet Orloff.

59 Sinks, "Paulus Never Hid from Fight."

60 Jewish Virtual Library, http://www.jewishvirtuallibrary.org/jsource/biography/Dayan.html.

61 Interview by Hansen, February 24, 2010.

62 Ibid.

63 Henry Richmond, McCall Legacy Award speech, given in honor of awardee Peter McDonald, March 1, 2013. Copy in possession of the authors.

64 Kanhaiya L. Vaidya, "Oregon Demographic Trends," Department of Administrative Services, 2012, http://www.oregon.gov/DAS/OEA/docs/demographic/OR_pop_trend2012.pdf.

65 Oregon Office of Economic Analysis Demographic Forecast, http://www.oregon.gov/DAS/oea/Pages/demo-graphic.aspx.

66 Vaidya, "Oregon Demographic Trends."

67 Expression appears in subhead of Brent Walth, *Fire at Eden's Gate: Tom McCall and the Oregon Story* (Corvallis: Oregon State University Press, 1994). Also appears on p. 289 in Charles K. Johnson, *Standing at the Water's Edge*, and Bob Straub's *Battle for the Soul of Oregon* (Corvallis: Oregon State University Press, 2012).

68 National Park Service, http://www.nps.gov/olym/naturescience/elwha-ecosystem-restoration.htm.

69 Inferred from interview with Bill Bakke, and NPCC website, http://www.nwcouncil.org/about/mission/.

70 Johnson, *Standing at the Water's Edge*, pp. 224–225.

71 Ibid., p. 225.

72 Organic agriculture program, Oregon State University Department of Horticulture, http://horticulture.oregonstate.edu/content/about-organic-agriculture-program.

73 The website ballotpedia.org lists partisan statewide offices and includes a nonpartisan office, filled by secretary of state appointment, called Oregon Audits Director (http://ballotpedia.org/Oregon_Audits_Director) as of 2013; in 2010 it was called Oregon Audits Division Director. There is no mention of such an office before 2010. Current officeholder is Gary Blackmer. Also there's a website under the secretary of state's devoted to audits: http://sos.oregon.gov/audits/Pages/default.aspx. It includes recently released audits and allows a user to search state audits and reviews and report government waste, fraud, and abuse. It provides municipal report forms and filing instructions, resources for local governments, and audit standards and practices. All this is evidence that Norma's reforms have been institutionalized.

74 Election results November 2014 on OregonLive, http://gov.oregonlive.com/election/.

75 Interview with Dave Frohnmayer.

Index

Note: Photographs and documents are indicated with an italic page number. Information from the Notes is indicated by an italic "*n*" and note number.